A Reluctant Hero

For Edward
28 June 1964
9 May 2007

A Reluctant Hero

The Life of Captain Robert Ryder, VC

Richard Hopton

Pen & Sword
MARITIME

First published in Great Britain in 2011 by
Pen & Sword Maritime
an imprint of
Pen & Sword Books Ltd
47 Church Street
Barnsley
South Yorkshire
S70 2AS

ISBN 978-1-84884-370-7

A CIP catalogue record for this book is available from the British Library

Typeset in 11pt Ehrhardt by
Mac Style, Beverley, East Yorkshire

Printed and bound in the UK by CPI

Pen & Sword Books Ltd incorporates the Imprints of Pen & Sword Aviation,
Pen & Sword Family History, Pen & Sword Maritime, Pen & Sword Military,
Pen & Sword Discovery, Wharncliffe Local History, Wharncliffe True Crime,
Wharncliffe Transport, Pen & Sword Select, Pen & Sword Military Classics,
Leo Cooper, The Praetorian Press, Remember When, Seaforth Publishing and
Frontline Publishing.

For a complete list of Pen & Sword titles please contact
PEN & SWORD BOOKS LIMITED
47 Church Street, Barnsley, South Yorkshire, S70 2AS, England
E-mail: enquiries@pen-and-sword.co.uk
Website: www.pen-and-sword.co.uk

Contents

Acknowledgements

I have been helped by many people in the process of writing this book. All of the following have helped me in one way or another; to each and every one of I am most grateful.

Dorothy Abel Smith, Mavis Ashton, Martin Bates, Oliver Bates, Duncan Beardmore Gray, Mark Bertram, Peter & Dinah Comins, Barry Cox, Hon. Librarian, RNLI, Mrs Peter Cracroft, Judy Faraday, Archivist, John Lewis Partnership, Mrs Didy Grahame, John Green-Wilkinson, Susannah Gurdon, Mrs Penelope Hatfield, Archivist, Eton College, Anne Head, Enid Henley (*née* Coulson), Diana, Lady Holderness, Andrew Imlach, of the CPA, Martin & Virginia Jolly, the late Bridget Lamb, Mrs Christine Leighton, Archivist, Cheltenham College, Sir Julian & Lady Loyd, Moira & the late John Marriott, Charlie Mayfield, Chairman, John Lewis Partnership, Lt.-Col. R.K. Montgomery MC, Francis Peel, Giles Peel, Mrs Francis Penley, Nigel Prescot, Major-General C.W.B. Purdon CBE, MC, Fergus Read, IWM, Andrew Rosthorn, Tim & Tuna Ruane, Olivia Ryder, Ralston Ryder, Peter Rymill, Victoria Schofield, Sheena Skjoldesbrand, Joanna Spencer-Nairn, the staff of the Hartley Library, Univ. of Southampton, Iain Stewart, Roderick Suddaby, Mark Tillie, the late Eric de la Torre, Selina Walker and Mary Wilkins.

I have quoted on p.202 from a letter written by Ian Fleming with permission of the copyright holders, the Ian Fleming Will Trust. Every effort has been made to trace the copyright holder in the papers of Vice Admiral John Hughes-Hallett and both the author and the Imperial War Museum, where the collection is preserved, would always be grateful for any information which might enable them to get in touch with the present owner of the copyright.

I am most grateful to James Dorrian who has kindly allowed me to reproduce his maps showing the harbour of St Nazaire in 1942 and the approach route taken by Operation *Chariot* up the estuary of the River Loire. They originally appeared in his *Storming St Nazaire* (1998). I am grateful too to Peter Rymill who has allowed me to reproduce the maps describing the BGLE from his father's *Southern Lights*. Glen Preece, artist extraordinaire, drew the map showing the route taken by the *Tai-Mo-Shan* during her epic voyage of 1933–34. He will be forever in my debt.

My greatest debt is to Robert Ryder's family, most notably to his son Lisle Ryder and his daughter, Mrs Martin Bates. They have answered endless questions, provided much constructive criticism and tolerated my intrusion into their family's past with great good humour. Most importantly, they have given me wholly unrestricted access to their father's papers. It is no exaggeration to say that without their help and encouragement, this book would never have seen the light of day. Needless to say, any errors of fact or judgment that remain are mine and mine alone.

The idea that I should write this biography came in the first place from an old friend of mine, Jonathan Peel. Johnny was Ryder's nephew and, therefore, a cousin of his son and daughter to whom he kindly introduced me. Sadly, he died suddenly in April 2009 at the tragically early age of 46. I miss him greatly and can only hope that he would have enjoyed this book.

Lastly but by no means least, I should like to thank Caro, without whose love and support nothing would ever get written in the Hopton household. To her, I owe it all.

Richard Hopton
Chittlehampton, Devon, October 2011.

Prologue

As the sun set on 28 June 1940, HMS *Willamette Valley* was at position 49° 19' N, 15° 15' W, 300 miles off the south-west coast of Ireland, seventeen days out of Gibraltar bound for the Canadian port of Halifax. She was a 'Q' ship, a tramp steamer converted with concealed guns and torpedo tubes for operations against enemy surface raiders and U-boats. Disguised as *Ambea*, a Greek merchant vessel, the *Willamette Valley* was commanded by Lieutenant Commander Robert Ryder, with a ship's company of about ninety men.

At about 2100, in gathering darkness and under a cloudy sky, the *Willamette Valley*, as she did every night, closed up to actions stations. At 2112 she was struck by a torpedo on the port side just forward of the bridge. It was too dark to see if the submarine had come to the surface. Moreover, the ship, silhouetted against the dying embers of the setting sun on the western horizon, presented a fine target for the U-boat's cannon shells.

The torpedo, luckily, had not caused too much damage. As the main engine was intact and still functioning, Ryder decided to continue with the normal drill. Accordingly, the 'panic party' in two boats – an apparently hasty evacuation of the ship, in the hope of luring the U-boat to the surface – was ordered away. Meanwhile, the concealed gunports remained closed, to preserve the disguise. After about twenty minutes one of the 'panic party's' boats, which had been damaged, returned to the ship. Ryder ordered the men on board to hide on the *Willamette Valley*'s decks so that they could not be seen were the U-boat to turn a searchlight on his ship. Ryder was at this stage still determined to continue the ruse in the hope of bringing the enemy to the surface where his concealed guns could get a shot at her. He had been crisscrossing the Atlantic for more than four months without making any substantial contact with the enemy. Now, finally, he had a U-boat in his sights.

Twenty-five minutes later, at around 2200, a second torpedo struck the *Willamette Valley*, smashing into the engine room on the starboard side. There was a blinding flash and a screech of tearing, flying steel. The engine room almost immediately burst into flames. Ryder ordered Michael Seymour, the First Lieutenant, to muster the hands he needed to tackle the fire, while the remainder removed as much unused ammunition as they could to safety. The centre of the ship was ablaze, great gouts of flame pouring from the engine room cowls and skylights. At one point a sheet of flame shot up the funnel, illuminating the whole ship. The fire main in the engine room was out of action so the crew fought the raging fire with buckets of water, sand and foam.

The crew was still fighting the fire, when, at 2216, the U-boat fired a third torpedo, which exploded under the *Willamette Valley*'s stern. Ryder, realizing that this was the killer blow, gave the order 'All hands on deck'. Less than a minute later the ship sank by the stern, rolling through 90 degrees as she did so. Her bows remained above the water for half an hour before sinking altogether. As his ship slipped beneath the waves, Ryder heard a small explosion, possibly of the detonator tank. Mercifully, the depth-charges had been set to 'safe' and so did not explode.

Ryder was thrown into the water as the ship sank, grabbing the lifebuoy from the bridge as he went. Buffeted by pieces of debris breaking loose and bursting to the surface as the ship went down, Ryder was able to keep himself afloat, thanks to the lifebuoy and the inflatable waistcoat he was wearing. It was pitch dark. He soon found a small baulk of wood, on which he was joined by one of his men. However, it was not sufficiently buoyant for two men, so Ryder swam off and found another, larger, piece of floating debris. This he clung to until daybreak. Ryder kept calling out and, for a while, voices answered from the darkness but gradually the replies became fewer and weaker until there was silence.

As the dawn came up Ryder found himself alone apart from the corpses of some of his men, floating face down in the water. In the light, he was able to haul himself on to the wreckage, which turned out to be a pair of wooden chocks for the ship's boats, joined by some broken planking. With the lifebuoy positioned as a seat, Ryder now had a raft, just substantial enough to keep him afloat, but not completely clear of the water. This makeshift raft was nevertheless perilously unsteady and liable to pitch Ryder into the water with the slightest loss of balance. He had also grabbed from the floating wreckage a 5ft length of planking, partly painted in red and white.

The sea was now much calmer than it had been the previous night. But as the sun rose the fuel oil in Ryder's eyes was starting to become extremely painful and it was becoming more and more difficult for him to see. However, at around 1000 he spotted the distant masts of a ship steaming towards him. She must have intercepted the *Willamette Valley*'s distress call; he would be rescued. Half-blinded by the oil in his eyes, he watched the ship come within perhaps 2 miles of him and stop for half an hour before steaming off to the west.

Not long after this disappointment, the heat of the sun and the fuel oil caused Ryder's eyes to become so inflamed and swollen that he was unable to see at all. Alone, covered in oil, wet and cold, hundreds of miles from land, with little chance of rescue – Ryder knew that since the fall of France the convoys were taking a course round the north of Ireland, well away from his position – apparently now blind, and without any food or water, he began to wonder whether he should not slip quietly off into the sea to drown. Unable to bring himself to do that, he tried to open an artery in his wrist with a bent, rusty nail from his plank. Then with the loss of blood he would loose consciousness painlessly. It proved more difficult than he expected to cut into the artery and he gave up. He steeled himself for his family's sake not to give in and prayed; indeed divine intervention seemed the only thing that might save him. Many years later, Ryder, who was an accomplished artist, painted a picture of himself adrift in the Atlantic. In the middle of an endless expanse of sea and sky is a figure, sitting hunched on a flimsy-looking square of wood, utterly alone, apart from a passing seabird. He entitled the picture 'Lord remember me in this vast ocean'.

Gradually, he drifted clear of the oil slick and was able to start trying to get the oil out of his hair and eyes. By the second morning, having bathed his eyes continuously throughout the night by using his handkerchief dipped in sea water, his sight had improved, although the glare of the sun on the water was still excruciatingly painful. With the return of his eyesight, Ryder's morale began to improve. Although he had no idea how long he might expect to survive, he began to allow himself hope. He might be picked up by a German U-boat. If he could hold on for six or seven days, the North Atlantic drift might carry him into Irish waters where he would be seen by a coastal patrol. He might be spotted by an aircraft on anti-submarine sweep, a Sunderland or a Catalina. This, Ryder felt, was his best, most realistic hope and so, with great courage, he prepared to wait.

While sitting on his tiny raft, hoping against hope for rescue, Ryder had much time to think. Before leaving England with the *Willamette Valley* he had become engaged. Now, with life itself in the gravest peril, he realized that she was not the right girl for him. He determined that, should he survive, he would break off the engagement.

The days were not so bad; Ryder was cheered by the improvement in his eyesight; he was warmed by the sun and, of course, there was always the chance of being sighted. The nights were grim – bleak and cold, with no hope of being seen. Shivering continuously, he prayed for the dawn. While adrift Ryder had some visitors: a small, hammer-headed shark circled him and a John Dory passed close by. A friendly little storm petrel fluttered around the raft, returning several times as if encouraging him to hang on. A less welcome passer-by was a large, 30ft basking shark which swam just beneath the raft. 'I drew up my feet', he wrote later, 'like Jeremy Fisher and was glad when he moved on.'

As time drew on, Ryder increasingly suffered from exhaustion: he would nod off, tipping up his precariously flimsy raft and slip into the water. He began to hallucinate too, as a result of hunger and lack of water and sleep. A small, white cabin cruiser would come alongside and a man in a white yachting cap would offer him a lift ashore, but as soon as he accepted he would wake up to the terrible reality of his situation.

At the end of the fourth day, as dusk was beginning to fall, Ryder experienced a different hallucination: a large ocean liner was steaming past him. At this point he came to, realizing that it was real. There were ships as far as the eye could see; it was a convoy. Frantically waving his red and white plank, he was soon spotted. The leading ship sounded four or five blasts on her horn but the column continued to steam relentlessly along, showing no signs of stopping. Perhaps, for the sake of one man, the convoy would not stop in waters where submarines were known to operate. Then Ryder noticed the last ship in the column, a tanker, pulling out of the line and slowing down. Eventually, at dead slow speed, she drifted close to Ryder, her huge sides towering over him, and threw down several ropes. One splashed down about 10ft from him and someone from the deck far above shouted, 'Swim for it'. Ryder leapt off his raft and made for the floating line. But in his weakened state he could not find the line nor regain the relative safety of his raft. His inflatable waistcoat had perished and so it now merely weighed him down. The tanker was drifting inexorably away. Then the huge propeller began to churn the water; the ship was steaming off. Would she return? Would she abandon him to his fate? Would she return in time? For Ryder, after his ordeal, was now very weak and could not survive much longer in the water. He knew that it would take a ship of that size at least fifteen minutes to gather way once more, come about and stop. As he was coming up to the surface for what he felt must be the last time, a line splashed into the water right in front of him. This time he grabbed the rope and was hauled alongside. A sailor came down one of the ship's lifelines to secure him in a bowline and he was lifted aboard. His ordeal was over. The ship was the SS *Inverliffy*, of the Bank Line, under the command of Captain T.E. Alexander.

Ryder had survived, alone on his tiny makeshift raft, without food or water, for three days and twenty-two hours.

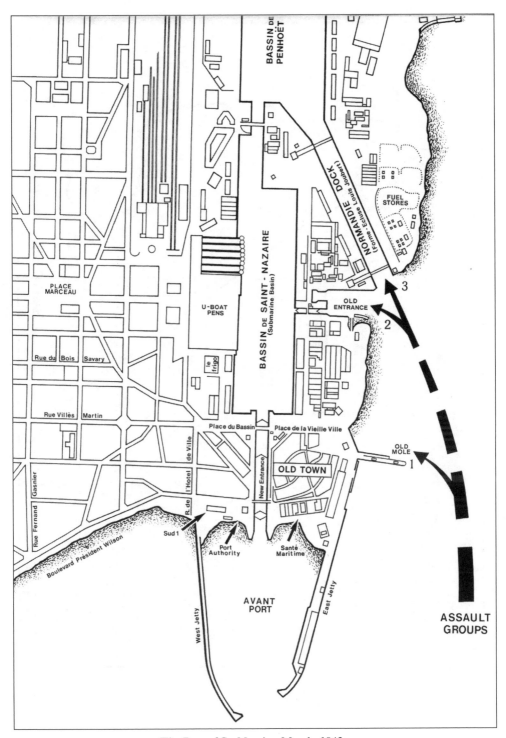

The Port of St. Nazaire, March, 1942.

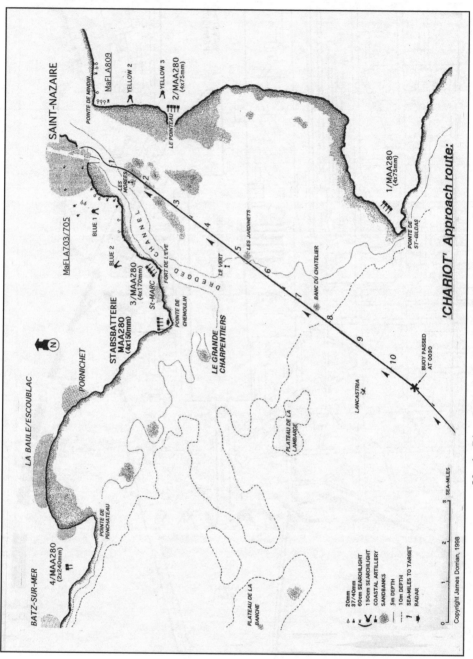

'CHARIOT' Approach route:

Up the River Loire from the sea: the approach to St Nazaire.

Copyright James Dorrian, 1998

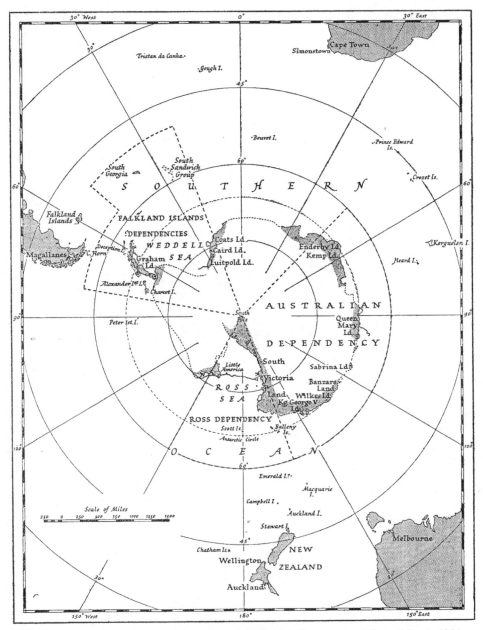

The Antarctic as it was known at the outset of the British Graham Land Expedition in 1934.

Graham Land as it was known before the sledge journeys of late 1936.

Graham Land as it appeared after the sledge journeys of late 1936 which proved that Graham Land was a peninsular of the Antarctic continent and that Alexander I Land was an island.

Chapter 1

Family and Childhood: India and England

Robert Edward Dudley Ryder was born at Dehra Dun in India on 16 February 1908. He was the third son and sixth child of Major (later Colonel) Charles Ryder, Royal Engineers, and his wife Ida (née Grigg). They had married in 1892 producing three daughters – Margaret (born 1893), Enid (1895) and Violet (1898) – and then three sons – Lisle (1902), Ernle (1906) and Robert, known by his doting parents as Bobby. At school he was known by some as 'Chippy'. Later in life, during his time in the Navy, he acquired, from his initials, the nickname 'Red' although thereafter most people knew him simply as Bob.

The Ryders were a distinguished family who numbered among their descendants an admiral and a bishop. The dynasty was founded by Dudley Ryder, the son of a nonconformist draper, who forged a successful career at the Bar and in politics, rising to become, successively, Solicitor-General, Attorney-General and, finally, in 1754, Lord Chief Justice. He was ennobled by George II in May 1756 but died the following day before the Letters Patent could be completed. His only son, Nathaniel, sat as MP for Tiverton 1756–76, before himself being, successfully this time, raised to the peerage in 1776. His son, Dudley, followed in his father's footsteps as MP for Tiverton, enjoying a distinguished political career as an ardent supporter of Pitt the Younger. Indeed, he was sufficiently close to Pitt to act as his second in the Prime Minister's duel with George Tierney on Putney Heath in May 1798. Having occupied a number of lesser government posts, Pitt appointed him Foreign Secretary in 1804. He was created Earl of Harrowby in 1809 and served as Lord President of the Council throughout Lord Liverpool's long administration.[1]

Charles Ryder, Robert's father, a distinguished surveyor and cartographer, was an important influence on his youngest son, passing on to him an adventurous spirit and love of exploration and map-making. Colonel Ryder had spent much of his career tramping the mountains, valleys, deserts and jungles of the Middle and the Far East, exploring and mapping. He had been a member of the Mekong Boundary Commission (1898–1900), joined the expedition charged with mapping the Yunnan province of China (1901–02) and took part, as mapping officer, in Francis Younghusband's notorious expedition to Tibet in 1904. After Younghusband's expedition, Ryder commanded a party of five which mapped 40,000 sq. miles of Tibet and the borders of British India. In the process the party covered 1,000 miles of inhospitable, mountainous terrain. For this remarkable feat he was awarded the DSO and the Royal Geographical Society's Gold Medal. In 1913 Ryder was appointed the Chief Surveying Officer to the Turko–Persian Boundary Commission, one of three attempts in the nineteenth and the early twentieth century to delineate the troublesome border between the two countries. By the autumn of 1914 he had surveyed the entire 1,180 miles of the frontier between the Persian Gulf and Mount Ararat.[2]

If Dehra Dun was a typical Raj garrison town, where life in the cantonment revolved around the club to the stifling rhythms of official protocol, Ryder was a typical child of British India. The much-loved and indulged youngest son of an extensive family, he was brought up largely by an ayah, who, by all accounts, greatly spoiled him. Families who served in British India endured as a matter of course prolonged separations nor were the Ryders any exception. As was the custom, young Bobby was packed off, aged six, to school in England with his brother Ernle. By November 1914 he was in England with his father, while his mother remained in India with the elder daughters. Charles was lodging in Eastbourne with his three sons, Violet and a French governess for the children. 'Darling', Charles wrote to his wife in India, 'it would do your heart good to see Ernle & Bobby rushing about the place, full of spirits & fun.'[3]

By the autumn of 1915 Ida was in England with the children while Charles had returned to India. The strain on Charles and Ida and their family imposed by the lengthy separations, made worse by the war, is evident from their letters. In April 1916 Charles's application for six months' leave was refused on account of the war. 'So that is the end of that', he wrote despairingly to Ida, '& when I shall get home or see any of you again God alone knows.'[4]

By then Bobby had joined Ernle at Hazlehurst School at Frant near Tunbridge Wells. He seems to have been an unexceptional pupil. His father, far away in India, scrutinized his reports with an eagle eye. 'Bobby I see for half-term is still bottom of his class. I fancy he is about the youngest; but all I want in his reports is "doing his best" or "trying hard" or something like that.'[5] But there were also encouraging signs: Bobby was showing distinct promise at drawing and had managed to get in the football XI. According to the Headmaster's wife, Bobby was 'really very good, he is our best back in spite of his size.'[6] In 1918 he won the drawing prize, an early sign of a talent that would develop throughout his life.

In March 1919 Charles Ryder took up his post as Surveyor-General of India, a fitting finale to a distinguished career. One of the conditions of his appointment was that he would agree not to take any home leave for the first year. As he had not seen his younger sons since 1914, this was not a condition he was happy to accept but he had little choice. 'It is an awful blow to me having seen so little of my boys, but I don't see that I could have helped it in any way.'[7]

In the summer of 1920 Charles, having completed his first year as Surveyor-General was at last allowed some home leave. Reunited with Ernle and little Bobby for the first time since 1914, he took them and Lisle off to the Brittany coast for a holiday. They had a wonderful time, fishing, drawing, playing on the beach, even having French lessons. The holiday also gave Colonel Ryder an opportunity to observe the sons he had not seen for five years as he reported to his wife in India:

> [Bobby] has two weak points: if he can't manage a thing he chucks it in the most utmost despair. Yesterday we were out fishing at Cancale & because he didn't get bites at one time he was in tears & waving his hands about in the most dramatic manner. Then he is dreadful at cards, if his king is taken by an ace he weeps ... The other great drawback is his selfishness.[8]

Ryder himself always claimed in later life that 'he was brought up to be a good winner.' But his youngest son had many redeeming features, too. 'What is delightful about him is his keenness & energy, his great love & knowledge of natural history & his love of painting. He is very good looking.'

In September 1921 Ryder followed his father and both his brothers to Cheltenham College. Being from an impeccably military background, Ryder entered the Military and Engineering side of the school, the preferred course for those intending to go on to Sandhurst or Woolwich. Ryder's family have the impression that he was not a particularly assiduous pupil: 'he needed motivation and, not getting it, he trundled along', his daughter remarked. This is not entirely borne out by his results at Cheltenham. In his first three terms he finished successively second, first and third in his year. Throughout his time at the school he never (with the exception of his last term when, presumably, he was concentrating on the Navy entrance exams) finished lower than eighth, in a class the average size of which was seventeen. He was always at the top of the class, or near it, for drawing and continued to do well on the games field. In 1923 his father recorded that 'Bobby [is] decidedly promising at games.'[9]

With their parents away in India – Ida did not return until the spring of 1923 – Ryder and Ernle were farmed out to relations during the holidays. Their favourite refuge was their uncle Wilfred's house, Gratnar, near North Bovey on the edge of Dartmoor. Here the two boys were able to run wild in the Devon countryside.

> [W]e took a young Wood pigeon from its nest and feed [sic] it on corn, which we had to force into its mouth one grain at a time, he was hideous when we got him but is getting prettier and prettier ... He now feeds himself which is a great relief.[10]

Gratnar was a home from home. As Ryder happily told his parents in January 1923: for 'our dinner we had Turkey & Christmas pudding which came in all flaming and we poured rum over it till it was blazing, when we ate it.'

Ryder seemed destined for a career in the Army: 'It had always been assumed that I would become a soldier', he wrote later. As he came from a formidably military family, this appeared to be a foregone conclusion. His father and uncle were serving officers; two of his mother's brothers were Army officers, as were both his own brothers, while his three sisters were all married to Army officers. His family background and his youthful memories of the Great War had profoundly affected the young Ryder. 'I was proud to be British and eager to serve my country.'[11] Meanwhile, Colonel Ryder, out in India, harboured ambitions that his youngest son might follow him into the Royal Engineers.

By then, however, Ryder's thoughts had turned to a naval career. At the age of fourteen or fifteen he had been taken sailing by his brother Lisle, who owned *Edith*, a converted fishing smack. They sailed from the Thames Estuary round the North Foreland to Dungeness and back, making a night crossing of the Thames estuary, then quite a rarity, in the process. During that trip they experienced 'just about everything – strong winds, fog and calms.' For Ryder it was an epiphany, the start of a love for the sea and sailing that was to last all his life. In old age he described the 'scintillating lights from the buoys and Light vessels, the fog horns, kedging when becalming off Walton, the sea fog setting in … all made a deep and exciting impression on my young mind.' He also discovered that, despite the rough conditions, he did not suffer from seasickness. 'I felt not a qualm which gave me a great advantage.'

A visit to HMS *Valhalla*, a destroyer lying at Devonport, further strengthened Ryder's thoughts of the Navy. Joining it would also allow him to leave school a year early, an added, and not inconsiderable, bonus. However, others were not so encouraging. His family were worried that he would not be able to live on his Navy pay and, moreover, that he would find it difficult to pass the entrance examinations, a sentiment firmly endorsed by his school. 'Back at Cheltenham my masters thought I had no chance of passing.' But Ryder was nothing if not determined and set himself to pass the exams. He sat the Public School Special Entry in November 1925, before facing an intimidating interview board consisting of 'a formidable array' of 'admirals, captains, civil servants and headmasters.' Asked the inevitable question, 'Why do you want to go into the Navy?', Ryder waxed lyrical about the joys of sailing across the Thames Estuary at night.

When the results were published, Ryder had come top. This came as a great surprise to his masters at Cheltenham. After all, his final report in English had described him as 'incredibly illiterate'. The head of the Military side of the school wrote: 'my heartiest congratulations. It was a very pleasant surprise to find … [you] at the head of the Navy List.' Lower down the list was a boy from Rugby, Sam Beattie, who was destined to win the Victoria Cross alongside Ryder at St Nazaire.[12]

Looking back many years later on his choice of career, Ryder wrote:

I don't think it ever occurred to any of us to go into business. We came from a military background and were really proud of it. The thought of working in a city office in the hope of being rich one day had little appeal to our adventurous instincts. We just took it for granted that there was no better way of serving one's country than in the armed forces of the crown.[13]

Chapter 2

Into the Navy (1926–31)

Ryder joined the Navy on 1 January 1926 and was posted to HMS *Thunderer*, a training ship moored off Devonport dockyard. For the new recruit the Royal Navy, steeped in arcane tradition, was an intimidating experience, with pitfalls at every turn for the unwary cadet. Ryder described his arrival at *Thunderer* in his first letter home.

[I] didn't know my way about the ship or who to ask; one has to be very careful to whom one speaks as it is a crime to speak to anyone on the lower deck, & it is not done to accost an officer. The Quarter deck is treated as hallowed ground; one is not allowed [to] walk on it, but only to double across it, & it has to be saluted whenever it is approached from any direction.[1]

However, Ryder soon acclimatized to his new life and, in this stimulating environment, began to blossom. 'I found navigation and seamanship of the greatest interest', he recalled. He also managed to do as much sailing as possible, gathering up fellow cadets for trips around Plymouth Sound. There were weekly whaler races too, in which Ryder occasionally managed to come second; they were almost invariably won by the King's Harbour Master. Occasionally he would take a cutter out of the Sound, round to Whitesand Bay.

His progress had been noted by the term Lieutenant, E.W. Bush, who arranged for Ryder and another cadet to crew on the *Jolie Brise* in that year's Fastnet Race. Ocean racing was in 1926 a sport in its infancy; the inaugural Fastnet Race had taken place only the previous August. As the *Jolie Brise*, a converted Le Havre pilot cutter, had won the 1925 race, it was both a great honour and a wonderful opportunity for Ryder to be invited to crew her. Nine boats started in stormy conditions at Cowes. However, during the course of the race the *Jolie Brise* was forced to heave to by the weather, allowing the *Ilex*, a yacht crewed by the Royal Engineers, to win. His boat may not have won the race but the experience had been thrilling. He had also made his mark, as George Martin, the owner of the *Jolie Brise*, told Admiral Phillimore, the Commander-in-Chief, Plymouth: 'Ryder was the best of them all. He said very little, but worked very hard. I think he will make a fine seaman: he is very keen.' Admiral Phillimore, passing Martin's remarks on to Colonel Ryder, added, 'I feel very proud of my kinsman.'[2]

In his third and last term Ryder was appointed Senior Cadet Captain and awarded the King's Dirk as the outstanding cadet of his year. He had made a better start to his career in the Navy than he could dared have hoped. On 1 January 1927 he was promoted Midshipman and, at the end of the month, joined his first ship. She was HMS *Ramillies*, a battleship of 29,350 tons, mounting eight 15in guns in four turrets, launched in 1916. When Ryder joined her she was refitting in a floating dock at Devonport. This gave Ryder a gentle introduction to life on a battleship as the ship's company was reduced to about two-fifths of its normal size. Judging by his midshipman's log of the period, Ryder and his fellow midshipmen were mainly occupied with lectures and courses, interspersed with drill sessions and the occasional game of hockey. They were also required to write descriptions of several new ships under construction in a basin adjoining *Ramillies*.[3]

Once the refit was complete, *Ramillies* joined the Atlantic Fleet for a summer cruise off Scotland before returning to Weymouth at the end of June for a regatta. Although *Ramillies* did not distinguish herself in the races, she did collect one consolation prize. In the sailing race for cutters crewed by midshipmen, the *Ramillies*'s boat, with Ryder in the crew, pulled off a most creditable victory. When the starting gun was fired the cutter was not only on the wrong side of the starting vessel but across the line as well. Having to beat back up to the starting line against the tide put her about five minutes behind the nearest boat. However, in very light winds, she was only about three cables (600yd) behind and steadily reeled in the leaders, before crossing the winning line comfortably ahead. The cutter, Ryder said proudly, 'certainly showed herself to be a fast boat in light airs.' The crew's prize was a cup presented by the Royal Dorset Yacht Club and lunch in the clubhouse the following day.

The highlight of the rest of the summer was Cowes Week in early August. Although Ryder seems not to have done any sailing, he was able to watch the races and drink in the atmosphere. His midshipman's log describes the comings and goings of the big yachts and the more exciting moments of some of the races. On the Thursday *Ramillies*'s officers gave a dance on board for 600 guests, comprising mostly parties from the yachts. The quarterdeck was hung with bunting, lights and greenery for the occasion, but the centrepiece was a salt-water fountain and pool alive with lobster. On the Sunday the King and Queen inspected *Ramillies*.

On 21 September *Ramillies* left Devonport bound for Malta, where she was to join the Mediterranean Fleet. Five days later she steamed through the Straits and into the harbour at Gibraltar, 'in time', Ryder noted, 'to see a wonderful sunrise effect on the Atlas Mountains.' From Gibraltar she made a stately progress east up the Mediterranean, putting in at the French colony of Bougie in Algeria. From Bougie Ryder took a motorcycle inland to the town of Serif. He was impressed by the 'very fine' Kerrata gorges and by the 'road cut out of the hill in many places'. However, on the return journey, the motorcycle's headlight failed so he had a fraught trip home, arriving back at Bougie, benighted, at 9.00 pm.

Having arrived at Malta, *Ramillies* began to prepare for her winter cruise in the tropics for which she departed, in company with HMS *Barham*, on 4 December. Ryder was not sorry to be leaving Malta, which 'is a rummy place & depends entirely on which way the wind blows, we have just had the rains & followed by the Scirocco, the latter makes one feel wretched.'[4] The cruise began eventfully, as Ryder told his parents. 'On leaving Malta we missed going aground & hitting the pier by a series of flukes … Well on passage we nearly ran down a tramp. The same evening our gyro compass broke down & we nearly rammed *Barham* who was on our beam.' But worse was to come as *Ramillies* came into Gibraltar:

> We actually crashed into the mole; it was grand [sight] the ship heeled right over & we smashed a few pontoons but in some mysterious way we failed to damage our stem. I wish we had it would have been great we should probably have returned to Devonport.[5]

Ramillies and *Barham* left Gibraltar on 14 December to cruise down the west coast of Africa, reaching Freetown, Sierra Leone, just before Christmas and Lagos on 2 January. As she steamed south so the weather improved, and with it Ryder's state of mind. 'I feel peculiarly fit in the Tropics', he told his parents from Lagos. 'I think it's because we play a very strenuous game of deck hockey at 1600 every evening and then plunge into our sail bath.' And there was an additional benefit, too: 'We have just steamed into the zone of extra pay, we get 1/- a day extra for 12 days.' He enjoyed the warm tropical evenings at sea, too, when 'we all sit back in deck chairs in pyjamas with the gramophone going, on the deck outside the gunroom.'[6]

During the passage north to the Mediterranean, *Ramillies* put into Accra in the Gold Coast where Ryder was able to see his brother Lisle who was serving there with the Royal West Africa Frontier Force. 'Lisle looked very healthy', Ryder told their parents, 'he is rapidly assuming the air of a regular "coaster" as they call them out here.'[7] On 6 February *Ramillies* berthed in the Grand Harbour at Malta.

Part of the Midshipman's training was a spell in smaller ships, so at the end of March Ryder left *Ramillies* to join HMS *Vanessa*, a destroyer attached to the Mediterranean Fleet's 2nd Destroyer Flotilla. On his third day in the ship he told his parents:

> the life is quite different from that of a battleship; it's altogether much more fun. Our captain – Hannay – is an amazing man – very fierce when on the bridge, very much the reverse in the wardroom and so long as one plays various games for the flotilla, and drinks one's quota in the evenings he is pleased.[8]

In later years, however, Ryder looked back on these months with a more jaundiced eye. 'It was bad luck too that during my four months in destroyers I was sent to a very hard drinking ship, *Vanessa*. I should have enjoyed this interlude but felt out of place in the gin drinking atmosphere of the wardroom.'[9] However, as *Vanessa* was cruising in Greek waters during June and July there were compensations. Ryder and a fellow midshipman took themselves off to explore the coast one day. We sailed, he told his parents:

> till we came to a bay, horseshoe in shape surrounded by sand dunes and guarded on either side of the entrance by cliffs and overlooked by the ruined castle and Nestor's cave. The water is wonderfully clear here & one can see the bottom at considerable depths and this bay is surrounded by lovely white sand.[10]

After an uneventful four months in *Vanessa* Ryder rejoined *Ramillies* in July. At the end of the Aegean leg of the summer cruise, *Ramillies* returned to Malta in the last week of August before setting off on 7 September for the second leg up the Adriatic as far as Fiume in Croatia. During this trip Ryder was able to get some sailing.

> I have been sailing twice here. The first time we had a good 2 reef breeze & a down pour of rain but the boat fairly shifted & it was great fun. We were pretty numb when we got back so we brewed cocoa and had hot baths. One of those occasions when it's worth being alive.[11]

Ramillies returned from the Adriatic to Malta where Ryder spent the remainder of the autumn and winter. As his time as a Midshipman was coming to an end, he was posted to HMS *Eagle*, an aircraft carrier, for a flying course. Although Ryder did not, it seems, fly an aeroplane himself, he did go up several times, making a number of deck landings on *Eagle*. His Midshipman's log ends on 21 March 1929; Ryder arrived back in England on 8 April. Recalling his time as a Midshipman in later life, he wrote:

> My time in my first ship *Ramillies* was less successful ... We had a dull and uninspiring captain, nor did I care for the two other midshipmen who were appointed to the ship with me. So I lacked companionship. The novelty and excitement of being in the Navy began to wear off. We were sent to the Mediterranean for some 2½ years with no leave and I found the heat in the summer oppressive. I was not used to it. At that age it seemed a long time.

Rather more of a setback was his failure to get a first-class certificate in seamanship. 'As it was really my best subject this was a disappointment.' All in all, Ryder remembered later, 'I returned to England rather disenchanted.'[12] However, his midshipman's logs give the impression of an observant young officer, keen to master the principles of his profession. The logs also bear witness to his burgeoning skill both as an artist and as a technical draftsman. Some of his pen-and-wash drawings of naval ships and other vessels are very accomplished for a twenty-year old. His technical drawings – usually details of pieces of the ship's equipment – are clear, painstaking and accurate.

Once Ryder returned to England he had a period of leave before starting on his Acting Sub Lieutenant's course at the Royal Naval College, Greenwich at the beginning of May. At once life improved, 'my spirits revived', he wrote. He played a good deal of rugby for the Naval College against some of the better London clubs. In one match against the Old Millhillians, Ryder was marking the England half-backs, Sobey and Spong. 'Spurred by this challenge', he remembered years later, 'I tackled Spong with such determination that he left the field.' Later in the season, playing for a United Services XV at Bath, Ryder scored 'a rather sensational try … that was reported on in *The Times*.' This caught the eye of the Navy selectors who came to watch Ryder in his next game but, carrying a slight injury, he played poorly. So 'that was the height of my rugger career.' Another advantage of the course at Greenwich was that he could spend regular weekends at home with his parents, who had bought a house near Camberley.[13]

For Ryder the highlight of 1929 was the ocean racing season. Having made a name for himself in the 1926 Fastnet Race, he was recruited by Harold Newgass as navigator in his boat *Grey Fox*. Her first engagement was the Fastnet Race, in which she finished in a slightly disappointing fifth place. The race was won by *Jolie Brise* in whom Ryder had sailed in the 1926 race. *Ilex*, which had won in 1926, finished second.[14] A week after the Fastnet, *Grey Fox* lined up for the Plymouth–Santander race, in which she finished third, having been becalmed twice, despite all the crew's efforts to get her moving. 'A great deal of heavy work was put in shifting sail & every combination of sail was tried but it was not until about 6.30 that we got under way again.'[15] *Grey Fox* won the prize for the longest day's run – 148 miles. This was entirely due to Ryder's accurate chart-keeping, for which he received official commendation from the Admiralty. A few days later *Grey Fox* took part in the Santander–Bilbao race in which she beat *Avocet*, navigated by Ryder's commanding officer, the Captain of Greenwich, 'which was another diplomatic success.'

> We have won three cups here already & I think that is ample … This is undoubtedly the place to come pot hunting. The Spaniard has so much cash that [he] can't think how to spend it and gives vast cups for everything.

There was fun to be had in the evenings, too.

> We have been having a very gay time. The best I did was just before leaving Santander when I did not get back to the ship till 0630 when we were just in time to hoist sail for the Bilbao race. Last night was quite good we were invited to a feast at the Real Club Maritimo, starting at 2200 after which we danced returning on board in driblets. I was the first back at 0715 and slept until 1600 …

Best of all, Ryder was now in demand as a navigator for ocean racing. 'I have had several offers to navigate in next year's ocean races, so I feel quite braced.'[16]

Ryder finished at Greenwich just before Christmas. His nine months there had been a success: he had been awarded a first-class certificate which made up for the disappointment of his failure in seamanship. He had enjoyed his rugby, too. 'I have been elevated to the 1st XV and have been put centre three-quarter, so I am happy at last. We had a great game against Woolwich and drew with them; I emerged feeling very sore as the ground was rather hard.'[17] In November Ryder, anxious perhaps to avoid a return to the longueurs of service in a big ship, applied for transfer to the Surveying Service, a branch of the Navy that would suit his independent spirit better. The Admiralty did not agree; his request was summarily refused.

After spending Christmas at home with his parents – something he had not done for three years – in the New Year Ryder started another series of courses at Portsmouth. He evidently applied himself as he finished the courses in June with first-class certificates in gunnery, pilotage and torpedoes. On 12 August 1930 he was promoted Sub Lieutenant with seniority from 1 March 1929.

By this time, the 1930 ocean racing season was getting under way. Ryder's first engagement was the Channel Race in Mr Maitland's *Freya*, a 12-ton, shallow-draught cutter built some thirty years previously. The race started at the Royal Yacht Squadron at Cowes on 1 August. Before the start, Ryder and his fellow crew members 'got the weather forecast on the wireless and it was pretty bum, forecasting strong winds.' And so it proved. By sunset on the second evening of the race *Freya* was off the French coast approaching the Cap d'Antifer when the wind began to increase and by the middle of the night she began to ship water badly. 'This necessitated pumping every ¼ hour, however the pumps became clogged with dirt out of the bilges and so we had to take the floor boards up & bail with buckets.'

There was no question of *Freya*'s continuing in the race: she was 'a very old & leaky boat', so they turned for the safety of Fecamp, to await an improvement in the weather. 'We were in the second smallest boat too so there was no shame in giving up'; commonsense had prevailed.[18]

For the Fastnet Race Ryder had been invited to navigate *Neptune*, a powerful 62-ton cutter, designed, built and crewed by Norwegians. Nine boats started the race in 'boisterous' conditions at Cowes. *Neptune* was leading the race by several hours when a bolt in her tiller sheared off, forcing her to abandon the race in order to seek shelter in Plymouth. Only four of the nine starters finished, the result being the same as in the previous year: first, *Jolie Brise*, second, *Ilex*. The result confounded those who maintained that the light winds prevailing during the 1929 race had favoured *Jolie Brise* and *Ilex*.[19]

The protracted finish of the Fastnet race delayed the start of the Plymouth–Santander race until 23 August, when *Neptune*, her damage repaired, took her place in the starting line-up. For Ryder and the rest of *Neptune*'s crew it was an exciting race. At sunset on the first day a 6ft split appeared in her mainsail, but the following day, thanks to a period of flat calm, Ryder was able to repair the sail.

This was no easy task & trying to coerce an unwilling sail needle through No. 1 American Cotton Duck was not made any easier when the boom swung into one's chest.

With the sail sewn and patched, by the second evening of the race *Neptune* was bowling along on a fine south-easterly breeze. However, as a result of her delay, she was now well behind; desperate measures were required. Having rounded Ushant, *Neptune* stood well out to the west in the hope of picking up a south-westerly breeze. As Ryder admitted, 'This we did as a long chance. We were obviously far behind and our only hope lay in sailing a different course to the leading boats.' The gamble paid off: *Neptune* continued to make good speed, passing *Ilex* on the fourth day. With *Neptune* rapidly gaining on her rivals, the race came to a exciting finish.

Then next day we picked up & passed *Jolie Brise*, sighting the mountains behind Santander about the same time as we took the lead. After this the wind fell light & finally died away altogether, leaving us about ¼ mile ahead of the *J.B.* and about a mile to the line. Swarms of motorboats came out to welcome us in, & we gathered that we were the leading boat. We eventually drifted across the line with *J.B.* about an hour behind.

Neptune had won the race, but Ryder could not join in the celebrations – the crews were invited to dinner by the King of Spain – as he had to return home for the start of his submarine courses. He arrived in the nick of time at HMS *Dolphin* at Gosport. As he told his sister Enid:

I then finished by coming home from Spain in a devil of a hurry by train & got here just in time for my course. I thought that I would be late & break my leave but I had to chance that as I won't be able to sail to Spain probably for some time.[20]

Ryder had decided to specialize in submarines because 'I liked small ships and needed the extra pay.' He was also inspired, as he later acknowledged, by accounts he had read of submarine operations during the Great War, notably Naismith's daring voyage through the Dardanelles.[21] The submarine course finished before Christmas and, after a few days' leave, Ryder was appointed to his first ship, HMS *Olympus*, refitting at Devonport. His first glimpse of his new ship was not inspiring: she 'is in a very sorry condition with dockyard mateys crawling everywhere.'[22] 'I have just … started on submarines', Ryder wrote to his sister, 'it is rather an anxious moment finding out whether I like my new job or not, but I think I shall.'[23]

Chapter 3

Hong Kong and the China Station (1931–33)

Ryder had barely had time for breakfast on his arrival in Devonport before he was whisked off to *Olympus* to take over from the officer he was relieving. He had been thrown in at the deep end: 'everyone is on leave & so I have *Olympus* and seven men on my hands', a situation made somewhat embarrassing by the fact that he had no uniform. Indeed, as the only officer on board, he had an array of job titles that would have delighted a panjandrum from Gilbert & Sullivan:

At present I have to do all the correspondence as well as my normal jobs but that and navigation is really Mowlem's job. I am in charge of the mess wine & tobacco; The Seaman's Division (30 men); I am also The Gunnery Officer; Signal Officer; Wireless Officer; Anti Gas Officer; Games Officer; Anti Submarine Officer, and Torpedo Officer.

The ship was in state of chaos: 'everything is topsy-turvy, odd bits of paper, pencil jottings lying about loose in all the drawers mixed up with all the Fleet Orders & letters from R/A Submarines.' Another, potentially embarrassing difficulty confronted Ryder in his capacity as officer in charge of the mess wine and tobacco: 'the Captain never by any chance pays his mess bills.' As a result the mess funds were nearly broke.[1] Gradually, as the other officers returned from leave, life in *Olympus* settled into a more regular rhythm. The refit continued slowly; there was a lot of work to be done before she would be ready to go to sea.

Although he was kept busy, Ryder had begun to enjoy himself with some of the other kindred spirits among the young officers at Devonport. The other sub lieutenant in *Olympus* was Oddie with whom Ryder immediately established a rapport. 'He and I', Ryder told his parents, 'have very similar views on life, he is also a devotee of the country & lives on the shores of County Down in Ulster where he sails a boat that he built himself.' They discussed sharing a boat although at this stage nothing came of it. Oddie sailed to Hong Kong with *Olympus* and later was part of the original crew of *Tai-Mo-Shan*.

There was also time that winter for Ryder to play a good deal of rugby. He seems for the most part to have turned out for Devonport Services 'A' XV. His letters referred to fixtures against the Cambourne School of Mines, Exmouth, the City Police, Teignmouth and Bath, to whom Devonport lost convincingly,

26–0. Ryder also tried his hand at golf but without much success: 'we both lost five balls in the heather & then chucked it.'[2]

He was also able to spend a weekend with his uncle at Gratnar, on the edge of Dartmoor, where he and Ernle had passed many happy holidays from school. He was thrilled to be able to revisit his childhood haunts : 'I find it quite unchanged, delightfully so'. He waxed nostalgic at the memories.

I particularly remember some of the trees; ones that I had frequently climbed …; I even found the Buzzard's nest exactly as I had originally found it with Ernle. It does seem strange to think of all the changes that have come over the country; Labour governments have come and gone & come into power again and yet that old nest hasn't altered one bit.[3]

By the end of February *Olympus*'s refit was nearly complete. Ryder had a week's leave in early March which prompted some morose thoughts about another prolonged posting abroad. 'I have no wish to leave England: I will miss seeing Ernle [who was expected home on leave from India], and miss my sailing and rugger.' But, nevertheless, he was looking forward to going abroad, 'a very good thing in many ways.'[4] Before he departed he was promoted Lieutenant, with seniority from June 1930. On 1 April *Olympus* left Devonport in company with HMS *Pathian*, another submarine, bound for Hong Kong. Ryder, having got himself appointed as *Olympus*'s navigating officer, was responsible, *Olympus* being the senior ship, for charting the course of both submarines, with only the barest supervision from his captain. He was looking forward to the challenge.

In the early 1930s the voyage from England to Hong Kong in a submarine was taken in leisurely stages, with stops at all the more important outposts of Empire along the way. *Olympus* and *Pathian* called at Gibraltar, Malta, Port Said, Aden, Colombo, Penang, Singapore and Hong Kong. As the submarines arrived in each port there was the usual round of hospitality: invitations from the governor and other local nabobs, tennis parties, drinks parties and dinners, invitations which *Olympus*'s captain reciprocated enthusiastically. Ryder, rather grouchily, complained that, 'When we get to harbour I find life rather trying as the captain is always throwing parties in the Wardroom, the temperature seems to double as soon as we stop …'[5] While the ship was berthed at Colombo Ryder was invited for a few days up to a hill station in the middle of the island. As it was 4,000ft up in the mountains, the atmosphere was a blessed relief from the humid heat at sea level, although Ryder did not make the most of the opportunity to refresh himself. 'Our four days stay was I regret no rest for me, I didn't go to bed before 0130 while I was there.' When he returned to *Olympus* it was 96°F in the wardroom.[6]

When *Olympus* had been at sea for three weeks Ryder told Neil Campbell, his brother-in-law, that, 'So far I am enjoying the voyage no end, and I find the Navigating keeps me fully occupied at sea …, and it leaves me free in harbour which is a very suitable arrangement.' Ryder was certainly kept busy while the submarines were at sea,. He described his daily routine:

> I am up on the bridge by 4.00 am, during the next four hours I enjoy the best part of the day and take my star sights & work them out. I am relieved at 8.00 am when I go & wind the chronometers, & have a hurried breakfast, so that I can take an altitude of the sun at 9.00 am; I spend most of the forenoon on the bridge either as Officer of the Watch or else in working out our future courses, tides or currents. I then take another Altitude of the Sun at noon & report our position to the Captain … In the afternoon, I write up the log after a quick lunch & generally have to sleep for an hour before I can make much headway; this takes me to tea time; after tea I wash and shave not having had time to do so before. At 5.00 pm I take an Altitude of the Sun. The next item of routine is at 6.30 when I fix the ship's position from Altitudes of the stars.

After a long, hot voyage, *Olympus* and *Pathian* arrived at Hong Kong on 6 June, exactly on schedule. This was a feather in Ryder's cap who, as the navigating officer, had set their course. Moreover, *Olympus* and *Pathian* had established a record: 'we have also come out here in a shorter time than any other submarine, so that we feel that we have accomplished something.'[7] Ryder was later formally congratulated by the Commander-in-Chief, China Station, and the Captain of his Submarine Flotilla for his 'conspicuous zeal and thoroughness' in completing his 'Navigating Officer's Remark Book' for *Olympus*'s voyage from England to Hong Kong. No sooner had he arrived on the China Station than his excellence at navigation had come to his superiors' notice. This would stand him in good stead in the months to come.

Ryder was immediately taken with Hong Kong. Within a week of his arrival he was telling his parents that, 'I think Hong Kong is without exception the most attractive place I have yet been to & am delighted with it.' The exotic colony, its seething Chinese port city, its junks and sampans, its sights and smells, all new and exciting to Ryder, made a great impression on him. One night in his first week he went to the top of the Peak after dinner. Laid out below him was

> the town of Victoria, the harbour & Kowloon on the far side all outlined with twinkling lights. One could hear all the sounds far away below as clearly as anything, & see the ships moving about the harbour, a mass of lights themselves with their reflections.

It was, he pronounced, 'one of the finest sights in the world.'[8]

When *Olympus* arrived in Hong Kong she was warmly welcomed by the other ships of the 4th Submarine Flotilla, to which she was attached. The 4th Flotilla's depot ship was the *Medway* where *Olympus*'s and many of the Flotilla's other officers were quartered. For Ryder this was the best of both worlds. The *Medway* was much more comfortable than a submarine and, with thirty or so junior officers on board, her wardroom had a lively, friendly atmosphere. Yet, at the same time, he had the stimulation of being on a small ship for much of the time. In these congenial surroundings, 'For the first time I made some real friends', among them two young fellow submariner officers from the Flotilla, George Salt and Philip Francis.[9]

Ryder threw himself wholeheartedly into all the amusements that Hong Kong had to offer a young officer. He was well-off, partly because of his submariner's pay and partly because the local currency had recently been devalued, virtually doubling his income. As he told his brother Lisle, 'Everything out here is ridiculously cheap.' A pair of good brown brogues which would have cost 30 shillings in England would be considered expensive at 7s.6d in Hong Kong. Moreover, his duties were far from onerous. Indeed, once *Olympus* began a refit in mid-October Ryder had practically no work: 'It's rather like getting a very diluted 3½ months leave,' he told his mother.[10]

It was a carefree, idyllic existence. Ryder and some brother officers gave a dance in June. The guests danced until nearly midnight, broke off for a treasure hunt before going swimming in Stonecutters' Bay. It was a memorable experience, as the water was 'really phosphorescent, & one swam along in a luminous patch, or splashing one sent out a shower of sparks, it was really very glorious.' Later, drying off, they sat on the bathing platform in the warm night drinking sloe gin and cherry brandy. On occasion youthful high spirits got Ryder into trouble, as when he was caught dropping an orange from a balcony of the Grand Hotel into the bell of a tuba in a brass band playing below. With a large and sociable expatriate community there was ample opportunity for eligible young officers to meet girls. There is a photograph from around this time of Ryder with a girl called Helen Campbell. They look decidedly friendly, although Helen perhaps looks as if she were enjoying the moment rather more than Ryder.

For the young officer Hong Kong was a sporting paradise. Ryder played rugby and hockey, swam and attended race meetings; a contemporary photograph shows him at the races, smartly dressed, very much the young officer around town. But for Ryder, as always, the main sporting attraction of Hong Kong was the wonderful opportunities it afforded for sailing. In early October he and two friends went sailing in a boat called *Tavy II*. It was a memorable weekend: in perfect conditions, with a full moon and a light breeze, they continued sailing by moonlight working their way up an attractive little creek. 'The following day we sailed off to some distant islands & found a little sheltered bay where we bathed in beautifully clear water.'[11]

During the autumn he had a dinghy built in a local shipyard, as he had done when in Malta as a midshipman. It cost £23, a sum equivalent to approximately one month's pay at the time. This gave Ryder even more scope for sailing, enabling him to race regularly – he and a few fellow enthusiasts had founded a dinghy racing club – and to explore the coastline around Hong Kong. As he fondly told his parents, 'I love my little boat, one can't help it: she always comes up to expectations.'[12]

However, by this time Ryder and his two new friends from the Flotilla, George Salt and Philip Francis, were hatching an altogether more ambitious plot: to build a yacht and sail her home to England. The earliest outline of the plan appears in a letter that Ryder wrote to his father on 15 October 1931. Even at this stage a good deal of planning had evidently already been done. Ryder told his father that the total distance would be approximately 14,500 miles taking, he estimated, seven to eight months. He added that it was not proposed to spend more than fourteen days searching for Ganges Island.[13] The yacht, as yet unbuilt, in which this epic voyage half way around the world would be undertaken, would be named *Tai-Mo-Shan*, after the highest peak in Hong Kong.

The plan to investigate Ganges Island originated with Ryder himself. He had noticed while correcting his charts in *Olympus* references to an island and a reef some 600 miles south-east of Japan. This was Ganges Island. As a result of a number of unsuccessful attempts over the previous twenty years to determine the precise position of the island, the charts had been annotated by 1931 'E.D.', for 'Existence Doubtful'. It was decided to include in the plan a proposal to establish definitively the existence or otherwise of the island. As Ryder candidly explained many years later, the reason for this addition to the expedition's plan was 'to elevate the proposal from a pure and undisguised yachting trip', in the hope that it would thereby be more attractive to their superiors.[14]

The proposal to search for Ganges Island has given rise to the glamorously romantic misunderstanding that the crew of the *Tai-Mo-Shan* were in some way involved in spying for British naval intelligence. The notion was elaborated by an article in *Classic Boat* magazine in 2007 and later taken up by a similar piece in *The Times*. The articles claim that the *Tai-Mo-Shan* was involved in a covert mission to visit the Kurile Islands, an archipelago between northern Japan and the southern end of the Kamchatka peninsular. The islands' significance lay in the fact that they were disputed territory between Russia and Japan and of considerable strategic importance; they were later used as the base for the Japanese attack on Pearl Harbor in 1941.

Ryder's planning notes for the expedition do indeed suggest exploring the archipelago as a possible object for the expedition, but more prosaic concerns intervened. The Japanese Foreign Ministry simply refused the *Tai-Mo-Shan* permission to visit the Kurile Islands. Ryder's detailed daily log of the voyage shows clearly that she never visited the islands. Furthermore, the British Commander-in-Chief in Hong Kong ordered the crew to omit the proposed search for Ganges Island, on the grounds that it would risk exposing the *Tai-Mo-Shan* to typhoons. Likewise the log shows that no attempt was made to disobey the Admiral's instructions. Ryder's most likely motive for raising the prospect of exploring the Kurile Islands was the same as his admitted motive for searching for Ganges Island: 'to elevate the proposal from a pure and undisguised yachting trip'. The whiff of espionage adds a dash of glamour to the voyage, but, sadly, it is not borne out by the facts.[15]

But what these proposals do show, however, is the difficulty the young officers thought they would encounter in getting permission from their superiors for the expedition. As Ryder wrote many years later, 'Getting approval was really more difficult than the actual voyage itself.' They had discovered that several previous applications from officers to sail back to England had been refused. The reason for the repeated refusals, it seemed, was that the voyages were to be made in junks, most unsuitable vessels for a round-the-world sea passage. Ryder and his friends, however, had two aces up their sleeves. The first was that George Salt, although young, was well connected: he 'had many friends', Ryder remembered, 'and played squash for the Navy. If anyone could wrangle anything it was George.' The second was Ryder's own experience of ocean racing. I felt, he wrote later,

> that with eight Ocean Races to my credit this would count favourably … I knew more about this kind of voyage than my superiors because few naval officers at that time had any experience of ocean sailing which has now become so commonplace.[16]

With all these considerations in mind, Ryder, Salt and Philip Francis decided that they should submit the most detailed proposals possible to maximize their chances of success. Ryder handed in his application to the commanding officer of HMS *Olympus*, Lieutenant Commander Hooper, on 16 October 1931. At first, Ryder told his mother, he 'asked me if I had gone crazy' but having read the proposal through became 'quite enthusiastic'. '"Well, that's very comprehensive indeed, Ryder", Hooper continued, "& I shall try & push it, and I shall be able to add in my covering letter that you are not altogether without experience in boat sailing, etc. having taken part in several Ocean Races."' As a result of this encounter Ryder's spirits rose: 'I am feeling quite elated.'[17] Salt and Francis put in identical applications.

At this early stage the three recruited a fourth member of the crew, Bertie Ommanney-Davis, of HMS *Bridgwater*, a naval surgeon. With the prospect of long sea passages in the deserted latitudes of the north Pacific, it was a sensible precaution to recruit a naval surgeon. Fortunately, his medical skills were not called upon to any great degree during the year at sea. Ommanney-Davis was distinguished by his mildly eccentric habit of sporting a monocle, even in heavy weather at sea. At twenty-seven he was three years older than Ryder, Salt and Francis.

Meanwhile, the crew's application made its way slowly up the chain of command. Ryder, Salt and Francis had clearly done their best to create a favourable impression among their superiors. On 18 November 1931 the commander of the 4th Submarine Flotilla, Captain H.R. Marrack, forwarded it to the Commander-in-Chief, China Station, remarking that the voyage 'appears to have been worked out in great detail and is considered to be fully feasible.' He added that:

They will have an opportunity for cultivating those essential qualities of practical seamanship, self-reliance and enterprise which the Service no longer offers to young officers, and the experience that they will gain will be of immeasurably greater value to the Service than anything that would come their way in the course of the performance of their ordinary professional duties during their period of one year's general service.

Marrack also took the opportunity to remind the Commander-in-Chief that Ryder had recently been specially commended for the 'zeal and interest' he displayed in navigating *Olympus* from England to China. A fortnight later, on 2 December, the Commander-in-Chief, Sir Howard Kelly, sent the application on to the Admiralty in London for favourable consideration, with a covering letter drawing attention to the 'refreshing' 'spirit of initiative and adventure shown by this application.'[18]

Now that their application had been dispatched to the Admiralty with a fair wind behind it, the crew could start in earnest planning the voyage. Money was, inevitably, the principal stumbling block. Ryder believed that the yacht could be designed and built for around £1,200 and that the expedition's running costs might amount to another £800, for a total cost of around £2,000. This would be met by the sale at cost of the *Tai-Mo-Shan* on arrival in England, that was £1,200. As the combined salaries of the four crew members on half pay in December 1931 would amount to perhaps £600 or £700 over the course of the voyage, they would be left to recoup only £100 through book royalties, the sale of photographs and so on.

At this juncture Ryder was still trying to recruit Oddie, his shipmate from *Olympus*. Oddie, 'with his knowledge of sailing, and his delightful company would be a great asset', with the added advantage that 'he would produce an additional £500'. Ryder was hopeful that he might succeed in persuading Oddie to join the party. 'He [Oddie] thinks it's a splendid scheme & is really very keen to come but his private affairs are the stumbling block, however, I think he will join up all right before long.'[19]

As it turned out, Ryder's optimism was misplaced. At the end of March 1932 Oddie announced that he would not be joining the expedition as it clashed with an important Navy course. For Ryder, anxious to recruit a fifth crew member for both nautical and financial reasons, this was 'a blow of the worst order'. However, at the same time, he heard that Martyn Sherwood, who had been in *Ramillies* with Ryder, was keen to join. Sherwood, visited by Ryder the following day, volunteered at once to join the crew as cook, despite being, at thirty-two and a lieutenant commander, much the oldest and most senior member of the expedition. Ryder was delighted, 'As he is the most amusing and delightful person I know I think it's splendid.' But even with the new recruit, Ryder still had lingering doubts about the expedition's financial soundness, 'Bertie and Martyn may be unable to raise the necessary funds.'[20]

In January 1932 Ryder began to search for a yacht designer; he needed someone who was willing to listen to his client but, most importantly, who would not charge an exorbitant fee. Ryder, the most experienced ocean-going yachtsman in the party, already had firm ideas about the type of boat that would best suit the expedition's needs. 'I am perfectly convinced that what we want is a long lean vessel that can be easily worked by a small crew', he noted. But, naturally, Ryder, who was at this point still only twenty-three, was hesitant about dictating to experienced yacht designers, not least because he did not want to 'end by cramping their style'.

By the end of the month Ryder and his friends had provisionally decided that they would entrust the construction of the yacht to the Hong Kong and Whampoa Dock Co. in Kowloon, whose managing director was a Mr Cock.[21] But before the crew could engage a designer, Ryder and the others needed the Admiralty's go-ahead for the expedition. They had asked the Admiralty to communicate its decision by signal so as to save time. By the middle of January, six weeks after Admiral Kelly had sent the application off to the Admiralty, Ryder was beginning to fret. 'I am waiting patiently to hear if the Admiralty are going to approve of our proposals and expect to hear by signal any day now. If we don't hear before Jan. 26 I think it means that it has been turned down', he told his parents.[22]

He was kept on tenterhooks for another two months until, at the end of March, the long-awaited news arrived out of the blue. As *Olympus* was casting off from HMS *Medway* a signalman leaned over the bridge to make 'S4 to *Olympus* – Admiralty have approved for Lieutenants Ryder, Francis and Salt to find their own way home.' Ryder was thrilled, 'For the rest of the day I was all a twitter.' Although formal confirmation of the Admiralty's decision did not arrive for another three months, Ryder and the others could now safely press on with getting the designs drawn up and the boat built.

At about this time Ryder was introduced to H.S. Rouse. It was to prove an inspired introduction. Rouse was by day an engineer in the Public Works Department but in his spare time an enthusiastic and skilful yachtsman. At the time he was Rear Commodore of the Royal Hong Kong Yacht Club, an influential figure in the local sailing fraternity with a considerable reputation as a yacht designer. He was also a close friend of Mr Cock of the Dockyard Co., an added bonus. On 2 April Ryder met Rouse for the first time and found him 'very keen on the show.' As Ryder later acknowledged, Rouse 'proved to be an incalculable asset.' Indeed, the 'success of the entire voyage was in great measure due to his constant help.'[23]

Things now moved quickly as the party was anxious to get the yacht built as soon as possible to allow the maximum amount of time for working her up before her long voyage. Ryder hoped to be able to persuade his designer and builder 'to dish up the design of some well-tried boat rather than try some scheme or theory of their own.' Two days later Rouse and Ryder met for dinner in order to discuss plans. They decided to base their designs on the lines of the *Dorade*, a new class of ocean-going yacht which had won the previous year's Fastnet race at her first attempt. She was the very latest thing in ocean racing at the time. They agreed on certain modifications to *Dorade*'s lines which Ryder hoped would make his boat better to windward in a strong breeze than *Dorade*, steadier on the helm and easier to heave to.

By the middle of May Ryder had received from Rouse the blue prints of the yacht's proposed lines; he was very pleased. 'I was delighted at the designs you sent up, it is just the type of boat I have had in mind', and asked him and Cock to 'forge ahead'. Ryder had other questions and suggestions to do with the arrangements of the deck fittings and the sail plans but was otherwise content to let Rouse press on.[24] What is striking is Ryder's knowledge, determination and confidence in dealing – on behalf of his friends – with Rouse and Cock, both vastly more experienced in the highly technical business of yacht design. We should not forget that he was still only twenty-four at this point.

While Ryder was refining the plans for the boat with Rouse and Cock, the rest of the crew busied themselves organizing other aspects of the expedition. George Salt was in charge of the finances; only he, Rouse and Cock were signatories of the joint bank account. With many competing demands and a strictly limited budget this was no easy task. Salt was also the ship's bo'sun, responsible for all the supplies and equipment she would need during the long voyage. Bertie Ommanney-Davis, as the ship's doctor, was in charge of mustering the required medical supplies.

Perhaps the most important practical challenge that faced the crew was feeding itself properly at sea for nine months. None of them could cook, so it would have been, as Martyn Sherwood put it, 'somewhat monotonous to live on boiled eggs for the best part of a year.' Sherwood, who had volunteered to join the party as cook, set about remedying this shortcoming. An advertisement appeared in the 'Tuition Wanted' column of the *South China Morning Post*: 'Gentleman requires cooking lessons, evenings four to six.' This caught the eye of a director of the Hong Kong and Shanghai Hotel Group, the owner of the largest hotel in the colony, who promptly invited Sherwood for an interview. 'The results exceeded our wildest expectations', Sherwood wrote, for he and Salt were taught to cook by the Swiss chef who presided over the Peninsular Hotel's kitchens. The tuition had a fiercely practical bent, for the chef had quickly realized that the two sailors would prefer to be 'able to boil a potato satisfactorily than produce a Lobster Meuniere'. Sherwood and Salt (now a cook as well as a sailor) were diligent pupils and were soon able to produce a varied repertoire of dishes without relying excessively on tinned food. Once at sea, almost all the cooking was done in a pressure cooker, a technique they were taught in the hotel's kitchen.[25]

Philip Francis was charged with training himself to operate the wireless set that would be installed on board. This was not a simple task with the primitive – by modern standards – equipment available in the early 1930s, but he was helped by an enthusiastic local amateur radio ham. He and Ryder visited him in November: we 'were both lost in a babble of call signs, [and] remarks like "I should most certainly have a double electrode pentode if I were in your position."' Francis also took responsibility for photography on the voyage and, equipping himself with a good, modern camera, began to practise his technique. That the *Tai-Mo-Shan*'s epic voyage was so well captured on film was almost entirely due to Francis's efforts.[26]

Despite all this extramural activity, all five of the crew had, of course, to continue to fulfil their naval duties. In February 1932, for example, *Olympus* departed Hong Kong for a four-day anti-piracy patrol along the Chinese coast. Piracy was a serious problem in the South China Sea and combating it was one of the Royal Navy's major tasks. In early January 1933 a Danish passenger vessel was hijacked by pirates a few miles out of Hong Kong on passage to Shantou. Three of the wealthier Chinese passengers were seized, taken off on to a waiting junk before being spirited away. A large ransom was then demanded for the release of the captives. This kind of incident was commonplace in Hong Kong waters and was a cause of considerable worry for the crew of the *Tai-Mo-Shan*.[27]

Every summer the Fleet moved 1,200 miles north to Wei Hai Wei to escape the heat and humidity of Hong Kong. Wei Hai Wei was a British naval base (acquired in 1898) on the eastern tip of the Shantung peninsular in northern China. Here the Fleet could carry out sea trials and exercises in comfort, away from the torrid climate of Hong Kong. As Ryder told his parents:

Wei Hai Wei consists of a bay with an island in it … it is to all intents and purposes English. The island is the only place on which one ever lands & it supports a club & a few shops & a 9 hole golf course with facilities for Squash & Tennis. The climate too is delightful & one sleeps under a blanket.[28]

Ryder had spent more than two months there during the summer of 1931; in 1932 *Olympus* had reached Wei Hai Wei by early May. For the crew it was a double-edged sword. It did mean that for long periods of the summer they were mostly together, and therefore able to discuss their plans regularly. On the other hand, it was much more difficult to maintain contact with Rouse and Cock, 1,200 miles away in Hong Kong.

As the summer wore on Ryder was beginning to chafe at the apparent lack of urgency in Hong Kong. He had hoped that the keel of the new boat would be laid down on 17 June, 'but, of course, not – delays – the curse of all expeditions, have begun already.' By early October Ryder, now back in Hong Kong, was at last able to see progress: the contract had been placed with the Whampoa Dockyard Co. and work would start in a few days. The construction of the yacht was expected to take four months. She would be finished by 10 February 1933 at the latest, leaving the crew three-and-a-half months to tune up *Tai-Mo-Shan* for her voyage. Gradually, the large sections of different timbers needed for the yacht arrived at the dockyard: Chinese fir for the masts, teak for the hull, camphor wood and ipol for the frames and yacal for the stern post. The keel was laid in the first week of November and by the end of the month construction was in full swing: 'The frames are now up, and in about a week I hope to see the planking started.'[29]

Ryder was now visiting the yard most evenings after work to inspect the work. By early January the steam-bent frames were installed and the planking complete. As the work progressed, Ryder remained closely involved in refining the design; the displacement of the finished boat, laden for sailing, was one concern, requiring much calculation and recalculation of weights, as was the sail plan. The fact that Ryder was prepared to engage with Rouse, the designer, Cock, the boat builder and the experts in the dockyard speaks volumes for his growing confidence and technical knowledge.

As the *Tai-Mo-Shan* began to assume a more recognizable shape on the stocks, her crew took every opportunity to get in as much sailing as possible. On Boxing Day Francis and Ryder sailed with Rouse in his 8-ton cutter *V and I* in the annual race to Macao and back, a distance of 70 miles. Pleasingly, they won; 'a great triumph' Ryder remarked. 'I think he [Rouse] thoroughly deserves his win as he sails his boat so much better than the others & generally seems to have all the bad luck with the winds.' Rouse had lent the crew *V and I* so that they could go out at night, as did Sherwood in another borrowed boat, *Wanderer*. Towards the end of January, the crew had a race round Hong Kong Island, Sherwood and Salt in *Wanderer* and Ryder in *Norseman*, a 4½-ton yawl. *Norseman* won.[30]

During the Chinese New Year work on the boat came to a halt, much to Ryder's frustration, but by the middle of February it had picked up again. By mid-March, he reckoned that about a month's work remained to complete *Tai-Mo-Shan*. 'This leaves us one month 23 days in which to tune the boat up for its 17,000 mile voyage, instead of six months as we should have had.' Ryder was uncomfortably aware of the maxim that 'fools build boats for wise men to buy', but could only hope that in their case it would not turn out to be true.[31]

On 23 April 1933 – St George's Day – after a final, frenzied burst of activity, *Tai-Mo-Shan* was launched. Ryder was delighted to see, after all the worry about her weight, that she floated well out of the water. After the long months of planning and waiting, it was for most of the crew an exhilarating moment; they were presented with a Blue Ensign by the captain's wife on the *Medway* and toasts were drunk to the success of the voyage. Typically – for he was not a gregarious fellow – Ryder recorded that 'These touching ceremonies unfortunately leave me limp.'[32]

Now that the *Tai-Mo-Shan* was afloat, the finishing touches could be applied and Ryder could reflect upon her genesis. Thanks to Cock she had been built at cost price with the result that 'we are getting a beautifully constructed vessel … at about half the price that it would have cost to build in England.' H.S. Rouse had put in a tremendous amount of unpaid work in his spare time on the boat, 'to him goes the credit for the design'. Ryder himself had played a major part in determining the *Tai-Mo-Shan*'s specification and was justifiably proud of what had been achieved. She had been designed 'for making fast passages over long distances', almost, Ryder believed, 'the first boat to be specifically designed for this.' Most racing yachts were designed to 'suit a rule or formula' but *Tai-Mo-Shan* was 'designed primarily to compete with the weather.' For all that, Ryder was painfully aware that the proof of the pudding lay in the eating. Whether the design was a success, a failure or somewhere in between, 'we will not fully know until we have sailed the boat and weathered some of the severe storms on the way home.'[33]

The one aspect of the design that the crew would live to regret was the decision to dispense with an engine, thereby leaving the boat entirely at the mercy of the winds and currents. In January 1933 Ryder reassured his sister Enid about the reasons for this decision:

> if I thought that we would reduce the time of our passages or increase the element of safety I should certainly install an auxiliary engine, but that the smell, vibration, weight, dirt, lack of reliability, space, and the danger in carrying large quantities of fuel have influenced me against auxiliary engines.[34]

In fact, Ryder was not being entirely straight with his sister. One of the most telling factors in the decision not to fit an engine was money. Engines were expensive and with funds very tight – Ommanney-Davis was unable to raise his full £500 and was compelled to borrow some of his contribution from Ryder – it was an economy that had to be made.

With only a few weeks to go until departure, there was one vital decision yet to be made: who was to command the expedition? This was a question that had been hanging in the air for a long while. Ryder, with some justification on account of his greater experience of ocean sailing, had clearly thought of himself as captain of the expedition from the outset. For example, his diary notes from November 1931, setting out tentative proposals for the allocation of crewing duties, state baldly 'Self – Captain, and in charge of the sailing and navigating of the boat'.[35]

In August 1932 at Wei Hai Wei Ryder had attempted to secure general agreement to his being in command. It was important, he said, that he was able to sail the boat as he thought best without recourse, as far as possible, to general discussions and votes, 'both of which might lead to serious rupture of friendship and disagreement.' He was of the opinion that 'generally the job of leading the expedition should be left to one mind.' This did not go down well with the others. Philip Francis and George Salt both attacked the proposals, Francis 'vigorously'; Martyn Sherwood, on the other hand, backed Ryder's point of view, albeit 'rather tamely', while Ommanney-Davis sat on the fence. All were agreed that it was an important point but, as it was clearly divisive, discussion was deferred until a later date.

However, on 23 May, barely a week before departure, Ryder was still trying to assert his authority as skipper. He remained convinced, and rightly so, that it was not 'possible to run the ship as a soviet.' 'I can count on the wholehearted support of three of the chaps' but not the fourth. It was presumably Philip Francis who continued to question Ryder's right to make all the decisions. This chimes with his sister's view, expressed many years later, that Ryder was the 'self-appointed skipper' of the *Tai-Mo-Shan*.[36] Ryder need not have worried. When, the following day the crew finally brought itself to discuss the question, his authority was confirmed, 'in the end I had everything my way and felt greatly relieved.'[37]

With the question of the captaincy resolved the crew threw themselves into the final, frantic preparations for departure. There was much to be done: stores to be bought and stowed, drinking water to be pumped aboard, the boat's equipment to be prepared and tested. One night the crew worked until 3.00 am bending the sails on to the rigging. But the most important priority was learning to sail the *Tai-Mo-Shan* in so short a time. The crew gradually worked her up, taking her out for longer and longer trips, around Hong Kong harbour and the island. All this hard work had to be carried out in very hot weather: 'Getting a show started at any time is a trying business, but with the tropical heat doubly so.'

With a week to go before departure, Ommanney-Davis finally joined the crew. He 'will fairly have to run around to get ready in time', with all his kit to buy and arrangements to make. As Ryder regarded him as the weakest member of the crew, with the least sailing experience, it was doubly unfortunate that he had missed some of the early practice runs. His first outing in the *Tai-Mo-Shan* took place on 25 May. Meanwhile, the relentless work in uncomfortably hot weather began to take its toll. By the final week Ryder reported that, 'Tempers are short and there is a general air of unrest with the crew.' The last thing Ryder wanted at this late stage was a mutiny; he could only hope that tempers would improve once they were under way.[38]

The date of the *Tai-Mo-Shan*'s departure from Hong Kong was a nice question of timing. The plan was to set off at the end of May as the first breaths of the south-west monsoon arrived in Hong Kong waters. This, it was hoped, would give the *Tai-Mo-Shan* a good start up the coast of China towards Japan before the typhoons associated with the monsoon could catch up and cause trouble. A later start would run the risk of encountering the typhoons.

Although the departure date had been set for the end of May, the crew tried their utmost to keep it and their sailing plans a secret. This was partly because of the Navy's traditional reticence – it was not known as the 'Silent Service' for nothing – and partly because the crew were anxious not to publicize their intentions for fear of making fools of themselves. As Ryder had noticed during a visit to the yacht club a year earlier, 'It is indeed amazing the number of fellows who were going to sail home, in fact have even got as far as the design and have then cancelled it.' 'I hope we don't join this crowd', was his only wish. But the most important reason for keeping their departure date and plans under wraps was the threat of piracy. The incident involving the Danish steamer already referred to was fresh in the memory, but another recent episode had starkly underlined the threat posed by the pirates. David Luce, then a Lieutenant Commander and a fellow submariner (later to serve with Ryder in Combined Operations during the war and rise to be First Sea Lord in the 1960s), had been kidnapped for ransom by pirates from a passenger steamer. The kidnap of a fellow officer was a grim reminder of the dangers lurking off the coast of China.[39]

To the crew's great annoyance, and despite their best efforts, news of their ambitious plans had already leaked into the press. In the middle of January an article about the voyage had appeared in the local press as a result of Martyn Sherwood's winning a race round Hong Kong Island. By the end of the month Ryder knew that the story had been picked up by the British press, too. '[S]o now the secret is properly out', he complained gloomily, 'we must expect to see some pretty good rot written about it and ourselves.' This was merely a foretaste of the interest that the voyage was to excite in the months to come.[40]

By the end of May the crew were longing to get away: 'This hanging about gets on everyone's nerves.' In the last week the crew attended four farewell parties and wrote their final letters home. With the final preparations coming to completion, everything was now ready. On 29 May the crew began keeping a close watch on the weather. The following day the wind was in the wrong quarter, but by the evening the forecast had improved: the weather for 31 May looked set fair, so the decision was made. The *Tai-Mo-Shan* would sail the following day at eleven o'clock in the morning.[41]

Chapter 4

The Voyage of the *Tai-Mo-Shan* (1933–34): Japan, the North Pacific and the United States

Tai-Mo-Shan slipped her mooring in Kowloon harbour at 1.30 pm on 31 May 1933, waved off from the quayside by a handful of friends and the staff of the Whampoa Dock Co. The morning had been spent hectically stowing the final stores and making innumerable last-minute adjustments to the boat's equipment and rigging. 'At last we are under way', wrote a relieved Ryder, as the difficulties of the last few weeks slipped astern in the breeze.

Tai-Mo-Shan's passage from Hong Kong to England has been described as 'one of the greatest blue water voyages of the inter-war years'.[1] It was a remarkable achievement, given the youth of the crew – Ryder, Salt and Francis were only 25 years old when they set off, Ommanney-Davis 28 and Sherwood 33 – and the fact that they had chosen to sail 'the wrong way round' the world, that is, against the prevailing winds, without an engine as insurance. Although they were all Naval officers, all young, spirited and adventurous, Ryder was the only one of the five who had had any worthwhile experience of ocean sailing. Added to that the fact that they were sailing a largely untried vessel of experimental form, gives one an idea of the magnitude of what they did.

The first leg of the voyage took them from Hong Kong north to Keelung, a port on the north-eastern corner of the island of Taiwan, or Formosa, as it was then known. Once out at sea, all the stress and irritation of the last, hectic, hot, few weeks evaporated. On the very first day at sea Ryder recorded in his log: 'Crew appear in [the] best of spirits, especially George, who is singing at the wheel at the moment.' The passage, which lasted five days and six hours, was a gentle baptism of fire for the crew. They enjoyed one excellent day's run in which they covered 195 miles – 'very encouraging' thought Ryder, but on two of the other days she managed only around 50 miles. Sherwood was badly seasick at the start but gradually acclimatized, while Ommanney-Davis had his first casualty to deal with when Francis slipped on deck, cutting his arm. Rounding the north point of Taiwan during the evening of 6 June in a force 7 wind, the crew had their first chance to try out the oilskins. We 'found them a great success', Ryder noted. Just after dark they sailed into Keelung, dropping anchor in Sendo Wan.[2]

At seven o'clock the following morning the crew received 'a tremendous ovation from the Japs' who came to welcome them. While the crew filled in countless forms, the officials drank whisky and Klim, a brand of powdered milk. When *Tai-Mo-Shan* visited Taiwan the island had been part of the Japanese empire since 1895; its officials kept a friendly but strict eye on the British yacht and her crew. While the rest of the crew were invited to visit the island's governor, Ryder remained on board 'under very close surveillance'.

After two days at Keelung, the crew bade farewell to their Japanese hosts and set sail for Yokohama, a port in Tokyo Bay, half way up the eastern side of Japan. The second leg of the voyage was, at an estimated 1,100 miles, about twice the length of the passage from Hong Kong to Taiwan. The first day's run from Keelung was poor: only 67 miles. However, the following day the breeze freshened resulting in a much more satisfactory run of 175 miles. For the next three days, in calm conditions, *Tai-Mo-Shan* made indifferent progress despite picking up the Kuro Shiwo current, which gave her an extra 20 miles a day.

Despite this slow progress, there was much to do and to admire. Passing the Pinnacle Islands, a large number of seabirds, mostly boobies and petrels, came close to the boat. The boobies, Ryder observed, were 'magnificent great birds of the gannet tribe ... but very foolish one is led to believe.' The calm conditions allowed the crew to bathe for the first time, enabling Sherwood to catch a Portuguese man o' war. The unfortunate creature was hauled aboard for inspection: 'quaint little things', thought Ryder. Nor was the calm weather wasted; on a sailing boat there is always work to be done, re-stowing ropes, mending rigging and making things shipshape. But there was time too for relaxation. 'This is a lazy life', wrote Ryder, 'we gently drift along, gramophone going, fishing lines out, periodically eating gigantic meals prepared by Martyn.'

Indeed, Sherwood, having now overcome his seasickness, was getting into his stride in the galley. A week out of Keelung he cooked 'a most wizardly' three-course dinner for the crew: cream soup, fish cakes and a pudding of oatcakes and golden syrup, which made 'the most excellent eating'. The standard of the cuisine was so high that Ryder was moved to observe that 'We have certainly fed better on this trip than any other boat I have sailed in, including ... the *Jolie Brise*.' All those hours in the kitchens of the Peninsular Hotel were now paying dividends. In rougher conditions the crew ate their food sitting on the cabin floor, each from his own large, china pudding bowl, 'our most treasured possessions', said Ryder. Food at sea he found very comforting: 'the feeling of a full stomach seems to offset the wet and later on the cold.'

By 18 June, after ten days at sea, the crew were starting to get excited about the prospect of arriving at Yokohama. *Tai-Mo-Shan* arrived off the breakwater outside Yokohama harbour at noon on 20 June, to be greeted by a launch full of reporters and press photographers, who, quaintly, filed their copy by carrier pigeon released from the launch. *Tai-Mo-Shan* was then towed to the quarantine berth where local officials came aboard. The crew were armed with a formal letter of introduction in Japanese, with an English translation, and signed by the Emperor's Foreign Minister; but this did not entirely quell the suspicions of local officialdom as to the purpose of *Tai-Mo-Shan*'s visit. It was difficult, with the language barrier, to get across the fact that the voyage was for pleasure. The Japanese were at a loss to understand this since, as Ryder remarked years later, 'We had no women on board and nothing to drink.' To them, spying seemed the only probable purpose of the journey. Eventually, after much sucking of teeth, the officials appeared satisfied and departed, having made several ineffectual attempts to seal up the cameras and the boxes of ammunition on board.[3] The Japanese 'obviously thought we were spies', Ommanney-Davis told a journalist from *The Times* ten years later. 'We were not, of course, but I don't deny we were interested in all we saw.'[4]

Once the formalities had been completed, *Tai-Mo-Shan* was towed to a better anchorage near the public gardens and the New Grand Hotel. Now the crew were free to explore all the delights that Japan had to offer. Sherwood and Ommanney-Davis went to Nikko whence they travelled up into the mountains by funicular railway, while Ryder visited Tokyo. There was time, too, for a little lotus-eating. They were given lunch by the British Naval Attaché in Tokyo, by the local yacht club and, for the first time, entertained on board *Tai-Mo-Shan*. The highlight of their stay, however, was a banquet given in their honour by the Japanese Master Mariners' Association. Sherwood recalled that 'five beautiful Geisha girls attended to the wants of each of us during the meal. They were certainly most efficient at refilling the glasses of sake.' Looking back on the evening, Ryder remarked drily, 'Nor were we the first to discover how friendly the women were.' 'It was', he concluded, 'perhaps as well that we had to press on with our voyage.'[5]

The *Tai-Mo-Shan* left Yokohama on 2 July. Even among this adventurous crew there were backward glances and, perhaps, not just at the geisha girls. As Ryder recorded in the log as Tokyo Bay slipped astern, the crew

are a little wistful – we seem to have made friends quickly, who entertained us well and turned out in force to give us a send-off. We have now put the fleshpots behind us for 100-odd days, and the realization of this gives one a strange affection for civilization, which I have never before experienced.

Nemuro, their next port of call, was a small fishing port on the northern island of Hokkaido. It would have been at this point in the voyage that *Tai-Mo-Shan* forged 600 miles or so out into the Pacific in search of Ganges Island, one of the objectives included in the original plan. However, in early April, two months before their departure from Hong Kong, the crew had been summoned by the new Commander-in-Chief, Sir Frederick Dreyer. He suggested that the proposed search for Ganges Island be abandoned for two reasons. First, the Japanese, by instituting an aerial search for the island, had disproved its existence and, secondly, that the timing of the diversion would necessitate *Tai-Mo-Shan* exposing herself needlessly to the risk of typhoons. The crew were happy to accept the Commander-in-Chief's advice.

The passage north to Nemuro was slow; on 9 July the boat managed only 12 miles in the whole day. There was also a good deal of fog which made navigation difficult. Becalmed and bored the crew amused themselves taking potshots at passing birds and porpoises. Francis managed to shoot an Arctic skua and another bird later identified as a Wilson's petrel, 'a very graceful little bird rather like a swallow with a white rump and yellow webs to its otherwise black feet', Ryder noted. Less successful was the first attempt to use the boat's harpoon: Sherwood fired it – presumably at a porpoise – but the ring gave way so the harpoon became separated from its line and sank. It 'now lies at 3,000 fathoms', Ryder noted, '… but we still have two left.'

Ryder also began a bracing early morning routine on this leg of the voyage: taking a seawater shower. He and Francis would throw buckets of water over one another. They began doing it on a sunny morning while the boat was still in the warm Kuro Siwo current; on a foggy morning in waters chilled by the Oya Siwo current, it was a different proposition. But Ryder was a hardy type: 'Certainly one feels on top of the world as one faces breakfast with a real glow on after a hard towelling.'

The approach to Nemuro was hazardous, particularly at night and in the foggy conditions that were likely to prevail in the area. Unsure of her precise position and shrouded in dense fog, the crew nosed through the narrow channel, past the shoals and reefs, into the harbour, mooring just after dawn on 10 July.

Nemuro was not an attractive place, 'taking its tone from the greyness of the fog', Ryder decided. The houses were wooden bungalows with slate and tin roofs, 'drab in the extreme'. The local customs officials once again took a close, if incompetent, interest in *Tai-Mo-Shan*, her crew and their equipment. Ryder and the crew stayed only four days in Nemuro before setting off on the most desolate leg of their voyage, across the northern Pacific to Attu, the westernmost of the Aleutian Islands.

The first seven days of the passage to Attu were marred by light winds, calm and fog. Ryder was tempted to put into one of the little harbours of Shikotan, one of the more southerly of the Kurile Islands, but, as they had been specifically refused permission to visit the islands, the risk of the boat being impounded was too great. Ryder's daily log of the voyage shows conclusively that they did not visit any of the Kurile Islands, let alone attempt any espionage or information gathering for the Admiralty during her passage past the archipelago.

After a week of drifting along in the fog, often in the company of whales, the wind at last picked up. On 25 July the wind reached force 4 for the first time since Yokohama so *Tai-Mo-Shan* began to make better progress. On 27 July the boat was overtaken by the tail end of a typhoon, so Ryder decided to heave to for the night to ride out the storm. How she would behave in such circumstances was an unknown quantity, but in the event Ryder was 'very impressed with her sense of comfort and security' in the rough weather.

On 30 July they picked up the snowy peaks of Attu in the distance, but soon afterwards the wind dropped and the fog descended once more. Unable to risk approaching land in thick fog, the *Tai-Mo-Shan* hove to to await an improvement in conditions. For nearly twenty-four hours they waited until, at 12.30 on 31 July, the fog suddenly rolled away to reveal the 3,000 foot peaks of Attu about 8 miles away. 'The brightness of everything after the fog was surprising', but the island looked spectacular, its bold, rugged coastline, snow-capped peaks and fog-filled ravines towering over the white-crested blue sea. 'No artist', Ryder knew, 'could have painted the picture before us.'

Chigahoff Harbour, the only settlement on Attu, had in 1933 an indigenous population of forty-nine and an American fur-trader from San Francisco called Fred Schroder, who also kept a small store in the village. The island's sole industry was the trapping of blue foxes for their fur. There were only nine houses here, their white walls and bright red roofs giving the impression of a model village. At one end was a square-towered church; at the other a new school building. Above the picturesque village the lower ridges of the mountains were covered with wild flowers, the higher ones with the remains of the winter's snow. Down at sea level flocks of puffins swooped over the water, the evening sunshine glinting off their coloured bills. It had much to recommend it to the yachtsman, too: 'This really is the most wonderful little anchorage' enthused Ryder.

Having listened to Fred talking about sea conditions in the Aleutian Islands, Ryder and the crew decided to revise their sailing plans. 'He strongly advised us not to sail along them as the gales and fogs, tide rips and currents make it hazardous even for steamers', Ryder recorded. Coming from a man who had spent a lifetime in the islands, this was good advice. *Tai-Mo-Shan* would sail direct across the Bering Sea, giving the islands' dangerous coastlines a wide berth.

Having made this decision, Ryder and Ommanney-Davis then set about surveying Holtz Bay, an inlet adjacent to Chigahoff Harbour. They spent two days surveying the bay, fixing the height and position of the more prominent features and taking soundings of the depth of the water in order to chart the anchorage. As cartographers and explorers often do, they named the bay's features after their own: hence, Ryder's chart has '*Tai-Mo-Shan* River', 'Davis Hill' and 'George's Knob'. The surviving notes reveal the painstaking attention to detail that went into the survey. The finished version of the chart is a neat, impeccably accurate piece of cartography, showing Ryder's burgeoning talent – no doubt inherited from his father – for surveying and map-making.

While conducting the survey Ryder was in his element. The wild, desolate landscape stirred his soul:

Viewing these snow-capped mountains over the blue water, with some covered in cloud, was to me a never-ending source of wonder, and seemed to hold one's gaze and conjure up all the photographs one has seen of Spitzbergen or South Georgia and the various polar expeditions.

That night he and Ommanney-Davis camped out under the stars at the head of the bay. The simple pleasures of camping, of self-sufficiency and self-reliance, of a feeling of being at one with nature, appealed deeply to Ryder.

> A glorious evening with the moon shining over the snowy hills, a blazing camp fire, a heap of drift wood to keep it going, our two selves with our heads protruding out of our sleeping bags ... and our pipes drawing evenly, made us realize what a great game all this is and how lucky we were.

While on Attu the crew discovered that puffin made very good eating, a welcome addition to their tinned provisions. One day Ryder and Ommanney-Davis managed to shoot three birds – albeit by firing no fewer than sixty rounds of ammunition – and trap two more. Sherwood, once he had discovered how to pluck them, then cooked the birds. 'They made the most excellent stew', he reported, 'and were not in the least fishy, having a taste resembling calf's liver.' Ryder declared puffin 'a real delicacy.'[6]

Now it was time for them to leave Attu for the voyage across the Bering Sea to their next port of call, Dutch Harbor, an American port in Unalaska. So far, the voyage had gone well, almost better than anyone could have hoped. As Ryder told his father, 'We feed like fighting cocks & are thriving on the cooler weather. Remarkably little quarrelling or bickering so far.' He added that 'I have a fine red beard at the moment.' As all his shipmates called him 'Red', he was now growing into his nickname.[7] Having replenished the boat's watertanks from a mountain stream, the crew weighed anchor at six o'clock in the morning of 10 August. As *Tai-Mo-Shan*, with a fresh westerly breeze pushing her along at 9 knots, headed on a wide semi-circular course for Unalaska, Attu disappeared astern in the mists and fogs of the Bering Sea.

The first three days at sea, with a gale blowing, were rough. As a result they sped along – on 12 August she did 171 miles – but the crew suffered badly from seasickness, all of them, that is, bar the skipper. 'Ryder was one of those amazing and fortunate people who remain quite unmoved however violent the motion', remembered Sherwood.[8] Although they were making good progress, the conditions were most dispiriting: 'The most cheerless place imaginable at the moment', Ryder recorded, cold, dank and foggy. Even Ryder, who had a deep affinity for the world's wilder, emptier spaces, felt isolated in these northern latitudes, 'one of the loneliest and most desolate seas of the world.'

Having made landfall on the north-west coast of Unalaska, *Tai-Mo-Shan* rounded Cape Cheerful, 'a most imposing sight.' The wind whipped round the tall black cliffs and down the gullies in violent squalls, blowing spray off the sea like sand. Cataracts of water cascaded hundreds of feet off the cliffs into the sea. Overhead, a host of seabirds wheeled and soared, 'their weird cries blending magnificently' with the storm. Once the boat had rounded Cape Cheerful, she sailed into the calm, blue, sunny waters of Unalaska Bay, mooring at a jetty off Uninlink Village. Looking back, the crew could see the gloom and murk from which they had so recently emerged. Cape Cheerful was well named.

'This is a most interesting place', noted Ryder, 'forming what might be termed the Singapore of the Bering Sea.' All ships visiting the Bering Sea and the Arctic Ocean stopped here, dropping off traders, trappers and prospectors bound for Alaska or the Aleutian Islands. It was the headquarters of the local US Coast Guard and, when *Tai-Mo-Shan* visited, the base of the Aleutian Survey Expedition. This far corner of the United States had a colourful history.

All these places, of course, witnessed tremendous activity in the days of the gold rush and now have many empty and deserted wooden shacks. Dutch Harbor is now completely deserted. The hurriedly built saloons and bars after riotous evenings of gambling and drunkenness, are silent testimonies of their heyday.

The crew were warmly welcomed by the Americans who quickly realized that Ryder and his men were urgently in need of baths after a week at sea in rough weather. Thereafter the Americans entertained their guests royally. After an amusing and restful week with the Coast Guards, the crew set off for Victoria, British Columbia, on 23 August. Laden with presents of fresh fruit, meat and vegetables from their new friends, they were towed out of Uninlink Harbour into a dead calm. On the second day out, *Tai-Mo-Shan* progressed only 2 miles. As Ryder remarked ruefully, 'beautiful sunny weather, just the stuff for bathing but no use to us.'

The first hazard awaiting *Tai-Mo-Shan* once the wind got up and she left Unalaska Bay was the passage from the Bering Sea to the Pacific. There was a choice of three passes to the east of Dutch Harbor: Akutan, Unalaga or Unimak Pass. All three were notorious for dangerously strong tides; sailing vessels were well advised to seek a tow through to the Pacific beyond. As the wind seemed favourable, Ryder decided to attempt the pass at Akutan. It was not a comfortable experience.

Nightfall saw us half-way through, being drifted back. With land all round us and a current reputed to run at 6 or 7 knots, we felt anything but happy. Unfortunately there was no wind, there was not much to be done except contemplate the possibilities of kedging.

By morning, the boat having drifted back into the Bering Sea, they decided to attempt Unimak Pass. Shortly after midday on 26 August the weather cleared, the sun came out and, best of all, a fresh northerly breeze sprang up. This was just what the *Tai-Mo-Shan* needed; with this breeze she reached through the pass at a spanking 7 knots and out into the Pacific. It had been a nasty moment, the first time on the voyage when the lack of an engine had seriously threatened the crew's safety. There had been previous occasions when the lack of an engine had been an inconvenience; for example, when they were becalmed; or an embarrassment, as when *Tai-Mo-Shan* ran aground on a mud bank coming in to Uninlink Bay in front of their American hosts. But this was the first time that it had posed a significant risk to vessel and crew.

For much of the 1,200 miles to Victoria the crew experienced splendid sailing conditions, with good reaching winds driving *Tai-Mo-Shan* along at 8 or 9 knots. On 5 September she covered 190 miles in the day, encouraging Ryder to hope that she might manage a 200-mile day. Even when progress was more sedate, life on board had its advantages.

> During this light weather the evenings are very pleasant. It is just cold enough to have the cabin stove on (49°F). After a good dinner we sit around with our mugs of coffee and pipes, listening to the wireless which is now coming through very well. Pleasant company and pleasant surroundings more than compensate for a slow passage.

Since entering the Pacific, *Tai-Mo-Shan*'s wireless, now expertly operated by Philip Francis, had been able to receive American radio stations. The first broadcast the boat's wireless picked up was from Oakland, California. It was playing 'Who's Afraid of the Big Bad Wolf?', a song they were to hear many more times during their voyage down the west coast of America.[9]

But with a good wind the sailing was exhilarating. 'Alone on the blue cresting sea', *Tai-Mo-Shan* sometimes did

> her nine knots with an ease and grace that is delightful to watch, at other times heeled over to a gust with water surging across her lee deck in a white turmoil of foam, even bubbling over into the companion. Then as she lifts the water pours back into the sea in little cascades …

At night 'the whole scene is bathed in moonlight and the wet decks glisten with a cold light.' Below deck, however, moonlit serenity was notably absent. The constant heeling over of the boat had deposited a thick sludge of porridge and tomato soup on the cabin floor, while the radio, blithely oblivious to the surrounding chaos, continued to thump out advertisements for Alka-Seltzer or emulsion paint.

After five good days, the wind slackened on 8 September, restricting them to a mere 35 miles. By the following day *Tai-Mo-Shan* was nearing the entrance to the Strait of Juan de Fuca, on the approach to Victoria. Frustratingly, becalmed and fog-bound, it took another three days to get there. On 10 September the boat managed only 6 miles in the day. Approaching Victoria in thick fog the crew endured several anxious moments from passing ships. One in particular, seemingly oblivious to *Tai-Mo-Shan*'s foghorn, came uncomfortably close, her lights towering above the yacht in the foggy gloom. Having survived these alarms, the *Tai-Mo-Shan* moored in Victoria harbour at noon on 12 September.

Tai-Mo-Shan was at Victoria for a fortnight while her crew enjoyed a break from the rigours of sailing the high seas. Salt and Francis visited Banff, while Ryder and the others remained in Victoria, where they stayed in the Royal Canadian Navy's barracks at Esquimalt. During her stay in Esquimalt *Tai-Mo-Shan* was, thanks to the generosity of the owner of Yarrow's shipyard, given a free overhaul, including having her hull repainted. Sherwood also took the opportunity to have a modern, gas-fired stove installed to replace the somewhat primitive Chinese equipment installed in Hong Kong.[10]

The crew found on their arrival in Victoria that they had, perhaps not surprisingly, become minor celebrities. They had, after all, crossed the Pacific in a small yacht, sailing more than 6,000 miles in the process; moreover, they were young, personable, good looking and British to boot. Ryder told his sister Enid:

> We are living in the R.C.N. mess here at Esquimalt B.C. & dine out or go to parties most nights & find ourselves very much in the public eye, till one gets tired of telling the same yarn over and over again ... Then one is continually showing people over the boat or competing with press reporters till one feels quite fed up. In the States of course it will be far worse.[11]

It was not just the unwanted attentions of the press that Ryder found wearing. He recalled being buttonholed by old ladies saying, 'I think you are so brave, you must come and have tea with us.' 'A necessary qualification for the ordeal', he concluded drily. He was also dragooned into giving a speech to a gathering of yachtsmen and delivered a lecture on 'Deep Sea Sailing' to the United Services Institute of Vancouver Island. True to character, Ryder grumbled to his sister, 'How one would like to do this sort of thing on the quiet. Petty fame I assure you is no joy.'

There was a lighter side to their stay in Victoria, away from press interviews, lectures and tea with old ladies. They were invited to a number of parties 'of a very amusing nature'. Here Ryder and the others noticed a marked difference between the chaperoned formality they were accustomed to at home and the more relaxed attitudes prevailing in British Columbia. 'The fairer sex here are a great institution and force back the beer in large quantities so that much amusement may be had by the passing opportunist.'[12]

After two weeks in Victoria, it was time to press on towards California and the Panama Canal. On 27 September *Tai-Mo-Shan* slipped her moorings, leaving Victoria 'with genuine regret'. The voyage south to San Francisco was an easy passage, with light winds, calm seas, fine, sunny days and moonlit nights. 'In this beautiful weather', Ryder confided to the log, making leisurely though steady progress, one has no worries, and feels at peace with all and sundry. It would be difficult to devise a more perfect existence. One can truthfully say that one envies no man.

However, even in this idyllic interlude, there was a tiny, almost invisible cloud on the horizon. 'Already the sneaking realization that the voyage is nearly half completed', Ryder wrote, meant that 'the time is now not far distant when we shall have to earn our livings once again.' During the evening of 6 October *Tai-Mo-Shan* sailed through the Golden Gate into San Francisco Bay, passing as she did so the foundations of the famous bridge, then under construction.

On the second day, *Tai-Mo-Shan* was offered a berth at the St Francis Yacht Club. This was a well-appointed establishment, with a fine view across the bay towards the Golden Gate and excellent facilities. The crew were very impressed by the club's 'complete little harbour with its own lighthouse, jetties and pens for the yachts.' *Tai-Mo-Shan*, however, looked out of place in the grand surroundings; 'a regular windjammer', her skipper thought, 'among the fleet of white and spotless yachts moored there.'

Their first visitors were journalists looking for a story. After their experience of the press in Victoria they were advised to prepare a straightforward, factual statement about the voyage. This they did; it seemed to do its job as the reporters, Sherwood remembered, were 'well satisfied'. The crew also made themselves available for photographs. A photograph appeared in the *San Francisco Examiner* of Ryder, Ommanney-Davis and Sherwood, under the caption 'On Daring Adventure'. Most pictures of the crew taken during the voyage are of all five of them posing on deck in sailing gear, shorts, rumpled shirts and deck shoes. In the *Examiner*'s picture the three crew members are smartly dressed for a night on the town, blazers, ties and cufflinks, hair slicked back, big smiles and lit cigarettes. Ommanney-Davis is sporting his monocle.[13]

Once *Tai-Mo-Shan* was securely berthed the crew could concentrate on sight-seeing and enjoying themselves. San Francisco made a lasting impression on the young British officers: they saw sky-scrapers for the first time and were amazed to find that 'the streets are so steep that you hardly walk up them without slipping down.' They had time for squash, a round or two of golf and the odd trip out into the country.[14]

In fact, the crew hardly had a moment to themselves: 'We have been so well entertained ... [in] San Francisco that [even] letter writing was out of the question.' They were invited to 'an incredible number' of parties. One of the crew confessed that 'I have attended more cocktail parties in 'Frisco than the rest of my life put together.' When they arrived in America, prohibition was about to be lifted; after 14 years it would once again be legal to drink alcohol. Much of the nation seemed to be straining at the leash, as Ryder and the others soon found out. 'The repeal of the 18th amendment is expected in a month or two & America is no longer pretending to be dry so that we came in for the first flush.'[15]

After ten memorable days in San Francisco, *Tai-Mo-Shan* departed for Los Angeles on 16 October. She sailed at noon on a Sunday, 'the fashionable hour' according to Ryder, seen off by a crowd of some thirty or forty people and escorted out of the Golden Gate by eight yachts. As when setting sail from Yokohama, Dutch Harbor and Victoria, the crew felt a certain wistfulness at departure.

> We left San Francisco with sadness as we had quickly acquired quite a circle of friends who all turned out to send us on our way with gifts of candy fruit cakes, etc., & waved a farewell to us off the jetty as we sailed out of the yacht harbour.

But in this instance there was a consolation: they were going to Hollywood. Francis, writing home from San Francisco, was evidently looking forward to the pleasures that lay ahead. The 'next time you hear from me', he wrote, 'I shall probably have Greta Garbo sitting on my knee!!'[16]

The passage down the Californian coast to Los Angeles was the shortest leg of the entire journey – no more than 300 miles as the crow flies – but with persistently light winds it nevertheless took the best part of seven days. Although progress was slow, the weather was good, which gave the crew a chance to work on the boat, to write letters, read and reflect on events. Two days after leaving San Francisco, Ryder was still 'sore at putting behind me what will probably be the happiest week of my life.'

> Although one has had more fun and excitement elsewhere, they have always been attended by worries of one sort or another. At S.F. everything went better than we had hoped. We stayed with the most delightful people who arranged parties for us every day ... We were able to put the boat into better trim than ever before. Settled weather on the next run, no worries about storms; the future prospect of Los Angeles; the sense of something achieved in crossing the Pacific; successfully avoiding publicity and speeches; tentative offers to buy the boat; they all made our stay in San Francisco one of the most pleasant recollections of my life.

By 21 October – Trafalgar Day – frustration was beginning to set in: 'Exasperating weather for sailing', Ryder wrote; '23 miles to Hollywood and it's Saturday night tonight.' But there was nothing he could do about the lack of wind. *Tai-Mo-Shan* eventually drifted into the harbour at San Pedro early in the morning of 22 October.

As in San Francisco, among the first visitors to *Tai-Mo-Shan* were the local journalists. Both the *Los Angeles Examiner* and the *Los Angeles Times* were eager for the story. The *Examiner* reported one of the crew saying that the voyage was undertaken 'just for a lark'. The *Times* told its readers that the voyage 'has so far been a unique mixture of battles against light and contrary winds, fogs, adverse currents and gales.' The papers carried similar photographs of the crew posing on *Tai-Mo-Shan*'s deck in yachting kit.[17]

The press disposed of, Ryder and the others were greatly looking forward to sampling the delights of Los Angeles and Hollywood. They were not disappointed. Their pockets crammed with letters of introduction, they threw themselves into Hollywood society. Ryder told his parents that:

> We are having a hectic time here – parties one after the other real Hollywood style. We seem to flit from house to house in Beverly Hills in high powered cars most of the time consuming large quantities of cocktails & every now & then posing alongside some film star for a photograph.[18]

To his log he was franker, admitting that some of the evenings were most amusing, others very drunken but all exhausting. 'America being a dry country', he wrote, 'liquor plays a very important part.'

Like many tourists, they were given tours of the more famous film studios, Metro-Goldwyn-Mayer, Fox, RKO and Warner Brothers, where they saw films in production – 'every sort from Tarzan to those stupid dramas or semi comedies one knows so well.' At Fox they were treated to a private screening of *Cavalcade*, a recent film partly set in London. As some of the film's scenery was still standing in the studio, the crew were able to pose in front of Nelson's Column. During the visit to the MGM studios, the first prop Ryder noticed, much to his amusement, was a copy of *King's Regulations & Admiralty Instructions*, the standing orders that governed every detail of life in the Royal Navy. At Warner Brothers, the boys were photographed with a languid, smoky-eyed Bette Davis. They did meet a number of well-known Hollywood figures during their stay, as Ryder, rather less than breathlessly, told his parents:

> The only real stars we were introduced to were John Barrymore, Wheeler & Woolsey, Maureen O'Sullivan a very charming girl & very easy to look at; We had one or two parties with the Talmadge sisters; we meet a large number of lesser stars, names one has vaguely heard such as Heather Angel, Florence Desmond, Madge Evans etc.

On the whole, he thought, they were very ordinary. So much for the star dust of Hollywood.[19]

Overall, Ryder was impressed with Los Angeles, 'a remarkable place', owing its existence to 'Oil and Films: the latter ruling the roost.' He was less enamoured of the gossipy, superficial chatter that seemed to be the staple diet of Hollywood life: 'actors and actresses are everywhere the first talk.' If he does not know the films or stars in question the visitor 'out of politeness to his hostess ... refrains from showing his ignorance or indifference.' Likewise, Ryder found that 'the conversation the next morning is monotonous ... the previous evening holds the field until the day is well advanced.'

So it might have been with some relief, at least to Ryder, never the most sociable of men, when the time came for *Tai-Mo-Shan* to continue her voyage. While in Los Angeles Martyn Sherwood had met Larry Kent, a leading actor and keen yachtsman. Kent, who owned *Audacious*, a large yacht with an auxiliary engine, wanted to accompany *Tai-Mo-Shan* as far as Acapulco and to visit Mexico City from there. The advantage for *Tai-Mo-Shan* in this arrangement was that *Audacious* would tow her in periods of calm. After the frustrations of the passages down the west coast from Victoria, this was an appealing prospect, although Ryder later, somewhat churlishly, claimed that 'this was the last thing that the rest of us wanted.'[20]

Chapter 5

The Voyage of the *Tai-Mo-Shan* (1933–34): Central America, the West Indies and Home

So it was that on 1 November 1933 *Tai-Mo-Shan* was towed out of San Pedro harbour by *Audacious*. Ryder and the boys had been showered with presents by well-wishers: whisky, chocolates, tobacco and food. Once clear, the crew hoisted the sails and steered south for Acapulco. With a fair wind in her sails, *Tai-Mo-Shan* soon had *Audacious* trailing far behind, 'a great triumph', thought Ryder. By evening, however, the wind had subsided; in due course, *Audacious*, cruising on her motor, caught up with *Tai-Mo-Shan* and took her in tow.

Audacious went on ahead, leaving *Tai-Mo-Shan* to make her own way south to an agreed rendezvous. Each morning the sun rose above the coast of Lower California, an 'arid, mountainous desert ... [v]ery blue and purple in the distance and rather alluring.' They enjoyed some more beautiful weather, too. One night particularly stuck in the memory.

> [T]he mountains of Cerros Island floodlit by the moon ahead, looking deserted and mysterious; the seals gambolling around our stern, making the sea phosphorescent with their splashes.

After an abortive attempt to rendezvous with *Audacious* at Cerros Island, *Tai-Mo-Shan* continued south at a leisurely rate, the California Current helping to compensate for the generally light winds. On 9 November, as *Tai-Mo-Shan* was for once running on a reaching wind, the port upper cross-tree suddenly snapped. This could have been disastrous but for prompt action by the helmsman in bringing her round into the wind and by the crew in hauling down the big 'ballooner' sail, which saved the top mast. Although immediate disaster was averted, the accident did reduce the boat's speed until the damage could be repaired.

As *Tai-Mo-Shan* sailed south the marine life became more interesting. On 5 November the crew saw their first shark swimming ahead of the boat and ten days later their first turtle. At one point a large shark swam close under the boat's counter, so close that the crew were able to examine its escorting pilot fish. There were three of these little fish about 6 to 8 inches ahead of the tip of the shark's nose. The following day, bored with their slow progress, the crew sighted three turtles, apparently in 'rather a compromising position'. 'Not waiting', Ryder wrote, 'to ascertain what particular perversion they were practising, we shot the middle one through the shell ... The luckless victim ... sinking in a red patch of blood.' The dead turtle was retrieved from the sea and cut up; turtle soup was a great favourite among the crew. The crew tried fishing, too, with mixed success. So far, Ryder reported, we have 'only succeeded in catching the log, sea-weed and jelly fish, and one small shark, having lost many different forms of bait.' On 22 November their efforts were at last rewarded when a fine 8lb tuna was hooked.

As *Tai-Mo-Shan* gradually worked her way south so the weather began to get hotter. By 25 November, at which point they were only 90 miles north of Acapulco, the midday sun was fierce, the temperature rising to over 80°: 'it was so hot during the day that we were compelled to spend our off-watch periods below deck.'[1] Finally, on 26 November *Tai-Mo-Shan* arrived off Acapulco, after twenty-six days at sea during which they covered 1,531 miles at an average of only 58 a day.

Rounding the last headland before Acapulco, the crew were delighted to see *Audacious* anchored close inshore. Larry Kent came out in a motor boat to tow *Tai-Mo-Shan* in where she anchored close to *Audacious*. The crew were delighted to be able to go ashore after nearly four weeks at sea and, it being a Sunday, there was little to do. 'In fact', Sherwood wrote,

> so great was the heat that we felt perfectly satisfied to sit outside the cafe and sip iced drinks, while we watched the inhabitants, who strolled or lounged about, in wide-brimmed hats and with pistols on their hips.

Acapulco has now long since acquired all the trappings of mass-market tourism but in the early 1930s the town was virtually untouched by the modern world. It stirred Ryder's imagination to reflect that it was 'much as Drake had left it, with only an old ruined fort and a few peasant huts clustering nearby.'[2]

Two days after arriving at Acapulco, *Tai-Mo-Shan*'s crew, accompanied by Larry Kent and another American from *Audacious* flew up to Mexico City. The flight, in a rickety old Fokker, was an alarming experience: 'As it was mountainous & hilly country all the way a forced landing would have smashed us up hopelessly. I think we will probably go down by car.' But the trip was interesting. They did some sightseeing, being particularly impressed by the pyramids at Teotihuacan, 'which date back 10,000 years & are reputed to be larger than the Egyptian ones', Ryder told his parents. They also watched a bull fight.[3]

It had been an enjoyable interlude for *Tai-Mo-Shan*'s crew, but by 4 December they had returned to Acapulco and rejoined their boat. On 5 December, *Tai-Mo-Shan* left Acapulco for La Libertad, in El Salvador. The passage down to El Salvador was a short one but the longer-than-anticipated stay in Mexico and the prospect of being becalmed for long periods in baking heat persuaded Ryder and the crew to accept Kent's offer of a tow down to Panama. The crew all had reservations, not least they could no longer claim to have sailed the whole way from Hong Kong to England.

Whatever the crew's deeper feelings, *Tai-Mo-Shan* left Acapulco on 6 December under tow from *Audacious*. In light winds and blazing heat, they made reasonable progress, thanks almost entirely to the tow. For the first six days of the passage four-fifths of the 630 miles *Tai-Mo-Shan* covered was in tow. By the sixth day, *Audacious*'s engine was starting to show signs of strain, so Kent suggested that the two ships made the final 70 miles to La Libertad under their own power. It was 'Quite a joy to be sailing again', wrote a relieved Ryder. The heat was terrific but swimming off the boat, even if it had been possible (which it was not under tow), was out of the question because of the sharks and barracudas. Instead, to provide relief from the heat, the crew flooded the well-deck between the cockpit and the hatchway with sea water. This enabled them to keep reasonably cool.[4]

Tai-Mo-Shan arrived off La Libertad on 13 December, joining *Audacious* at anchor in the open roadstead. It was an exposed anchorage; the heavy swell running towards the shore made landing difficult except at the pier, where passengers were hoisted in a cage by crane from their boat. The crew were met by the British Vice-Consul who provided cold beer and laid on a car. Larry Kent and his friend had gone up to the capital, San Salvador, which was about 25 miles inland from the coast, so the crew decided to join them. Ryder, worried by *Tai-Mo-Shan*'s exposed position, decided to remain with his vessel. I 'hustled the others up there & spent a night by myself on board', he told his parents. 'I found it rather a relief.' He had a shower at the Vice-Consulate, ate supper on board and 'lay smoking and listening to the roar of the surf for some two hours.'[5]

At this point it became clear from Kent that *Audacious* would not be able to tow the *Tai-Mo-Shan* any further. So it was with mixed feelings that the crew weighed anchor in the afternoon of 15 December to continue their voyage to Panama unaccompanied. Ryder admitted that 'it has been very good of him to tow us as far as he did'. Since Los Angeles, *Tai-Mo-Shan* had been towed for a total of 590 miles, which, Ryder reckoned, had saved about four-and-a-half days' sailing. But that was not the whole story. As Ryder put it as they left La Libertad, 'it was with a considerable feeling of relief that we weighed [anchor] at 15.30 to rely on the wind and not on the vicissitudes of Larry Kent.' Privately, Ryder told his parents that 'half of us didn't go much on the American party who treated us very casually.'[6]

For the first fortnight of the passage *Tai-Mo-Shan* made only moderate progress, dogged by light winds.

This is a peculiar existence progressing at 50 miles a day for weeks on end … we seem to have been doing it for months & months … One reads quite a lot but it is rather hot for writing one has to have a rag tied round one's brow to prevent the drips from falling on the paper with a splash.

Although it was hot, the atmosphere was also stormy, which made for anxious sailing: 'heavy cloud, rain squalls, lightning etc., make a depressing sight when the wind drops.' Ten days out of La Libertad the crew celebrated Christmas afloat. It was not an occasion that Ryder enjoyed, as he told his parents:

> Christmas eve was the worst I can recall – no snug fireside – no stocking to hang up – on the contrary heavy cloud & intermittent lightning … About midnight instead of thinking longingly of home your youngest son was prancing about on deck in the pitch dark – stark naked and very cold. A heavy rain squall struck us & brought us tumbling up on deck to shorten sail.

Christmas Day itself was more relaxed. A bottle of red wine was opened, cigars produced and, with the gramophone wound into action, the crew spent 'a cheery half hour' before the threat of squalls forced them to pack up.[7]

The last part of the passage across the Pacific, the approach to Panama, was the most troublesome. *Tai-Mo-Shan* arrived off Cape Mala, the westernmost point of the Gulf of Panama, on 29 December, with high hopes of being at Panama for the New Year. However, the combination of the prevailing northerly wind and the strong south-westerly current – setting directly away from Panama – meant that *Tai-Mo-Shan*, unable without a motor to make headway against the elements, was obliged to work round to the eastern side of the Gulf. Here, with the current now in her favour, she was able to run into Panama, arriving in the early hours of the morning on 5 January. The passage from El Salvador to Panama was the slowest of the voyage so far, at an average of only 41 miles a day.

Arriving in Panama was something of milestone for *Tai-Mo-Shan* and her crew. They had together sailed nearly 10,500 miles, which was considerably more than half the total expected distance of the voyage. They were leaving the Pacific after more than seven months. The light winds which had so hampered their progress down the west coast of America were now behind them. Indeed, the sailing in the Caribbean and the Atlantic was likely to be altogether more lively.

Once the crew had collected their post, the first letters they had received since Los Angeles more than two months previously, the main task was to negotiate a free tow through the canal. This, after a good deal of toing and froing, was arranged, saving the expedition the £40 tow fee. On the morning of 8 January, what Ryder could 'only describe as an enormous floating heap of bananas came alongside.' This was *Tai-Mo-Shan*'s tow. A line was thrown down and, with two huge bunches of bananas as fenders, she was towed through the canal.

Having been towed through the Panama Canal, *Tai-Mo-Shan* berthed at the US Fleet Air Base at Coco Sola, where she was given a substantial overhaul. As well as the usual cleaning and refitting, Ryder did as much as he could to reduce her weight to improve her performance during the long passages to windward that awaited her in the Caribbean and the Atlantic. While the crew relaxed with their American hosts and worked on *Tai-Mo-Shan*, Ryder reflected on the course of the voyage so far. He confessed to his parents in a letter from Panama that 'The shares of the expedition are at a low ebb at the moment. I feel full of self reproach & feel that I have been a most unenterprising leader.'

Ryder's guilt arose from the failure, as he saw it, of the expedition to visit any out-of-the-way places or to do any worthwhile surveying. They had, he felt, spent too much time in the fleshpots of the big cities to the detriment of the more ambitious objects of the expedition. All the brave talk during the planning stages had come to naught: 'We have really accomplished little except our Meteorological record, a rather poor sketch survey of Holtz bay and a rather poor intelligence report.' In fact Ryder's pessimistic self-denigration was overdone. The 'rather poor sketch survey' of Holtz Bay was commended by the Royal Geographical Society in the judging for its Shadwell Prize in 1935.[8] He even reproached himself for the fact that *Tai-Mo-Shan* had, as he saw it, not 'sailed well'. Given the weather prevailing for much of the voyage, this self-criticism seems unduly harsh but speaks volumes for Ryder's ambition.[9]

Tai-Mo-Shan left Coco Sola on 18 January, arriving at Kingston, Jamaica, a week later after a long beat to windward against the trade winds. The crew were guests of HMS *Danae* at Kingston, living in her wardroom where they were well looked after. *Tai-Mo-Shan*, too, was taken in hand by the Navy, 'we also scrounged a very good refit ... and had our bottom scraped by natives diving.' Meanwhile, the crew, according to Ryder, were 'living fast and dangerously'; 'we had a very hectic time with dances, dinners, etc & picnics.'[10]

On 3 February *Tai-Mo-Shan* left Kingston with the intention of exploring and surveying some small anchorages on the islands of the southern Bahamas. To reach these, *Tai-Mo-Shan* had to pass through the Windward Passage, the channel running between Cuba and Haiti. Three days out from Kingston, as *Tai-Mo-Shan* approached the southern entrance of the Windward Passage, the weather grew threatening: it was, Ryder logged, 'quite the darkest and most forbidding-looking sky I had yet seen.' Great masses of dark, heavy rain clouds swirled overhead.

> For the next twelve hours we were subjected to drenching rain, varying from steady English rain to tropical downpour. The wind meanwhile veered and backed to most points of the compass, and our discomfort was not lightened by finding ourselves in a tide rip and bounding about like a pea on a drum.

Once the weather relented, *Tai-Mo-Shan* reached through the Windward Passage, by which time the crew had decided to head for Little Inagua, a small uninhabited island about 8 miles long and 5 miles wide. On 9 February the boat arrived off the small anchorage on the south-eastern corner of Little Inagua. As the anchorage was uncharted, Ryder took every precaution: Philip Francis and Martyn Sherwood were sent on ahead in a dinghy to buoy the entrance to the reef harbour and to take soundings while Ryder himself went aloft to keep a look-out for submerged hazards. He immediately took to the island, 'Little Inagua is one of those completely desolate and barren places that have such a strange fascination [to me].'[11] But they soon realized that surveying the anchorage was not practical. Not only did the lagoon pose too great a risk to the boat but any worthwhile survey would have taken far too long. So, their good intentions frustrated, they edged out of the lagoon and set sail.

On 11 February, strong winds forced *Tai-Mo-Shan* to take refuge at Portland harbour on Crooked Island. Not liking the look of the harbour – another reef anchorage – Ryder decided to anchor away from the harbour, in the lee of the island. Although the anchorage was open to the west, the land afforded *Tai-Mo-Shan* shelter from the freshening north-easterly trade winds. It was an attractive spot with a long beach of clean, white sand descending into beautifully clear water, 'which from the shore seems to be laid out along the coast in parallel bands of various shades of green, getting darker as the water deepens.' While *Tai-Mo-Shan* rode at anchor in 4 fathoms of water, the crew eagerly went ashore to explore the island.

The following day the wind began to veer round, which, taken in conjunction with the synoptic weather map, warned of a westerly wind. As the boat was completely exposed to the west, this put Ryder on the alert. However, as the crew was dispersed ashore, *Tai-Mo-Shan* remained at anchor until dark. The crew returned aboard but as a considerable quantity of kit was still ashore, including Ommanney-Davis's medical equipment, Ryder decided, rather against his better judgement, to stay put. If need be they would leave during the night.

Then disaster struck. 'At midnight a light breeze sprang up from the west giving us a lee shore.' Ryder called all hands on deck, put up the mainsail and started to weigh anchor. However, without a motor and with the wind against them, they were, despite frantic efforts, unable in the dark to manoeuvre the boat off the beach. The crew tried to push her bows round with a pole in the hope of being able to tack away from the shore but this failed, as did attempts to haul the bows round with a kedging anchor. The keel bumped and then stuck in the sand and soon *Tai-Mo-Shan* was stranded. Realizing that the boat was now stuck – she had heeled over at an angle of about 40 degrees – the crew decided to haul her up the beach to stop her breaking up in the surf. Each time the boat lifted on the tide the crew managed to haul her a little further up the beach to safety on a rope secured by an anchor. The onshore wind had freshened considerably and by daybreak the rollers began breaking against the side of the stranded *Tai-Mo-Shan*, dousing everyone and everything with spray. 'With no sleep', Ryder recalled, 'wet and cold it was the most miserable moment of our lives.'

However, despite the desperate circumstances, the crew remained positive: 'if we could stop her breaking up all might be saved.' To this end, with the help of the locals, they shifted every movable object from the boat and secured the rudder to prevent it from being smashed. The following day they started trying to refloat *Tai-Mo-Shan*. This was no mean task. She was now high and dry on the beach, all 25 tons of her. Her deep draught was a great handicap to any chance of refloating her as was her lack of movable ballast.

On the second and the third day the crew made two unsuccessful attempts, with the help of the entire population of the village, to haul *Tai-Mo-Shan* off the beach. In each case their efforts were frustrated by the soft coral sand which would not hold the anchors. Then suddenly, like a mirage in the desert, the crew sighted the funnels and masts of a large steam yacht approaching the island. 'As far as we were concerned', Ryder recorded in his log, 'she seemed to be sent from heaven and we pictured ourselves being hauled off in an hour or two.' The yacht was *Vagabondia*, owned by a scion of the Mellon family and 'quite the most luxurious yacht I had ever seen fitted with everything up to automatic steering.'

Waving frantically, shouting and sending semaphore messages, the crew managed to attract the *Vagabondia*'s attention. Ryder, donning a naval uniform coat over his beach shorts, went out to the yacht to plead his case. Much to his disappointment, the skipper declined to attempt to haul *Tai-Mo-Shan* off; the mirage had vanished as abruptly as it had appeared. *Vagabondia* did, however, offer the services of her two powerful launches and some heavy equipment. This the crew gratefully accepted, spending the rest of the day preparing for an attempt to haul *Tai-Mo-Shan* off with the evening tide. Despite the combined power of the launches, she remained defiantly stranded. It was a thoroughly depressing end to Ryder's twenty-sixth birthday, 'What a miserable birthday.' *Vagabondia* recalled her launches, departing for Haiti the next morning.

The crew made another attempt with the help of the locals to refloat *Tai-Mo-Shan*, again unsuccessfully. Worse, the ship's big anchor snapped under the strain; now, with no anchors left, they had no means of hauling the boat off the beach. There then followed two days of back-breaking labour, in which the crew attempted to build a breakwater around *Tai-Mo-Shan*. This was a thoroughly dispiriting task as each high tide at least partly washed away their work.

Conditions for the crew on the beach, too, left much to be desired, despite having pitched tents (which leaked) and built a fire for the evenings. 'We are all feeling weary and sore', Ryder recorded.

> Small cuts in the feet get sore through being continually wet, and sand gets into them like everything else. The weather is alternatively [*sic*] very chilly and scorching hot. I think it's the sun burn on one's feet that make them so sore.

Adding to their discomfort were the ubiquitous sandflies. These got so bad at one point that Francis, Salt and Ommanney-Davis experimented with sleeping in dinghies anchored 50 yards off the beach to avoid them. This proved a failure as the dinghies leaked.

On 20 February the mail boat *Alisade* arrived, making another abortive attempt to haul *Tai-Mo-Shan* off the beach. The situation was now desperate, several attempts to refloat her had failed; a more powerful boat and heavier tackle were now the only answer. Moreover, as *Alisade* was keen to be under way, the crew decided, after a lengthy discussion that Ryder would accompany her to Nassau to summon help.

Two days after Ryder had departed for Nassau, the schooner *Louise* arrived equipped with jacks, rollers and planks to make another attempt to bring *Tai-Mo-Shan* off. Captain Colley, her skipper, was a local man with much experience of salvaging beached vessels. 'He seems most capable and confident of success', wrote Sherwood. There was the added incentive that any help Ryder might succeed in getting from Nassau would undoubtedly be expensive.

On 23 February Captain Colley and the crew got to work. After two days of titanic effort with jacks, rollers, and ropes they had hauled *Tai-Mo-Shan*'s bow round so that she faced out to sea. As one of the high tides fell during the night, much of the work took place by moonlight. The sweated toil and nervous strain of the salvage operation were in marked contrast to the serenity of the tropical nights, as Sherwood remembered, 'The starlit sky and silvery sea, the long stretch of yellow sand and the palm trees silhouetted against the sky' made a memorable backdrop to the work.[12] On the fourth day, 26 February, the combined efforts of Captain Colley's men and *Tai-Mo-Shan*'s crew at last got her off the beach into deep water. Thankfully, the damage was not great: one plank on the port side had been crushed in and some of the coppering worn away. Once the hole had been patched, she would be able to sail to Nassau. Ryder was cabled with the good news.

While the others were struggling to refloat *Tai-Mo-Shan*, Ryder was on *Alisade* making his way towards Nassau. *Alisade* was 'dirty, smelly and infested with mice.' Her cargo was decidedly mixed, too, 'a row of turtles, about five sheep, some poultry, a cow, a pony, and this morning I was awakened by the grunts and squeals of a fat porker being hoisted inboard.' The five days Ryder spent aboard *Alisade* gave him ample opportunity to reflect on the near-disaster that had befallen his ship. Before leaving Hong Kong Ryder had been determined to be acknowledged as leader of the expedition and skipper of *Tai-Mo-Shan*. His shipmates had, after long discussions and with varying degrees of willingness, fallen in with his wishes. So clearly the responsibility for *Tai-Mo-Shan*'s predicament was Ryder's. As he confessed to his parents, 'as leader of the expedition it [the stranding] is a sad blow to one's prestige'.[13]

There were, however, mitigating circumstances for Ryder's failure to set sail once the westerly wind threatened to put *Tai-Mo-Shan* on a lee shore. His first instinct, when a light westerly got up, was to leave at once. However, the fact that some laundry and equipment was still ashore and that the wind had dropped, persuaded him to stay put and keep a sharp eye on the weather. Also some other members of the crew thought that he was perhaps panicking unduly. 'By half past seven', Sherwood wrote, 'there was only a gentle breeze blowing, and everything seemed satisfactory.'[14] But ultimately the safety of the boat and crew was Ryder's prime responsibility. He should have put to sea if he felt that the weather posed a significant risk.

Alisade arrived at Nassau at noon on 26 February, whereupon Ryder was handed a message telling him that *Tai-Mo-Shan*'s prospects had improved and suggesting that he await events before arranging (expensive) salvage. The following day Ryder received the eagerly-anticipated news that *Tai-Mo-Shan* had been refloated and was making for Nassau. He then had 'two thoroughly miserable days kicking my heels … with nothing to do but wait.' Nor did the news from Crooked Island do much to improve his morale: 'The unexpected arrival of the gear & the magnificent effort of the others in refloating *Tai-Mo-Shan* in my absence only makes me feel more miserable about things.' Moreover, as the wind had been blowing hard, gusting to force 8, over the previous two days, Ryder feared for her safety.

But, after dark on 1 March, *Tai-Mo-Shan* arrived at Nassau after a rough passage. Ryder, who had been in bed, immediately got dressed and joyously rushed to the quayside to rejoin his shipmates. He found them very weary but in good spirits. The following morning, when the boat was hauled up on to the slipway at a shipyard, the news was even better: the damage to the hull was only minor. The estimate for the repair was £41. In total, therefore, the cost of the *Tai-Mo-Shan*'s misadventure came to about £120: '£40 for getting her off, £41 for repairs to hull, and £40 for odds and ends.'

By 12 March the repairs were complete. The crew were keen to get away: 'I think', Ryder reported, 'that we are all fed up with Nassau … It is purely a tourist dump; … The inhabitants are a scurrillous crowd, sharp as needles and most unhelpful.' To make matters worse, it was exorbitantly expensive, too. Their departure was delayed by Francis who, having fallen ill with a septic ankle and a high temperature, was now recuperating. The privations of Crooked Island had been exacerbated in his case by an accident involving a heavy cable while they were mooring on arrival at Nassau.

While *Tai-Mo-Shan* was waiting at Nassau for Francis to recover there was an incident from which she was extremely fortunate to escape without serious damage. One day a powerful wind got up, causing the boat to strain at her mooring. The crew, having decided to move to a more sheltered berth, weighed anchor. No sooner had they done this than a combination of the wind and a strong tide sent her careering down the harbour. Unable to bring her under control, they dropped anchor but, much to their horror, it failed to hold. *Tai-Mo-Shan* swept on down the harbour towards *Vamarie*, winner of the recent Miami–Nassau race. As *Tai-Mo-Shan* surged towards *Vamarie*'s beautifully-varnished hull, glistening in the sunshine, her crew held its breath. By great good fortune, a collision was avoided before a tug came to their rescue.[15]

This episode was another stark reminder of the pitfalls of being without a motor. Almost certainly had *Tai-Mo-Shan* had a motor she would not have run aground on Crooked Island. Sherwood, when he came to write the story of the voyage, thought 'that this and similar incidents during our voyage made one realize that an engine would be of great use.' The cost of the damage caused to the boat at Crooked Island alone would have justified the extra expense of the motor.[16]

On 23 March, Francis having recovered sufficiently to rejoin the boat, *Tai-Mo-Shan* slipped her buoy and left Nassau bound for Bermuda. As the wind was from the north-east, at least for the first part of the passage, *Tai-Mo-Shan* was obliged to beat against the wind, which did not make for a comfortable voyage. Ryder, however, characteristically derived a visceral, almost masochistic pleasure from it.

> There is something about sailing a boat to windward which appeals to those who love sailing for its own sake … There is a semblance of achievement and of conquering the elements, in working against them, that no amount of downwind work conveys.

When *Tai-Mo-Shan* left Nassau the crew had not fully recovered from the ordeal on Crooked island: 'I think', Ryder wrote, 'that we are all in poor health.' By the fifth day of sailing in good weather Ryder recorded in the log that, 'Spirits and general health on board show visible signs of improving.' During the morning of 1 April while negotiating the tricky approaches to Bermuda, the crew received a friendly welcoming signal from the Commander-in-Chief, West Indies Station, Sir Reginald Plunkett-Ernle-Erle-Drax. In mid-afternoon she entered the dockyard basin and made fast astern of HMS *Norfolk*, the Admiral's flagship.

Ryder and the crew had intended to spend only three days at Bermuda since the stranding and the longer-than-expected stay in Nassau had put them behind schedule. However, as Francis had not fully recovered he was again admitted to hospital on arrival in Bermuda. After a week reports from the hospital indicated that he would not be fit to sail until at least 20 April. It was decided to wait for him. As the crew was worried that the Admiralty might look askance at a further delay, Ryder cabled the news of Francis's illness and the revised sailing plan. The reply was encouragingly positive:

> Officers of the *Tai-Mo-Shan* should be informed that their Lordships have watched with great interest the progress of their voyage. Tenacity and initiative appear to have been shown…

The signal added that the Admiralty approved the plan to wait for Francis to recover before sailing for home.

'I am getting frightfully impatient to get home & chafe under this enforced delay', Ryder told his sister after less than a week in Bermuda. The others were likewise anxious to press on, but there were compensations in their enforced delay. Naturally, the crew felt sorry for Francis but 'inwardly we were rather pleased, I think, at the excuse for staying in Bermuda that his illness gave us.' Indeed, there was much to do and much fun to be had while they waited for him to recover. The presence of a number of Royal Navy ships meant that there was a band of like-minded young officers on the island. Having sailed *Tai-Mo-Shan* from Hong Kong, Ryder and the others had a certain celebrity, while the yacht herself was in constant demand for day trips around the island for picnics and bathing. One day, Ryder reported, 'we took *Tai-Mo-Shan* for a short sail with a party of beauties, Lady Drax and a daughter were aboard.'[17]

Indeed, Ryder seems to have enjoyed himself immensely, not least because, as he confessed to his parents, 'I have lost my heart to a girl who is staying in the house.' Sadly, we have no clue to her identity but it was not the first time on the voyage that Ryder's eye had strayed from the business of sailing. As he told his parents, 'This is the fourth time this voyage.' In Nassau he had fallen for a married woman. This gave his morale a much-needed boost but had its complications: 'unfortunately her husband was a veritable giant & so I had to walk delicately.'[18]

Kicking his heels in Bermuda with the *Tai-Mo-Shan* adventure almost over, Ryder had plenty of time to think about what the future held for him. Indeed, the question of what to do once *Tai-Mo-Shan* reached England had been exercising his mind for many months. As early as August 1933 he was already thinking beyond *Tai-Mo-Shan* to the next 'show'. He told his father in a letter written from Attu that he hoped to organize and lead an expedition to the Canadian Arctic. The following month he confessed to his sister Enid that: 'I have been wondering to myself if I shall ever be able to settle down to pacing the quarter deck of some battleship. The feeling of freedom & of being one's own master grows on one ...'[19]

Once Ryder reached Bermuda his despondency at the prospect of a return to regular naval duty, probably in a big ship, was palpable. 'I shall', he told his parents, 'be in a wretched state of anticlimax & nothing except the prospects of organizing another show in the near future will give satisfaction.' Feeling restless and unsettled and dreading the prospect of returning to ordinary, peacetime naval duty, Ryder contemplated resigning his commission, particularly as he had heard that the Admiralty was offering officers of his seniority a bounty of £1,200 to leave the Navy. Nor was he in the mood for compromise: 'If I am allowed to plan another voyage well & good but if I have got to foot slog for promotion in a groove with all the rest, it's not so attractive.' This was not an attitude likely to endear a lieutenant of less than four years seniority to the Admiralty.

Then, out of the blue, on 20 April came an Admiralty signal calling 'for one Lieutenant capable of commanding & navigating a 112ft topsail schooner for a three-year voyage to the Antarctic.' Ryder was thrown into a frenzy of excitement; here suddenly was his salvation from the prospect of the drudgery of naval duties. He sent his name in at once. Guessing that the vessel was to take John Rymill's expedition to the Antarctic, Ryder was ecstatic. He wrote to his father: 'I think it is the biggest show ever. You simply must get me chosen for it.'

He was also, in his desperation to be selected, beset by anxiety: 'I am afraid the competition will be very hot ... hundreds of names will be sent in all backed by Admirals, explorers & generals galore.' He was worried that his relative lack of seniority would count against him.[20] But Ryder did have some advantages, his successful leadership of the *Tai-Mo-Shan* expedition – and the Admiralty's high opinion of it – being the most obvious. This was not something that any of the other candidates would be able to include in their applications. He was also well connected at the Royal Geographical Society under whose auspices the expedition was being mounted. Ryder himself had been elected a Fellow in 1930. His father, also a Fellow and a past winner of its prestigious Gold Medal, was a well-known figure in the Society. Most importantly, Ryder enjoyed the patronage of Admiral Sir William Goodenough, who had been a Fellow of the Society since 1897, had served on its council in the 1920s and had only the previous year retired as its President. With such strong support there was every reason for Ryder to hope that his application would be successful.

This new, unforeseen opportunity made Ryder even more restless. 'It makes me feel desperate held up here – simply chafing to get a move on but we are still waiting for Francis.' On 25 April Philip Francis was at last discharged from hospital for a few final days' convalescence at home with the chief medical officer. This gave Ryder fresh hope for an imminent departure.[21]

At last, on 1 May at 10.00 am *Tai-Mo-Shan* slipped her moorings to be towed clear of the reefs by an Admiralty tug where the crew set sail for England and home. The five members of the crew had been in Bermuda for exactly a month, during which time they had been royally entertained. 'In spite', Ryder recorded in the log, 'of a real keenness to get on our way, we left Bermuda with many a backward glance.' Passing HMS *Danae* the crew waved farewell to the Commander-in-Chief and Lady Drax who, together with a large party from Admiralty House, had come to see *Tai-Mo-Shan* off.

For the first ten days out of Bermuda, *Tai-Mo-Shan*, in glorious sailing conditions, made splendid headway. On three days she covered more than 200 miles, prompting Ryder to comment on 6 May that she was 'Rolling home like a clipper'. After ten days *Tai-Mo-Shan* was more than half way across the Atlantic, allowing the crew to start thinking of making the passage in record time. But it was not to be. The winds died and *Tai-Mo-Shan* slowed almost to a halt. On 12 May Ryder reported scarcely a breath of wind and glassy seas. On 15 May she made only 15 miles in the entire day. Two days later the wind picked up again and with it the crew's spirits. Ryder, lying in his bunk, could once again hear the heartening swish of water against the ship's sides as she sped along, 'things look rosier', he thought. By 19 May with Dartmouth only 830 miles away 'The excitement of getting home after three years abroad, grows as each mile slides under the keel.'

But light winds frustrated the crew's hopes of a quick passage. On 26 May the wind veered round to the north-east, much to Ryder's irritation. '[J]ust when we thought we might be getting in in a couple of days, the wind sours on us and now Dartmouth distant 324 miles seems as far off as ever. Too disgusted to write much.' However, as *Tai-Mo-Shan* ran towards the Western Approaches, the number of birds, gulls, kittiwakes, gannets and swallows, harbingers of home, reminded the crew that England was getting ever closer. The amount of shipping too, trawlers and merchantmen, the crew sighted increased as *Tai-Mo-Shan* sailed towards the Channel.

At noon on 30 May the crew sighted land for the first time, 3 miles to the west of the Lizard. The crew enjoyed a memorable final day's sailing as they came up the Channel towards Dartmouth, as Ryder noted in the log:

> the wind remained in the east to the bitter end [and] blew freshly; however, we felt in a reckless mood and sailed *Tai-Mo-Shan* hard with all sail set and held our own against a small German steamer for quite some time, although we were close-hauled.

At 8.30 pm, *Tai-Mo-Shan* came into Dartmouth, picking up a tow once the wind died in the entrance to the harbour.

> Here we certainly had an amazing reception, starting with what at first appeared to be a boat-load of trippers but which on closer inspection turned out to be the Ryder clan … Here as far as the eye could see were hundreds of small boats manned by the Cadets, not to mention the band which made us feel completely foolish by playing patriotic music …

For the crew it was a heady experience. There was the sense of achievement in having sailed home from China and the delight of being reunited with family and friends after three or more years abroad.

> [A]s may be imagined, from the moment of leaving Hong Kong we started to conjure up the supreme moment of arriving, and as each of the 17,000 miles went by, the matter became more and more of a probability and less of a possibility, and here we jolly well were exactly a year out from Hong Kong, almost to the hour.

Once *Tai-Mo-Shan* had moored to a buoy 'there was a pandemonium of relations, Commanders, Lieutenants, and even the Captain of the College, who had come to welcome us.' The voyage had caught the imagination of the Navy's top brass. The Commander-in-Chief, Admiral Fullerton, came from Plymouth to inspect the boat; Admiral Sir Dudley Pound, the Second Sea Lord, travelled down by train from London to welcome the crew home. Ryder was summoned to interviews at the Admiralty with the First Lord of the Admiralty, Sir Bolton Eyres-Monsell, and the First, Second and Third Sea Lords, an unusual privilege for a mere Lieutenant. On the evening following the crew's arrival, a dinner was given in their honour in the College.

Congratulations flooded in from all sides. A plethora of admiring Admirals wrote offering their congratulations. Lady Drax – who was evidently very taken with Ryder – wrote from Admiralty House, Bermuda to tell him of the moment the news came through of *Tai-Mo-Shan*'s safe arrival at Dartmouth.

> Scene: A.H. Dinner party in progress. Lull in Conversation as Steward is seen to give signal to C-in-C, whose face lights up as he reads it. He immediately rises & reads out the glad news of the safe arrival of the *Tai-Mo-Shan* at Dartmouth. A roar goes up & we clap & cheer & I offer up a silent prayer of thankfulness that all is well with you all. Bless you Red, it's a magnificent achievement.[22]

Most unexpected of all was the telegram from the King. 'H.M. the King wishes to welcome the officers of the *Tai-Mo-Shan* on their safe arrival home after their eventful voyage from China.'

* * *

Once the brouhaha had died down, the crew had leave to look forward to before restarting more conventional naval duties. Ryder, Philip Francis and Philip's father sailed *Tai-Mo-Shan* to Gosport where she was left at the yard of Camper & Nicholson to be sold. As Ryder wrote in closing his log of the voyage, with wistful pride, 'a grand and staunch little vessel for some lucky person'. Martyn Sherwood retreated to Ireland where he wrote his account of the voyage with commendable speed; it was published in March 1935 as *The Voyage of the* Tai-Mo-Shan. By 1942 it had been reprinted twice.

Financially, too, the voyage proved a success. George Salt's eagle-eyed control of the costs during the construction of *Tai-Mo-Shan* meant that the boat had been built to budget. The Admiralty's purchase of *Tai-Mo-Shan* on her return to England reimbursed the crew the costs of her construction. The crew also received from the Admiralty the cost of a standard passage home – then around £70 each. When the royalties from Sherwood's book and the fee for an article that Ryder wrote for *The Times* were added in, the five members of the crew had lived for an entire year and enjoyed a great adventure for a mere £90 each. As Ryder was quick to acknowledge, the crew had received much free assistance from the American and the Canadian Navy during the voyage, help that did much to keep costs under control.

All in all, the voyage was a great success. The crew sailed halfway round the world, against the prevailing winds, in a boat without an engine. Ryder and his shipmates had one serious mishap, from which *Tai-Mo-Shan* escaped with only minor damage. The crew handled their vessel, under Ryder's skilful direction, with consummate efficiency, often in difficult conditions. Ryder's navigation and seamanship were, throughout, of the highest calibre. The crew had a great deal of fun, both afloat and ashore. And perhaps most importantly, the five remained friends; there were no serious rows or disagreements. As Bertie Ommanney-

Davis recalled when interviewed about the voyage ten years later, 'They were a grand crowd, and I think it is a great tribute that we were all as good friends at the end of the trip as we were at the beginning.'[23]

The voyage had marked all five of the crew out as resourceful, intrepid and adventurous young officers. Important men at the highest levels of the Service had taken note. This reputation was to be more than justified during the war to come when between them the crew won a Victoria Cross and no fewer than four awards of the Distinguished Service Order, Francis and Sherwood each winning a DSO and Bar for their bravery in command of submarines.

Chapter 6

The Voyage of the *Penola* and the British Graham Land Expedition (1934–37): The First Year

'Almost as soon as I landed I received a letter from Rymill informing me that I should be commanding his ship', wrote Ryder. His fears that the Admiralty signal inviting applications for the post would attract a large number of applications were well founded: more than 200 young officers sent in their names. However, Ryder's leadership of the *Tai-Mo-Shan* expedition, combined with some judicious string-pulling on his behalf won the day. It emerged, for example, that Admiral Drax, with whose family Ryder had made such a mark, forwarded his application from Bermuda with a strong official recommendation. Ryder was thrilled. On receiving the news 'as may be imagined my joy knew no bounds.'[1]

John Rymill (1905–68) was the leader of the British Graham Land Expedition (BGLE). An Australian, Rymill was, at 6ft 4in, enormously tall, 'a giant of a man', a modern Viking ranging over the world's frozen wastes. But he was also, as an obituarist who knew him well wrote, 'slow and methodical ... and utterly reliable.'[2] While studying in Cambridge, Rymill had been invited by Gino Watkins to join his British Arctic Air Route Exploration to Greenland in 1930–31. During that expedition he navigated the party that rescued Augustin Courtauld after five months alone in a tent. The following year Rymill returned to Greenland with Watkins to continue the work started during their previous expedition. Tragically, only twelve days after the expedition had arrived in Greenland, Watkins drowned while kayaking; Rymill took over as leader of the expedition until its return to civilization in 1933.

While in Greenland Rymill had begun to formulate plans for an expedition to the Antarctic. Having discussed his ideas with two of the leading British authorities Rymill decided to mount an expedition to explore the Western Antarctic. To the west of the Weddell Sea was an area known as British Graham Land. Exploration of the east, the Weddell Sea, coast of Graham Land was made very difficult by pack ice, but on the west coast the prevailing currents tended to push the ice away from the shore, making access to the coast by ship easier – in theory. In 1934 Graham Land was largely unexplored south of latitude 65°. As a result of Sir Hubert Wilkins's pioneering flight of 1928, it was thought to be an archipelago jutting north from the Antarctic continent towards the tip of South America. North of latitude 65° the coast was better known, having been the province of whalers and explorers for many years.[3]

Rymill's plan was approved by the Royal Geographical Society at the beginning of 1934, which made him a grant of £1,000 towards the costs of the expedition. His attempts to raise the necessary funds were hampered by the poor state of the world's economy during the Great Depression and his own relative obscurity. He was no Captain Scott. Eventually, the Colonial Office, anxious for political reasons to promote Britain's claim to that part of Antarctica, then known as the Falkland Islands Dependencies, agreed to contribute £10,000 from whaling royalties. Rymill managed to solicit a number of private subscriptions, from the Corporation of London and Lord Leverhulme among others. In total, Ryder estimated, the expedition did not have more than £20,000 at its disposal.[4]

£20,000 was in 1934 a ridiculously small sum of money to finance a major polar expedition. As Colin Bertram, the BGLE's biologist wrote many years later, 'We were poor indeed in the midst of the world economic slump.'[5] In more prosperous times, thirty years earlier, Scott's Antarctic Expedition of 1901–04 had had more than £100,000 at its disposal. The British government alone had contributed £20,000 to the coffers of Scott's second expedition in 1910–13. Inevitably, this chronic lack of funds affected every aspect of the BGLE.

The earliest and most enduring manifestation of the shortage of money was the expedition's ship. A three-masted Breton fishing schooner she had been built in 1908 for Atlantic trawling. By the time she came into the expedition's hands she was in poor condition, reflected in the fact that Rymill paid £2,200 for her against an asking price of £9,000. She was 112ft long and 24ft across the beam, with a carrying capacity of approximately 200 tons. She was equipped with two 50hp engines. On deck she carried twelve 'dorys' – small rowing smacks – of the type described by Kipling as 'dropping away like bees from a crowded hive' on the Grand Banks in *Captains Courageous*. Originally called *Alcyon*, Rymill changed her name to *Penola*, after his family's sheep station in South Australia.

Penola was repaired and refitted at Southampton, where her bows were strengthened both internally and, by the addition of sheathing, externally in order to protect her against the Antarctic ice. Other changes included the removal of partitions to create a hold for cargo, the fitting (at Ryder's insistence) of guards for the propellors, the installation of an echo sounder and a heating system. The engines were completely inadequate for a vessel of *Penola*'s size and weight but, with money so tight, Rymill could not afford replacements. So, effectively, *Penola* would have to rely on sail power and the skill of Ryder and his crew to reach Antarctica.

These French fishing boats may have been, in Ryder's words, 'picturesque old vessels, very comfortable at sea', but *Penola*, with her strengthened bows and often heavily laden, performed poorly, especially to windward.[6] Indeed, Ryder later described her as 'a very rotten, defective and unhandy ship, possibly worse than any other that had been South.' The contrast with Scott's ships, the purpose-built *Discovery* and the whaler *Terra Nova*, both well suited to Antarctic conditions, could not be more marked. It was Ryder's onerous responsibility, as *Penola*'s captain, to ensure her safety, and that of her crew, in the hazardous waters of the Antarctic.

To sail *Penola* Ryder had a crew of six. His First Mate was James Martin, a man of many parts, an eccentric maverick but an experienced and reliable seaman. Born in 1900 Martin, had attended Harrow School and been commissioned in the Grenadier Guards at the end of the Great War, before working in the City. By then the call of the sea had become too strong and he abandoned his career to sail the oceans. By the time he joined Rymill's expedition he was renowned for his sterling qualities as a seaman. He had also, importantly, experienced polar conditions aboard a Norwegian whaler and during a voyage to the Canadian Arctic. He was, Ryder wrote, a 'Jekyll and Hyde, one moment being a dapper Guard's officer about town and the next with beard, dungarees and cloth cap a regular Cape Horn Shellback.'[7]

> As the mate of a sailing ship Martin was admirably suited for the position … Slow and methodical, he had everything in good and dependable condition when it was required. He was by instinct a seaman of the very highest standing … One did not appreciate his thoroughness until some dark and stormy night with its moments of anxiety put matters to the test.[8]

The two men forged a strong partnership during their three years together in *Penola*, one that was crucial to the ship's smooth running and efficiency. J.M. Wordie, a polar expert, wrote of Ryder and Martin that, 'I doubt if a more successful combination of abilities and dash and mutual trust had been known in the Antarctic.'[9] They also became great friends. At the outbreak of war Martin joined Ryder's Q-ship but was drowned when she was torpedoed in June 1940. 'I lost a greatly valued friend', wrote Ryder.[10]

By the time Ryder met Rymill on *Tai-Mo-Shan*'s return to England, James Martin had already been signed up for the expedition. Ryder was allowed to choose one other person to man the ship. He considered recruiting George Salt or Philip Francis but the Admiralty would not release either of them so he chose his eldest brother Lisle, a captain serving in the Norfolk Regiment. After some string-pulling, he was given leave by the War Office and joined the ship as Second Mate. He was a very experienced sailor – it was in his boat *Edith* that Ryder had first caught the sailing bug as a school boy – and an accomplished carpenter. 'It was', Ryder wrote many years later, 'very sporting of him to come and serve under his youngest brother and wonderful for me to be able to count on his loyal support.' Lisle's skills as a carpenter proved very useful in the Antarctic. He was a popular member of the expedition, too: Brian Roberts called him 'one of the most generous-minded and good-humoured of men.'[11]

Three others made up the crew: Lieutenant Commander Hugh Millett, Colin Bertram and Norman Gurney. Millett was a Royal Navy engineer officer, whose unenviable task it would be to keep *Penola*'s antiquated, inadequate engines in working order for three years. He did a brilliant job in often very trying circumstances. Bertram was the expedition's biologist. Bertram was only twenty-two when the *Penola* left England but had already taken part in two Arctic expeditions while at Cambridge. The 1933 expedition was transported to its destination in Greenland by the celebrated French polar explorer Dr J.-B. Charcot in his ship *Pourquoi Pas?*. As Charcot had visited Graham Land in 1909, Bertram learned much that would stand him in good stead during the BGLE. The sixth and youngest member of the crew was Norman Gurney. Gurney successfully applied to join the *Penola* at the end of his first year at Trinity Hall, Cambridge. Despite suffering from seasickness almost every day on the outward voyage, he was a 'doggedly conscientious and cheerful sailor who never missed a watch.'[12]

The other half of the expedition constituted the shore party, responsible for accomplishing the BGLE's scientific objects and the surveying. The scientists were all Cambridge men, most of whom had had some experience of polar conditions. The core of Rymill's team had been with him in Greenland on Watkins's expeditions. Rymill himself, according to Ryder, had only a limited interest in science. 'He was more in the Amundsen tradition, a splendid traveller. He went for the fun of it.'[13] The second-in-command was W.E. Hampton, a Cambridge-educated, aeronautical engineer and pilot who was responsible for flying and maintaining the aeroplane that the expedition took to the Antarctic. Rymill had complete confidence in him for, as he wrote in his account of the expedition, 'it would be impossible to get a better man for the difficult position of second-in-command of a prolonged polar expedition.' Quintin Riley, had also been with Watkins in Greenland, volunteered to join the BGLE at the very start as meteorologist and commissariat officer. Short, dapper and possessed of a lively character, he did much to keep spirits up in the harsh conditions of the Antarctic. As one of his fellow explorers wrote, 'No expedition with him as a member could ever be dull'. It was entirely typical of him that, where all the other members of the expedition described themselves as 'surveyor' or 'biologist', he simply entered 'gentleman' against his name. Riley brought with him his motorboat *Stella*, which was to prove invaluable for forward reconnaissance and as *Penola*'s tender. She also stood in as a tug for *Penola*, helping her manoeuvre in the more confined and rock-infested anchorages.[14]

Alfred Stephenson and Ted Bingham were the two other members of the party who had been with Rymill in Greenland. Stephenson was the surveyor to the expedition, responsible for surveying and mapping the hitherto uncharted southerly reaches of the coast of Graham Land. Lieutenant Commander Bingham, a naval surgeon, was in charge of the expedition's huskies. He had had a good deal of experience with sledging and huskies in Greenland and Canada and assembled a large team of dogs – at one point there were more than a hundred with the expedition – for the sledging journeys.

Two other Cambridge scientists, a wireless operator and an engineer, made up the shore party. Brian Roberts was the expedition's ornithologist. He had taken part in expeditions to Iceland and Greenland where he had experienced polar conditions. His effectiveness on the BGLE was curtailed by a continuing appendicitis, which eventually required his removal to the Falkland Islands for treatment. The expedition's chaplain and geologist was Launcelot Fleming, Chaplain and Fellow of Trinity Hall, Cambridge; he had taken part in two previous polar expeditions. He and Ryder became lifelong friends. Lieutenant Ian Meiklejohn of the Royal Corps of Signals joined the expedition as its wireless operator and Jim Moore, a Cambridge engineer, as second engineer.

The entire expedition was to sail in *Penola* to the Antarctic. During the voyage the scientists of the shore party were required to help the six-man crew sail the boat and perform all the tasks, some menially unpleasant, necessary to keep an elderly, wooden sailing vessel in trim. The scientists were required to fulfil this role as lack of funds (and space) precluded the employment of a full professional crew. It was Ryder's job to knock this amateur crew with little or no sailing experience into shape. Ryder intended to run the *Penola* on naval lines, 'with the usual ship discipline'. This arrangement gave rise to a certain amount of ill-feeling between the ship's party and the scientists of the shore party, particularly once the *Penola* had arrived in the Antarctic. As Alfred Stephenson, the surveyor, wrote many years later: 'Ryder proved a strict disciplinarian, engendering a feeling among non-service members of the expedition that discipline could have been relaxed when not at sea.'[15]

Ryder himself foresaw that his determination to adhere to naval discipline might prove divisive. In the event, the issue flared up while the *Penola* was still at sea. On 12 January 1935, during the passage south from the Falkland Islands, Ryder wrote in his diary:

> The scientists requested again to be excused scrubbing & cleaning ship. They are fully prepared to do the work necessary for the safety of the ship but they feel that their scientific work is more important than mere cleaning. The request has been turned down as it is hardly possible to differentiate between all the various sorts of work on board.

Ryder did later concede that perhaps he had been guilty of over-zealousness in enforcing naval standards of discipline on the party. 'I was a keen young naval lieutenant chosen out of two hundred applicants.' Ryder felt that the Admiralty would be looking to him to maintain the high level of efficiency traditional in the Royal Navy. The Cambridge scientists, however, were not accustomed to service discipline: 'they adhered to the view that everyone should be free to get on with jobs as they pleased.' The fault line in the expedition between the ship's crew and the shore party remained, although, for much of the time, their co-existence was fruitful and amicable. Nor were Ryder's misgivings about the scientists entirely justified; as he admitted, when called upon they were prepared to work long and hard.[16]

Once *Penola* had been strengthened and refitted at Southampton Ryder and a skeleton crew left on 26 August for St Katherine's Dock at London where she would be loaded. *Penola*'s shortcomings as a sailing vessel became immediately apparent, even on a short cruise up the Channel coast. 'With an auxiliary & a light head wind, one can really neither sail nor steam.' Ryder also reported that half the crew were incapacitated by seasickness. Neither development boded well for the big seas and high winds of the Southern Ocean that lay ahead for *Penola* and her crew.

On 1 September *Penola* arrived at St Katherine's Dock. The following ten days were spent loading the ship, an immense task for a three-year voyage. Stowing the lower hold with eighteen drums of fuel oil and eight tons of anthracite took a day in itself. By 9 September the cargo was stowed. Part of the stores, the crated-up aeroplane and sections of the base hut had already left for the Falkland Islands, with Hampton, Stephenson and the huskies, in a cargo vessel. Despite this, 25 tons of cargo were stowed on deck. In photographs *Penola*'s deck looks so crowded with piles of cargo lashed down against the weather that one wonders how the crew had any room to move about let alone work the sails. As well as the general stores the ship had some live cargo: two kittens, several crates of chickens and two pigs, Dennis and Gladys. In fact, although the little ship looked overloaded her loading marks were well clear of the water.

On 10 September with the cargo now stowed and both engines in working order at last, *Penola* was ready to set sail. An hour before departure the Bishop of Gibraltar came aboard and, in full fig, blessed the expedition and the ship. In mid-afternoon, *Penola* set off. She looked like a ship from another era, practically a museum piece in 1934, as she made her way down the Thames. Her antiquated rigging and her square-rigged foremast suggested the age of Nelson rather than the 1930s. The *Penola*'s outdated appearance merely served to emphasize the hybrid nature of Rymill's expedition. In some respects, it was a modern undertaking, equipped with an aeroplane and two tractors; yet they intended to use dogs for sledging, as Amundsen had, and made their way south to Antarctica under sail. Nor did they have any of the advantages of modern transport that later, postwar expeditions were to enjoy. It lay on the cusp between the heroic age of polar exploration, exemplified by Scott, and the modern expeditions of the 1950s and 1960s.

The voyage south was uneventful. The amateur crew, once it had shaken off its seasickness, began to learn the ropes, while Ryder mastered *Penola*'s foibles. He fretted about her unhandiness when sailing to windward, but was more worried to discover that she leaked. 'I am very disappointed to find that we have to pump the ship every watch now, which is a poor outlook for the future.' Pressing on south, *Penola* slowed as she passed through the doldrums but nevertheless crossed the Equator on 18 October. On 30 October Ryder saw the first albatross of the voyage, a sign that they were reaching the southern latitudes.

On 11 November the *Penola* reached Montevideo, where Ryder discovered that Bingham and the huskies had gone on to Port Stanley. Montevideo did not appeal to Ryder nor his crew, 'a rather dirty port town', he decided. *Penola* left Montevideo on 16 November for the Falkland Islands. Two days out she ran into the first fog she had encountered since leaving the Channel. There was much to keep the naturalists aboard busy, too. On 18 November Ryder reported sightings of seals, dolphins, Magellan penguins, Cape doves, Cape pigeon and albatross, as well as a variety of different petrels. As the ship sailed south so conditions became colder. On 22 November Ryder reported that 'This is pretty bum weather ... the strong wind & driving rain soon chills one down', although the radiator in the saloon was now working so 'Down below all is snug and attractive'.

On 29 November *Penola* reached Port Stanley after a tricky approach in fog and strong winds. She spent a month there, longer than had originally been intended. As a result, Ryder and the crew were able to get the ship well in order. Most importantly, *Penola*'s rig was altered to make it better adapted to working in ice. The only fly in the ointment was the parlous state of the engines: 'Snag after snag seems to crop up with these', first the gearbox, then the drive shafts and so on. Characteristically, Ryder was taken by the islands: 'The Falkland Islands are one those places that attract me instinctively. They resemble in appearance the upper reaches of Dartmoor or the north of Scotland and are treeless.' In view of the length of time he was destined to spend on the islands before the BGLE was over, this was just as well.

Having enjoyed the Christmas festivities, which included two days' racing and five dances, at Port Stanley, *Penola* left the Falkland Islands on New Year's Eve for the last leg of the journey to the Antarctic. Before leaving the crew was strengthened by the addition of Duncan Carse from the oceanic research vessel *Discovery II*. He became the BGLE's youngest member. *Discovery II* also took on board much of the expedition's equipment, including the aeroplane and the huskies, that had come south in a cargo vessel. This lessened Ryder's fears of his ship being overloaded in the stormy Southern Ocean. However, the ship had barely got clear of the islands before first one then the other engine broke down. As they had both been refitted during *Penola*'s stay at Port Stanley, this was most unwelcome news. Rymill, Millett and Ryder decided to return to harbour to examine the engines and attempt to repair them.

As it was now late in the season – the Antarctic summer was already half gone – Rymill was anxious to push on to Graham Land. Ryder, on the other hand, with responsibility for the ship his prime concern, was worried about the state of the engines. 'The voyage out has shown the ship to be unduly unhandy ... and in my opinion she is inadequate for the programme before us without reliable engines.' As Millett had found that the trouble had been caused by the engines shifting, it was decided to take on cement with a view to fixing the engines' beds when the opportunity arose. With time pressing and money scarce, it was decided to proceed south under sail alone. Henceforward, at least until they could be properly repaired, the engines would be used only 'for ice work or in an emergency'.

So on 6 January 1935 *Penola* finally left the Falkland Islands. Three days later Ryder, already worried about the lack of reliable engines, made another alarming discovery: the foremast was rotten at deck level. Lisle, the ship's carpenter, set to work to rig up a temporary repair. Meanwhile, *Penola* sailed slowly south. On 20 January Ryder made his landfall at Smith Island, north-west of Graham Land. Alfred Stephenson, the expedition's surveyor, was not alone in appreciating Ryder's skill as a navigator. 'Having crossed Drake Strait, to our amazement he found Smith Island in a fog exactly where he expected.'[17] It was a dramatic sight, too: 'massive great cliffs some 5,000 feet almost a sheer drop'. Shortly afterwards Ryder saw his first iceberg, 'very impressive and a lovely shade of pale green'.

The following day, *Penola* arrived at Port Lockroy on Graham Land's west coast. Ryder's first sight of the Antarctic left an indelible impression on him. The coast seen for the first time was 'quite the most impressive scene I have ever witnessed and quite defy the writer's pen or the artist's brush. Peaks & ranges rise almost sheer up from the sides of the straits to heights of 3 & 4,000 feet … so that one almost feels as if one were steaming down a grand canyon.' The beauty of the scenery did not, however, blind Ryder to the dangers facing *Penola* here. 'From a navigational point of view this appears to me a most hazardous part of the world.' For *Penola*, lacking adequate engine power, strong winds would make navigation all but impossible; in a storm, Ryder noted, she would be in 'a pretty tight corner'. Her only hope would be to thread her way downwind through the channels to the relative safety of the open sea. The hazards of navigation in these waters were compounded by the difficulty of picking out the channels and islands in good visibility; in poor conditions, it was virtually impossible. Furthermore, the frequently very deep water removed the expedient of anchoring 'on which sailing vessels so much rely'.

The anchorage dignified by the name Port Lockroy was in fact nothing more than a cove nestling beneath cliffs of ice. What it did offer, once the ice had dispersed from the anchorage, was shelter and calm waters. *Discovery II* had already landed Hampton, Stephenson and Bingham together with large amounts of fuel, the crated-up aeroplane and all the huskies. Once *Penola* arrived, Hampton assembled and rigged the aeroplane. Living in a tent on the bare beach, amid frequent snow flurries and against an almost constant roar of ice falling from the glaciers into the sea, he patiently put the little De Havilland Fox Moth biplane into a serviceable state. The Fox Moth flew at around 90 mph with a range of about 450 miles in calm conditions. For service in the Antarctic, it was equipped with both wheels and floats.

By 27 January the Fox Moth was ready and, after a successful trial flight, Ryder and Rymill joined Hampton to fly south in search of a suitable winter anchorage. The plane flew down the coast of Graham Land, which was discouraging, 'grim, uninviting and almost inaccessible', thought Ryder, not at all promising for a secure anchorage. Then, as the three explorers were beginning to despair of finding a suitable refuge for *Penola*, they noticed just off the coast in the Argentine Islands a narrow channel between two islands, which gave into three different bays. 'It was the place of our dreams', wrote a relieved Ryder. The following day, he set off in *Stella* with Rymill and Riley to investigate the anchorage. They made the 36 mile trip in just over six hours. Seen from sea level, it looked even better than it had from the air. 'The warm sun, fine weather, together with hundreds of seabirds, the moss and red lichen seemed to give the place quite a summery aspect; very different from Port Lockroy or any of the coast we had passed.' It looked as if their prayers had been answered. They christened the anchorage Stella Creek. The three men climbed to the high point of the island and ate lunch in their shirtsleeves before returning home.

The following day *Penola* and *Stella* took the first consignment of stores to Stella Creek where the crew spent five strenuous days unloading the ship's cargo. On 4 February *Penola* left Stella Creek for Port Lockroy but got stranded on a shelf of smooth rock, floating off with the tide in the early evening. She continued up the coast through the night which, according to Ryder, 'at this time of the year is just dark enough to be unpleasant.' Ryder directed the ship through these treacherous waters from aloft. 'Up in the crow's nest one is very snug, & the sight of the ship twisting & turning below in accordance with one's hand signals is pleasing to watch.'

Once *Penola* had returned to Port Lockroy the members of the expedition threw themselves into loading the rest of its stores and equipment aboard. This took four days of hard work after which the *Penola*, delayed by poor weather, did not reach Stella Creek until 14 February. By this time the ice had all gone from the creek so the ship was put into her winter quarters at once. Meanwhile Lisle and Jim Moore started building the base hut, a job that took three weeks. The site chosen for the base was a flat rocky outcrop on the shore about 250 yards across the creek from *Penola*'s berth.

While Lisle and Moore were busy with their saws, hammers and screwdrivers, the scientists too were getting down to work. Stephenson erected the meteorological observation station on the summit of the base island while the others prepared to begin their own studies. On 28 February Hampton and Rymill took off on a reconnaissance flight. This convinced Rymill that the expedition's sledging expeditions would have be confined to the western coast of Graham Land until *Penola* could be wintered further south. This was because of the glaciers and cliffs preventing the sledge teams penetrating inland.[18] The delays in England before departure, in the Falkland Islands and the slow passage south had cost the expedition dear. The failure to get further south for the first winter meant that the BGLE's main objects were curtailed if not postponed for a year.

On 5 March the shore party was able to move into the hut, which was now finished. This meant that, as Ryder put it, 'we could spread a bit' as they settled down for the winter. Under Stephenson's supervision, and assisted by Lisle, Ryder began to chart the miniature archipelago in which the *Penola* was berthed for the winter. '[W]e spent', he recalled, 'some happy days rowing round with a plane table, compass and lead line.' He also helped Stephenson with his theodolite observations of the outer islands. While Ryder was absorbed in this interesting work, the more junior members of the crew were saddled with the mundane chores, collecting ice, cleaning the ship and so on. On 12 March Ryder took part in a practice skiing run but 'came a real cropper & can hardly write in consequence of a bruised & stiff shoulder.' It was not all work, though. On 13 March the expedition celebrated Rymill's birthday. It was evidently quite an evening. 'The mixture', Ryder reported, 'of schnapps, sherry, Russian stout & port was most disastrous & one member of the party took a header down the ladder & stunned himself completely & is lucky not to have cracked his skull.'[19]

With the expedition settled at its winter base, Ryder had time to reflect on the make-up of the party. Its members could, he thought, be divided into three types:

On the one extreme there are those who are accustomed to earning their living & working with troops or seamen in the services or in merchant ships. On the other extreme come the university elements, represented by the scientists. In between are the remainder largely represented by those who were with Watkins & Rymill before & being university educated for the most part tend mainly in that direction.

The extremes had been present on most previous polar expeditions which had, Ryder surmised, 'generally succeeded in living on pretty unfriendly terms.' This he attributed to the fact that the university-educated members tended, albeit largely subconsciously, to regard the servicemen as intellectually inferior.

During the BGLE's first winter this divide was potentially exacerbated by the fact that at Stella Creek the two halves of the party were living apart. The ship's crew, who were, broadly, the 'service element' of the expedition, lived aboard *Penola*, while the shore party, broadly, the 'university element', lived ashore 250 yards away in the hut. 'Living in two different camps has a peculiar psychological effect; in that one always fancies that the other party are a crowd of bums & doing no work, pinching the best of everything & altogether having a good time.' Sensibly, in order to prevent such ideas gaining any currency the ship's crew visited the base hut as often as possible.

By the end of March 1935 the Antarctic winter was drawing in apace. On 27 March Ryder reported that for 'the first time we have ice on deck all day.' Two days earlier the first sledging practice had taken place, with Rymill and Bingham, the doctor, each taking a sledge and a team of dogs. It was the first time that Ryder had witnessed sledging with dogs; he was 'very impressed'. The training of the dogs into teams which would be capable of pulling the sledging parties across the ice was fundamental to the success of the BGLE.

The next important task was to gather food for the coming winter. It had been decided that as an economy measure once it was in the Antarctic, the party would live off the land, rather than carry with it expensive tinned and preserved food. In Graham Land, this dictated a diet of seal meat. In the second week of April Ryder joined James Martin and Colin Bertram in a party led by Alfred Stephenson charged with collecting the winter's supply of seals.

The operation took a week during which time they killed around a hundred seals, which were then gutted, flensed and taken by boat to the meat larder that had been cut in the ice above the base hut. In that part of the Antarctic, the commonest seals were crabeaters and Weddells. The crabeater, it was soon discovered, made much the better eating; the Weddells were left for the huskies. The local bird population joined in enthusiastically, as quickly as the men killed and butchered the seals, the skuas and petrels would descend to feed on the carcasses.

The sealing expedition was Ryder's first experience of camping in polar conditions; it proved a rude awakening. The islands on which the four men camped were exposed and inhospitable and for two days they were confined to their tents by a snow storm. Ryder had, as he confessed to his diary, always been puzzled how people slept on 'snow or ice without melting it & getting wet'. He soon found out: 'The answer is simple – one gets wet.' It made life miserable: 'Both our sleeping bags are wringing wet', Ryder moaned, nor was there any way, until the weather improved, of drying them. Recalling the sealing episode in later life he remembered that 'In our tents our body heat soon melted a puddle in the ice below so that we were cold and wet and uncomfortable.' This might have been avoided but the 'best equipment was ... being kept for the main sledging expeditions.'[20] However, three days after returning to *Penola*, he wrote:

> In future years I shall always look back on our sealing camp with the greatest pleasure. The discomforts even now seem remote, but our camp on the little group of islands 15 miles out from the coast with their little channels & boat harbours not to mention the magnificence of the surf were impressive at the time and will remain so.

As conditions around the base camp grew steadily more wintery those members of the expedition without polar experience had to learn the tricks of the trade. On 1 May Rymill took Ryder out on to the ice to show him 'the ways & advantages of using an ice spear & ice techniques generally.' There were considerable risks involved in walking over the ice; moreover, it could be somewhat alarming: 'One can see it bending under one's weight [and] the question of falling through has to be thought out in advance.' Ryder decided that, on the ice, he would carry two 'short, daggerlike knives' for pulling himself out should he fall through into the water. Before long he was using his newly acquired skills in his surveying work, taking soundings through the ice on the creeks.

The beauty of the scenery, particularly on crisp, sunny days and moonlit nights, stirred Ryder's imagination. On two successive evenings in the middle of May Ryder and his brother Lisle skied across the sea ice in the creek to one of the islands where they walked along the foreshore. 'It is full moon & the snow sparkles as if it had been strewn with countless diamonds and precious stones', he rhapsodized. All around are mountains and the 'odd grotesque shapes' of the icebergs, bathed in luminescent moonlight. The splendour of the surrounding scenery also inspired Ryder to take up his paint brushes. His spare, descriptive watercolours give a good idea of the Antarctic landscape seen from the sea.

Rymill had decided that the BGLE would use dogs to pull the sledges. It was a lesson he had absorbed from Gino Watkins's two expeditions to Greenland. The Norwegian Amundsen had beaten Scott to the South Pole by using dogs and men on skis, whereas the British had relied largely on ponies and man-hauling the sledges on foot. The dogs were, therefore, of prime importance to the success of the BGLE. Of the original consignment sixty-five huskies came from Greenland and some additional dogs from Labrador, but a bad outbreak of distemper among the Greenland dogs killed all but fifteen of them. These were hurriedly replaced by thirty-five dogs of lesser quality from Labrador.

Ted Bingham, the expedition's doctor, was in charge of the dogs. Thanks to the distemper and the fact that a number of the dogs were elderly – at least some of them died of old age while in the Antarctic – there was a pressing need to increase the expedition's stock of huskies. This Bingham set about doing through a judicious breeding programme. The fact that the BGLE had failed to penetrate as far south as had been hoped in its first year gave him time to build up the dog numbers. During the winter and spring spent at Stella Creek, eight families, comprising no fewer than forty-five pups, were born. His skill and attention to detail were amply rewarded: 'these youngsters were the backbone of our teams during the long sledge journeys the following year.'[21]

With *Penola* snugly berthed and the Antarctic winter closing in, the time had come to set about repairing *Penola*'s defective engines ready for the summer's work. This unenviable task fell to Hugh Millett, the engineer, assisted by Jim Moore. Colin Bertram remembered the work, 'In the dank chill of the small and silent engine room, it was their lot, crawling like animals on their bellies, to fit iron bars and a network of wires between the thwart-wise timbers that composed the engine beds.'

Once this was complete, Martin, Gurney and Carse had to excavate several tons of aggregate from beneath the ice to be mixed with the cement brought down from the Falklands to make concrete. This was then poured into the reinforcing steel skeleton to form a solid base for the engines. At the same time a great deal of work, supervised by Lisle, was put into a proper, lasting repair to *Penola*'s rotten foremast. Ryder himself spent a good deal of time repairing sails in the ship's hold.

In the middle of May Ryder was informed that he would be accompanying Rymill in one of the two long sledging expeditions planned for the coming winter. He was thrilled to be selected, nor was it a compliment he had expected. By the end of May the ice in the channels was strong enough to allow the dog teams to be driven over it for the first time. Before he could drive dogs Ryder had to learn how to use a whip. The expedition was equipped with 20ft Australian stock whips, which were not to be trifled with: as Ryder wrote many years later, 'The difficulty was to avoid hitting oneself.' As one 'had to lash out boldly', he donned oilskins and a sou'wester as makeshift armour until he had mastered the technique. On 7 June Ryder had his first attempt at sledging. During the morning Rymill coached him in the art of driving a team of dogs; in the afternoon Ryder was allowed to go off on his own. He quickly became very proprietorial, writing after his first afternoon's sledging that 'Actually my team is I think the best of the bunch & consists of seven Labrador dogs, Hector, Rogue, Spot, Spider, Snow, Imp, and Gin. They are in fact the only large and intact team.'

He found the process exciting as well as absorbing: 'Seeing dogs driven for the first time is really quite thrilling.' He quickly realized that there was a great deal more to it than met the eye. 'The good driver will reel off a thousand miles & the bad driver will exhaust both himself & his dogs after 150.' After his first two runs Ryder took his dogs up and down Skua Island, tiring himself out in the process: 'Sprinting in the soft snow shoving up the slopes, wielding a 20ft whip and shouting is appallingly exhausting.' He had much to learn.

Training the teams continued apace during the months of June and July, weather permitting. On 2 August five sledges with their teams of dogs set off from base camp along the coast. Ryder was bringing up the rear, which on ice of sometimes doubtful quality was potentially a hazardous position. Several people went through the ice during the run including, up to his knees, Ryder. It was, he wrote, 'A very instructive day for me & an imposing sight seeing five teams trotting along one after the other.' It also brought home to Ryder the vital importance of the leader who even on a short sledging run has continually to make decisions. 'On these occasions', he wrote, 'Rymill comes into his own & one can see that he knows what he is doing.'

Rymill was now very keen to get the sledge parties away. On 4 August he and Hampton flew 50 miles down the coast, from which it seemed that the ice was good enough for the sledging parties to be able to make a start south. On 8 August Ryder recorded that we 'Have been working feverishly to be ready by today.' The sledging parties were in a high state of anticipation but their hopes were dashed by the weather. The following day Ryder noted that 'it has been blowing hard from the north to north-west all day. Temperature up to 37°F. Thawing hard.'

These were not the conditions in which any sensible expedition would venture out on to the ice.

The poor weather continued for another ten days, while among the party spirits sank. However, on 15 August Rymill and Bingham sledged a few miles south and reported that the condition of the ice had improved. So, on 18 August, four sledges set off southwards. Rymill's plan was to explore as far down the coast of Graham Land as the ice allowed. The advance party, consisting of Bingham, Martin and Moore with two sledges, was to establish a landing ground for the aeroplane at the north-east end of Adelaide Island, approximately 140 miles south of Stella Creek. They could then assess the prospects of further southerly progress. Rymill and Ryder would join the advance party for the first 50 miles in order to establish a supply depot to be used by the returning sledge parties. A third party, consisting of Stephenson, Bertram, Millett and Fleming, would accompany the others as far as Beascochea Bay, where they would carry out a survey and other scientific studies.

The first day's objective was the depot at the Berthelot Islands, only 8 miles from the base. Around the outer islands the party encountered some very thin ice so the leaders made their way gingerly ahead, constantly testing the ice with their ice spears. Even so several of the dogs fell through the thinnest parts of the ice. For Ryder the great adventure had not got off to a good start: 'Stubbed my toe badly while leaving the creek & fell flat on my face.' On the second day the scientific party split off leaving Rymill, Ryder and the others to make their way south. They were now travelling through unexplored country. As Rymill explained in *Southern Lights*, his account of the BGLE,

> although the mountainous coast had been seen many times from ships some 30 to 40 miles out to sea, no one had, to the best of my knowledge, ever landed anywhere on the mainland south of a point opposite the Argentine Islands.[22]

It was nearly a year since the expedition had left London, but now, at last, it was entering unknown territory.

For the next two days the sledges made excellent progress south in good conditions. On 20 August they covered about 18 miles in total, the following day, 23. Ryder reported that the 'dogs [are] warming up to it' and that the weather continued very fine. So far during the journey, the temperature had ranged between zero and minus 15°F. By the afternoon of 21 August the party had reached a point about 50 miles south of the base. Here Rymill decided on a change of plan. Moore was suffering from mild frostbite on his feet which made walking very painful so Rymill decided that he, Martin and the incapacitated Moore should return to base. This left Ryder and Bingham to continue south on their own.

So on the morning of 22 August, Ryder and Bingham set off. After a good day's run of about 21 miles, despite encountering some poor ice along the way they camped in a small cove just north of Cape Evensen. Ryder, to whom the responsibility for surveying this uncharted coast had now devolved, was 'Much puzzled by the appearance of the coast and the inaccuracy of the charts.' That night, lying in their tent, the two men listened to 'the almost continuous roar of vast avalanches cascading down the precipitous sides of the cape'.[23]

After the previous day's good run Bingham and Ryder had high hopes of reaching their objective, Adelaide Island, in good time. However, their hopes were soon dashed. Once they rounded Cape Evensen it quickly became apparent that the ice ahead was dangerously thin and rotten. Indeed, looking south they could see open water, with flocks of birds, penguins, gulls, petrels and shags basking in the sun. They returned to camp close to the spot where they had spent the previous night. Although the ice around their camp was sound their position was far from secure. There was, they knew, open water to the south and bad ice to the north. Moreover, there was no possibility of gaining the relative safety of the mainland, which was well defended by cliffs.

The following day, 24 August, Ryder and Bingham prospected on foot before sledging out to the westernmost of a chain of islands that ran out from Cape Evensen on the north side of the Pendleton Strait. Climbing to the island's low, snowy summit, the two men had a splendid view south to Adelaide Island, perhaps 60 miles away. The ice in the Strait looked bad, and was laced with patches of open water. Some further investigation of the ice, on skis and roped together, confirmed the point, 'it was quite hopeless.' Admitting defeat was the wise course of action. As Ryder recorded in his diary, 'it was obviously very risky to continue though not impossible and one certainly couldn't camp on it.' There was also the risk that they could 'lose a sledge, tent & primus & the wherewithal for keeping alive in one fell swoop.' It proved to be the southern limit of the expedition's sledging journeys that year.

Next day, Ryder and Bingham retraced their steps back to a group of islands to the north-east of Cape Evensen, where, having pitched camp, they laid out flags on the ice to indicate a landing strip to Hampton, the aeroplane's pilot. Rymill had promised to fly south on the first practicable day after he had returned to the base. 26 August dawned foggy but both Ryder and Bingham were in better spirits. At about one o'clock, as the sun was beginning to come through, they heard the drone of the Fox Moth overhead. Ryder and Bingham at once took to the ice in order to make themselves conspicuously visible to Rymill and Hampton in the plane.

Once the Fox Moth had landed it transpired that Hampton had been following the sledge tracks, 'which showed up like a white ribbon lying across the darker shade of undisturbed snow.'[24] Before landing they had made a reconnaissance of the area covered by Ryder and Bingham from which it was obvious that the sledging route south was impassable. It was a great relief to both Ryder and Bingham to find that Rymill agreed with their decision not to persevere with attempts to push south of Cape Evensen. The four men then agreed a new plan: Ryder and Bingham would work slowly northwards surveying the coast and the outlying islands as they went. At the same time, Rymill in company with Stephenson and Fleming would work south until the two surveys met. Before the work could begin, some surveying kit had to be brought down in the Fox Moth.

After four days the weather relented sufficiently to allow the Fox Moth to deliver the surveying kit. On 1 September Ryder began taking solar observations for fixing latitude and longitude but was hampered by problems with the time signal radio set. On 3 September they broke camp, having been in the same place for over a week, to begin the journey northwards. That evening they pitched camp in the shelter of Sphinx Island's dramatic northern ice cliff. After four days' enforced idleness thanks to the weather, Ryder was able to start surveying again on 8 September. Two days later the temperature had risen to 32°F, but the weather had closed in once more. Ryder was beginning to get frustrated: 'Waiting for one good day only', he wrote.

The next day Ryder managed to take a good set of observations, despite light ground fog. In the afternoon he and Bingham heard the baying of dogs to the north which, it turned out, heralded the arrival, like a ghost out of the fog, of John Rymill. The return journey to the base at Stella Creek – where they arrived on 16 September – was a tough, unpleasant trip. On 12 September Ryder reported a 'Strenuous day – pretty wet with sweat.' Poor ice and rough conditions underfoot made the journey hard work. On 14 September Ryder, noting that towards the end of the day's run he had to run alongside his sledge, complained of 'treading continually through a weak crust – very tiring.' The final day's run into Stella Creek was 'Very rough and unpleasant.' 'In fact', he concluded, 'I hated it.'

> Going at a half run over frozen brash, a continuous jumble of hard ice blocks soon bust up my toes so that one dreaded putting [a] foot to the ground. I had in fact kicked one nail right off and loosened up the other so that I will loose it soon.

Looking back on his sledging experience, Ryder decided that it 'varies from the extremes of exhilaration to complete misery'. 'I loved the good going', he wrote, 'Outward bound when we had cloudless skies, a good surface and flat ice ... passing the most impressive scenery imaginable, I found it hard to beat.'

Added to which their equipment was excellent, the tents and sleeping bags warm and dry and the rations good. Ryder found the daily morning rush less to his taste; he was someone who preferred a leisurely start to the day. Many years later he remembered well:

> Leaving one's warm sleeping bag. Dressing in a cold tent with frost flowers sprinkling down one's neck and in a cramped space. A hurried breakfast, loading up the sledge and unravelling the dogs, with numb fingers and indigestion.[25]

Ryder 'positively hated' the rough going or travelling on snow with a weak crust, as every second step 'one sinks in up the knee' which was very tiring. In these circumstances the dogs and the sledge fly over the thin crust of the snow, while the driver 'stumbles along cursing & swearing.' In later life – and also at the time, for the most part – Ryder was inclined to think that, on balance, 'dog sledging really is the finest of all winter sports. It is sad to think that this is now virtually all mechanised.'[26]

The Voyage of the *Penola* and the British Graham Land Expedition (1934–37): The Second and the Third Year

By the time the sledges returned to Stella Creek in the middle of September 1935, the onset of the Antarctic spring made further expeditions impossible. Equally, until the winter ice cleared properly, it was too early for the *Penola* to navigate the coast of Graham Land safely. By now, however, there had been a major change in the expedition's plans. Brian Roberts, the ornithologist, had been suffering from a grumbling appendix throughout the winter. Indeed, in July the party, under Bingham's direction, with Ryder cast in the role of anaesthetist, had been ready to operate on Roberts but the crisis passed. Rymill and Bingham decided that he should be taken to the Falkland Islands have his appendix removed in a proper hospital. Then there was the question of the state of *Penola*'s engines. Although Millet and Moore had managed to bed the engines more firmly into the ship, they were still in need of a complete overhaul. Vital spare parts had been ordered over the wireless; it was hoped that they could be fitted and the engines significantly improved during a visit to the Falklands.

So it was decided that *Penola* would go north to the Falklands during the coming summer and spend the winter refitting at Port Stanley. First, however, she was to go to Deception Island, a disused whaling station about 100 miles off the north coast of Graham Land. Here she was to collect a load of timber, spotted during the passage south, with which to build the base hut for the second winter. Rymill had realized that it was not possible to take the first hut apart and rebuild it elsewhere. Once the wood had been gathered up, *Penola* would then return to the Argentine Islands and embark the shore party before sailing south down the coast of Graham Land to establish the expedition's base for the second winter. *Penola* would disembark the shore party and its equipment and supplies before sailing north again for the Falkland Islands.

The change of plan was a great disappointment to Ryder as it ruled him out of the sledging expeditions planned for the second winter. These, it was hoped, would be the major journeys of exploration that would constitute the BGLE's achievement and secure its place in history. It also involved a considerable extra mileage for *Penola*, but Ryder was reasonably confident that, after Millett's work, she was up to the task. And, of course, *Penola*'s refit was badly needed. It was nevertheless an unwelcome turns of events but, as Ryder realized, 'There was little alternative really.'[1]

With the change of plan now agreed, there was much to be done to prepare *Penola* for sea. Before anything else could be done there was, Ryder estimated, 60 tons of compacted snow and ice on her deck which had to be removed. The rigging needed to put back into working order after the winter. The ship had to be scrubbed, painted and varnished. There was a vast quantity of stores and equipment that needed to be stowed in the holds.

Penola also had to be released from her winter quarters. As Stella Creek was so sheltered, there was little prospect that the ice would break up of its own accord in time for the ship to sail, so it fell to the crew to cut her out. Starting at the seaward side, the crew laid long lines of ash on the ice to harness the sun's power in melting long cuts. Then, using ice saws, slowly and painstakingly, a channel was cut to allow *Penola* to reach open water. As each pan of ice was cut free, the crew poled it out on the ebb tide. In all around 300 yards of ice around 4 feet thick was sawn. As Colin Bertram remembered, 'Sawing ice was a one-man job and a tough one requiring strength, vigour and high motivation … In ice the friction is much less than in wood, and the saw is pulled up loosely and does its work by downward pressure and its own considerable weight. The activity can be wet and chilly, but soon warming with the muscular effort when ice is a few feet thick.'[2]

By 28 December Stella Creek was clear of ice. The next day the crew warped *Penola* – that is, pulled her with ropes – from the cove in which she had spent the winter out into the neck of the creek. The anchors which had held her fast during the freeze-up had to be dug out of the hard ice. Once the warps were laid the entire manoeuvre was carried out by hand without any mechanical assistance. With the ice receding, crabeater seals had started coming back into the creek. This was most welcome as 'On board we get the brains, heart, liver & tongue as they don't like them ashore.'

Ryder spent the afternoon and evening of 2 January 1936 in the motorboat *Stella* looking for a clear passage out to open water. The next morning the crew weighed anchor at 10.45 and were under way an hour later. *Penola* shoved her way through the broken ice which clogged the channels between the islands before setting a course for the open sea to the north-west. There were some anxious moments on the way. 'We passed any number of reefs and one or two shoal soundings that made things anything but pleasant.' Eventually, after 'boldly steaming between two reefs hoping for the best' *Penola* was in open water. She then set a course for Deception Island, keeping about 10 miles offshore to avoid any submerged hazards, arriving late in the evening on 5 January.

Deception Island is a breached volcanic caldera whose vast flooded crater offered a sheltered anchorage for passing shipping and refuge to countless seabirds. The entrance was, picturesquely, called Neptune's Bellows. The volcano was not then in an active phase, but the volcanic ash composing the beaches steamed continuously. Dotted along the shore were the abandoned steel and corrugated iron buildings of a disused whaling station. When *Penola* arrived in 1936 the place was utterly deserted; the crew were alone in the dramatic, steep-sided lagoon apart from several million seabirds.

The size of the bird colonies on Deception Island beggared belief. Colin Bertram had seen other very large bird colonies but 'these penguins of Deception were yet a mightier throng.'

'The noise was tremendous, astonishing, overwhelming and ever more so as we entered their domain, stepping with care between the nests, the eggs, the chicks. The penguins' cries of disapproval rose to an ever greater crescendo. And suddenly a new determination came among them: as a body, vast numbers seemed to approach us, pecking at our knees.'[3]

Penola's main purpose at Deception was not ornithological but more prosaic: to load up with wood and coal. The expedition had permission from afar to take whatever materials they might find useful further south. Ryder had high hopes of the booty – rope, paint and stores – that Deception Island might yield but was forced to admit that 'This eldorado of the Antarctic was disappointing.'

The crew worked hard for a week bagging up coal and collecting timber. For much of their stay on Deception the weather was bad, strong winds blowing in snow, sleet and rain. As Ryder tersely remarked, 'Shovelling wet coal dust in this weather is not to be recommended.' Nor were they helped by the fact that for much of the time the rough weather forced Ryder to post one member of the crew on anchor watch. This reduced the labour force to just six men. Nevertheless, they managed to load 343 bags of coal and a large amount of timber on to the ship. By 23 January, the work was done, *Penola* loaded; it was time to return to collect the shore party.

Penola's passage down to Stella Creek, which should have been quickly accomplished, was delayed by poor weather and high winds. This compelled Ryder to seek shelter in various isolated anchorages along the coast. It was an uncomfortable time for the ship and her crew, exposed to all the hazards of inshore navigation in poor weather in Antarctic waters. On 26 January, three days after leaving Deception Island, the crew had just turned in for the night when an iceberg suddenly threatened the ship, causing a flurry of activity. It was, Ryder remarked, a 'Heavy great sod [that] came slowly at us on the tide & ground against the side but three of us shoved him along till one of his long prongs fouled our cable. However, after more shoving he went off.'

The final leg of *Penola*'s long-drawn-out journey back to Stella Creek was the passage down the De Gerlache Strait on 30 January. It was typical of the hazards that could – and regularly did – face ships in these waters. *Penola*, lacking engines powerful enough to carry her away from trouble, was especially vulnerable. 'The prospect', Ryder wrote, 'was indeed dismal … the straits are about ¾ of a mile wide with towering cliffs & mountains on either side rising to 3,000 or 4,000 feet. The North easter was blowing strongly in gusts with driving snow & poor visibility – which together with the numerous bergs & growlers to be avoided was not pleasant.'

Once or twice snow storms blotted out everything. Ryder, who was navigating his ship from the crow's nest, admitted to feeling lonely up in his eyrie, unable to turn back to safety, because of the wind, and intermittently unable, because of the snow, to see what lay ahead. In the end the weather relented, giving Ryder and his crew a period of reasonable visibility in which to enter Stella Creek.

For the next seventeen days *Penola* lay anchored in Stella Creek while the crew loaded her with all the stores and equipment the expedition would need during the coming winter. It was back-breaking work, even for *Penola*'s tough crew, made worse by persistently bad weather, rain, sleet, snow and fog. This was the hard graft that underpinned the glamour of polar exploration. The crew were also constantly on the alert for growlers – large chunks of ice that had spilt off ('calved') from glaciers or from other, much bigger icebergs. At this time of the year, towards the end of the polar summer, they were an active menace to ships, even when at anchor in a sheltered creek. For example, at 3.30 in the morning on 3 February a 'growler came with a thud under our counter'. It took an hour, in the middle of the night, to push it off. Four days later, this time at 2.30 in the morning, the same thing happened again: 'a small growler drifted into our stern with a crash.' Later that day, fed up with the nocturnal disturbances, Ryder used the motor launch to tow several growlers out of the creek. We 'hope we will have a quiet night in consequence.'

On 16 February Hampton and Ryder made a reconnaissance flight southwards, flying from headland to headland along the coast. From the Fox Moth's cockpit Ryder could see a 'tolerably broad channel' as far as Larrouy Island some 50 miles to the south. Beyond that he could see a mass of little islands down towards Pendleton Strait. By 2 pm the two men were back at the base.

Meanwhile *Penola*'s crew had been making the final preparations for sailing. In the late afternoon the crew weighed anchor and, with *Stella* acting as a tug, *Penola* slipped out into the sound beyond. There she anchored again, ready for an unimpeded departure in the morning. The majority of the shore party had rejoined the ship as temporary crew, bar Hampton and Stephenson who would remain behind to fly the Fox Moth south. Rymill and Bingham were also still ashore as they were to be responsible for loading the dogs. This they planned to do during the night before sailing.

By now, thanks to the success of Bingham's breeding programme, the BGLE had seventy-six dogs to load on to *Penola*. As many of these were young dogs not used to being handled by humans Rymill and Bingham had considerable difficulty getting them out to the ship. In lots of about twenty, they were ferried the three-quarters of a mile or so out to *Penola* in a motorboat before being handed up the side. The dogs were then chained together in family groups on top of the deck cargo.[4] Such was the volume of this cargo that the decks were now higher than the level of the rail.

With the last of the dogs loaded by about 4.30 in the morning, *Penola* set sail an hour and a half later. Taking advantage of the information gleaned from the two reconnaissance flights, Ryder steered a course inside the coastal islands where there was 'a good wide channel'. He navigated from the crow's nest, from where he had a better chance of spotting reefs and other submerged hazards. These frequently rose too steeply in the water to be identified by the echo sounder in time for *Penola* to take evasive action. While Ryder guided his ship from aloft, the scientists took advantage of the clear, sunny weather to survey the coast and its off-lying islands. 'A most successful day', thought Rymill.[5]

As Ryder had observed during the reconnaissance flight, once south of Larrouy Island the waters became more hazardous. However, with her skipper on watch aloft and the echo sounder scanning the depths, *Penola* arrived off a small island about 10 miles south of Larrouy Island at around 8.30 in the evening. The island's potential had been spotted from the air, and now, from sea level, 'it appears to be quite a handy anchorage.' Ryder suggested calling it Mutton Island, a name which took him back to his early days in the Navy at Devonport. As always when approaching an unknown and uncharted anchorage, Ryder sent *Stella* in ahead to look for rocks and take soundings.

The intention had been to continue the following day with *Stella* leading *Penola* through the more hazardous waters that lay to the south. However, come the morning, as the weather was evidently deteriorating, Ryder decided to stay put. For the next two days *Penola* remained in the sheltering lee of Mutton Island. On the third day, with an improvement in the weather, Ryder decided to continue south. This was potentially the worst part of the voyage, but Ryder, following a channel seen from the air, was able to take *Penola* past the islands and reefs without mishap. He then altered course, taking the ship out through the Pendleton Strait into the open sea. At once *Penola*, with her heavy deck cargo and high centre of gravity, began to roll badly in the swell.

The huskies, most of whom had never been to sea before, were badly affected by the ship's motion. A seasick husky was a pitiful sight: 'All the colour left their mouths and lips', Rymill observed, 'the nearest they could get to having pale faces, and they lay about looking utterly miserable.' Their misery also had, unfortunately, a rather more tangible physical consequence, diarrhoea. As the huskies were chained together on the timber covering the deck cargo this, added to the slime of the sea air, made the crew's work extremely unpleasant particularly, as Ryder noted, 'in the dark when crawling about on all fours to prevent falling overboard.'

At first light on 24 February *Penola* was nosing her way through thick banks of fog. By noon the ship had rounded the southern tip of Adelaide Island and, passing Jenny Island, stopped a mile or so short of the Léonie Islands. By now, the fog having cleared, it was a beautiful day, the best of the year, according to Ryder: 'Bright sun, clear & cloudless sky, the sea looking very blue, & the many bays showing up brilliantly in the sun.' Five miles to the south was a strip of brash ice some 15 miles wide forming a coastal barricade. That apart, Marguerite Bay was clear of ice as far the eye could see. Rymill, Bertram and the two Ryders then set off in a dory with an outboard motor to find a suitable anchorage for *Penola*.

After several hours searching they found 'a very small land-locked harbour ... with 2 to 3 fathoms' of water on the north-east side of the Léonie Islands which seemed to fit the bill. Rymill noted that it had 'a difficult entrance and very little room inside, but just enough water over the bar at high tide.' They returned to the ship, hoisted the dory in and motored up to the entrance of the bay. Here *Stella* was lowered into the water to tow *Penola* into this very confined anchorage. Rymill described the operation.

Using the *Stella* in this way proved most useful on many occasions and enabled Ryder to manoeuvre the ship into [the] most impossible-looking places. He would direct operations from the crow's-nest with various flag signals: one set of signals for Riley in the *Stella*; another for the man at the wheel; another for a man stationed at the engine room hatch, who passed the instructions down to the engineer in charge; and still another for Martin, who was stationed forward ready to let the anchors go. I was always amazed that he was able to give the right signals to the right man, especially when things were happening quickly.[6]

This account of the ship's manoeuvre speaks volumes for Ryder's seamanship and his skill in handling *Penola* in such difficult waters. Ryder's own account of the same operation is, completely characteristically, brief to the point of terseness: 'hoisted out the launch & towed in, securing about 1630.'

The following day, 25 February, the Fox Moth was at last able to join the rest of the party. Stephenson and Hampton, on receiving their summons, boarded up the base hut – painting 'This House to Let, season 1936–37' on the door – and took to the air.[7] Rymill was anxious to see how much further south *Penola* could be taken. Strong winds delayed flying for a day but on 27 February Hampton and Rymill flew over Marguerite Bay. They established that the open channel was navigable as far as Neny Fjord, about 50 miles south of the base in the Léonie Islands. Rymill and Hampton then returned to base, Hampton later flying Ryder down to inspect the potential harbours and plan a route.[8]

Having found a suitable harbour, *Penola* was under way early the next morning, 28 February. Weighing anchor at 5.45 am, Ryder immediately ran into difficulties. Before the ship had even left her berth the crew 'had a barging match with a growler which had drifted over our anchor.' Then the ship grounded slightly leaving the anchorage for at low tide there was only barely enough water for her to scrape over the bar. Once out, *Penola* had to negotiate a great number of icebergs and some patches of loose pack ice. This was water that had looked, from the air the previous day, clear but the ice had come in overnight from seaward. After careful navigation, *Penola* reached her intended new berth at 5.00 pm and secured.

The following day, Rymill found what he considered a more suitable site for the new winter base, about a mile from where *Penola* was moored. As always, Ryder prepared carefully before moving the ship: 'Spent most of the forenoon up the mast in the launch examining a route to this island and also the proposed anchorage.' At noon *Penola* weighed anchor and, with *Stella* acting as tug, steamed slowly to her new mooring. To reach it Ryder had to guide the ship through a narrow gap in a reef before negotiating a cut between two islands that was no more than 50 feet wide. As *Penola* measured 24 feet across her beam, this left little room for manoeuvre. The anchorage itself was well-protected if small: the ship had to be securely moored as she had only 30 feet in any direction in the constricted space with a strong current running. These six little islands, none of which was more than 200 yards in length, were named the Debenham Islands, after the six children of Frank Debenham, the Professor of Geography in Cambridge who had done so much to get the expedition off the ground.[9]

With *Penola* secured, it took four-and-a-half days of hard work in strong winds and frequent snow storms to unload her cargo. Not for the first time, Ryder felt that his crew was left to do the lion's share of the work. On 1 March, the first day of unloading, he noticed that after a while there was only one member of the shore party helping with the cargo. All its other members were somehow otherwise engaged.

Once the cargo had been unloaded the crew started putting *Penola* into shape for sea, clearing and cleaning the decks, stowing gear and refitting rigging. Meanwhile, the shore party began to build the new base hut. Although it had already been decided that *Penola* was to return to the Falkland Islands during the coming winter, no date for her departure had yet been fixed. This was because Rymill still hoped that she would be able to penetrate further south before the winter freeze started in order to lay a depot of supplies on the shelf-ice for use by subsequent sledging parties. Bad weather prevented any reconnaissance flight until 10 March, but when Rymill and Hampton did manage to take off it soon became evident that *Penola* would not be able to push through the belt of sea ice to reach the shelf-ice. As a result, Ryder noted, 'it would not be possible to land the depot on anything secure.' As the *Penola* now had no further role to play in Graham Land, it was time for her to set sail for the Falklands before the coast froze for the winter. Accordingly, on 11 March the crew unloaded the would-be depot supplies. Those who had not been up in the Fox Moth were taken for a spin.

At first light the following morning the anchors were weighed and the warps brought in. At about 7.30 am *Penola*, with *Stella* as her tug, nosed her way through the ice that had drifted into the islands. Once out in the bay the ship slipped her tow and set off up the coast. By nightfall, she was almost out into the open sea, but as there were still growlers she hove to until daybreak.

* * *

'We had a good send off by the shore party who turned out in force', Ryder recorded in his diary. It was the last the ship's crew would see of their fellows in the shore party for the best part of a year. The passage up to the Falklands, helped by good winds, was quickly accomplished. Ryder recalled that, 'In all however we were lucky and made a good run back to Port Stanley 997 miles in 12 days.'[10]

After six days *Penola* reached the region of the westerly winds to the south of Cape Horn. Now running before the strong prevailing winds she made good progress, averaging a hundred miles a day. The weather was grey and gloomy with squalls of hail and high seas but *Penola* was sailing well. Then, on 23 March, as the ship drew abeam of Beauchene Island, to the south of the Falklands, the weather relented. The sun came out: 'Our spirits rose spontaneously,' Ryder remembered. The heavy seas were still rolling up astern, but now, instead of looking grey and threatening, they shone blue and magnificent in the clear morning air.

> The numerous albatross and Cape pigeons gliding gracefully down the advancing slopes seemed to share in our sense of enjoyment as we dried ourselves in the warmth of the sun ... In the humdrum life of a steamer one misses the rare sense of elation and satisfaction that comes with the passing of a storm; such joys are peculiar to sailing ships and will disappear with them.[11]

At dusk that day the crew could smell the peat smoke of Port Stanley fully 70 miles up wind of the ship. The following morning, 24 March, *Penola* entered port after an anxious, three-hour tussle with a freshening headwind, anchoring at noon. The next day *Penola* berthed at the government jetty, making fast with wires and cables. It was a welcome relief to be freed from the constant vigilance to which Ryder had become accustomed in the Antarctic. He gave the crew a well-deserved week's leave but busied himself getting estimates for the repairs to the ship and, more pleasurably, renewing acquaintances from his five-week stay over Christmas 1934. As he recalled, 'The friendliness of the Falkland Islanders on our return impressed us all, and greatly added to the joy of our arrival.' The crew were showered with presents of eggs, milk, vegetables and flowers.[12] On the second night at Port Stanley, the crew gave a party on board *Penola*, 'with the young things, all hands attending.'

Arrangements were made for Brian Roberts, the ornithologist, to be admitted to hospital for the operation to remove his appendix. Meanwhile the crew, after their leave, got down to work refitting the ship. Keeping an elderly ship like *Penola* in working order required a great deal of effort, but relieved of the daily chores of gathering ice and meat the crew made good progress. Ryder spent much of his time repairing sails in the Town Hall, which doubled as an excellent sail loft. Other members of the crew constructed extra accommodation on the ship and installed another stove. Millett toiled away endlessly at the engines.

But despite the friendly welcome and the gentle pleasures of life in Port Stanley, this was, Ryder wrote, 'a worrying and unhappy time for me.' It had become evident that a great deal more work was needed to make the ship seaworthy for the return to Graham Land. The engines were (as ever) particularly in need of attention. Hughie Millett gave Ryder a written report stating categorically that the *Penola* would need to be docked to rectify the engines' faults. The expedition had been offered the free use of a dock in South Georgia together with considerable help in her refit by the Vestfold Whaling Company. With the BGLE permanently short of funds, this was a welcome offer, but it would entail a winter voyage in the Roaring Forties from Port Stanley to South Georgia. This was not something that any responsible sailor would wish to undertake in a vessel that was in any way unseaworthy.

On 5 April, ten days after *Penola* had arrived at Port Stanley, Ryder telegraphed Jimmy Scott – de facto chairman of the expedition's committee in London – with the news that the estimate for the required refit was £790. The main items of expense were the docking charges and the cost of a new foremast and engine spares. In November 1935 Ryder and Rymill had had a discussion about the state of the ship. They talked about the need for a new foremast and the possibility of taking on paid crew at South Georgia. 'He [Rymill] gave me carte blanche to raise funds for the new mast, etc.'

It must then have come as a shock to Ryder to receive the reply to the estimate from Jimmy Scott in London, 'Money not available so incur no expenses other than survey without sanction from expedition attorney or you might be held personally responsible stop.' Rymill's reply went even further: 'Please read my instructions to you I did not authorize survey on *Penola* stop Send all messages to Scott [in London] via this office or I can be in no way responsible for expenses stop.' These, as Ryder told his sister, were 'pretty rude replies both from Rymill & our committee.'[13] Ryder's frustration stemmed from the fact that he had always felt that Rymill had never been interested in the ship, regarding it purely as a means of transport. On 1 October 1935 Ryder had written in his diary that 'Rymill has only been over to the ship about twice since we have been here & I feel is disappointed in the ship, dislikes the ship, dislikes the way she is being run ...'

With the earlier promise in mind, it is easy to understand Ryder's irritation at Rymill's curt reply to his messages about the cost of repairs to *Penola*. Ryder vented his frustrations in a letter to his sister from Port Stanley,

The expedition seems to be in a pot mess, no funds and so on we don't know if we are to go south again or back home. The uncertainty is really quite trying. I am in many ways in a very unenviable position, the expedition is run on the most chaotic lines, Rymill doesn't like my methods & really gives me no support, he is opposed to all form of discipline & so that although I am in command of this ship it's a doubtful distinction one has no means of enforcing one's orders.

Ryder felt that Rymill should not have doubted his professional opinion about the state of the ship; he and the committee should simply find the funds for its repair. Ryder backed up his demands with a threat: 'I would not go south unless my demands were considered more seriously & that I was quite prepared to resign my command if I hadn't got their confidence.'[14] He telegraphed Rymill on 18 April to that effect.

During May and June the telegrams continued to wing their way, with increasing acrimony, between Ryder in Port Stanley, Rymill in Graham Land and Scott in London. Although Ryder was unhappy with the expedition's attitude to its ship, he did admit, many years later, that

I felt sorry for John [Rymill]. The expedition had not yet achieved much and it was always worrying to be in debt. He was moreover in the middle of organising his sledge parties. What distressed me was that he seemed to blame me in some way, for being overcautious I suppose.[15]

Nevertheless, by the end of June, Ryder confided to his diary that, 'The situation at the moment seems to me to be almost hopeless.' He could not see any realistic prospect of raising the required money nor did he consider that *Penola* was in any fit state to be risked in the rough seas of the Southern Ocean in winter.

While this game of slow-motion, transcontinental, telegraphic ping-pong was playing out Ryder and the crew were quietly getting on with what work they could on *Penola*. There was a peaceful rhythm to life in a distant outpost of Empire like Port Stanley.

Most of my time is spent up in the town hall repairing sails, the dance floor there is a splendid place to spread[;] on dance nights we have to roll up our gear. We work from 8.00 to 1700 after which I contrive to play badminton or go for a run, followed by a good soak in the public baths which are excellent here, plenty of hot brown peat water & very clean. They are a joy to us.

In the mid-1930s Port Stanley had a population of around 1,200, including half-a-dozen government officials and the manager of the Falkland Islands Company, 'although the gentry are few & far between, being the station owners out in the camp'. However, none of this prevented Ryder and the others from having a good deal of fun, 'There are about four girls here whom we take to dances occasionally & neck rather more frequently.' In the middle of May Ryder told his parents that 'What with one thing and another I seemed to have changed my life of Polar explorer to lounge lizard.'[16]

During *Penola*'s protracted stay at Port Stanley, a boxing competition and sailing races were organized; there was an amateur performance of *The Middle Watch*, a popular comedy of the period, in which Ryder took a role.[17] He was invited to dinners and parties and there was the occasional invitation to Government House. Indeed, by the end of July things had evidently warmed up socially as Ryder recorded in his diary: 'Considerable social activities late nights most evenings rather exhausting.'

On 13 July, by which time *Penola* had been at Port Stanley for three-and-a-half months, the impasse was finally broken by a telegram from Scott in London, 'Have arranged an advance of five hundred pounds so can approve expenditure not exceeding this stop'. Rymill cabled his authority for Ryder to spend up to this amount and gave his consent for the recruitment of extra hands for the forthcoming voyages to South Georgia and back to Graham Land. By the time this telegram arrived *Penola* was practically ready for sea. On 27 July the Governor inspected the ship and was 'very impressed with everything he saw', according to Ryder.

On 1 August *Penola* cast off her moorings and slipped out of Port Stanley bound for South Georgia. Ryder had recruited two young Falkland Islanders, Hennah and Barnes, as deck hands working their passage back to England and a cook, Halliday. The ship made her way out to sea 'The grey-brown hills of the Falkland Ids. slowly fading astern.' For much of the voyage *Penola* made solid progress in good winds. A week out from Port Stanley she encountered two days' of head winds which, with the current, resulted in the ship being pushed back about 50 miles over the forty-eight hours. 'It was', Ryder wrote later 'the coldest passage we had experienced to date; the spray for the first time froze on the ship, coating the sails, decks and ropes with ice. The days were grey and cheerless, with little sun and a tendency to sleet and fog.'

Ryder's principal worry was arriving at South Georgia, 'not a particularly pleasant landfall for a sailing ship.'[18] It is a crescent-shaped island, concave to the western side which is exposed to the prevailing wind. This was a dangerous lee shore, foul with hazards, and to get stuck here would be serious indeed. On the other hand, were the ship to miss the island and be carried to leeward it might take her weeks to work back to windward to make the island once more. 'So what it amounted to was that a dead accurate landfall was essential on the North-West point of South Georgia.'[19] Even for a navigator as skilled as Ryder this was no easy task: fog and poor visibility could be expected to make navigation difficult and so it proved. 'We had few opportunities for a sun sight and virtually no stars.' Fortunately, the weather cleared for long enough for Ryder to identify Cape Buller on 11 August.[20]

Having sighted land that morning, Ryder decided to run for Prince Olaf Harbour, which, being 20 miles closer than Stromness, he hoped he could make in daylight. However, by the time *Penola* reached the harbour night had fallen, and, in the dark, Ryder missed the entrance. The ship had, it appeared, turned into the wrong fjord where the crew spent a nervous and very uncomfortable night. 'It was certainly', Ryder wrote, 'one of our most anxious moments, we had land in close proximity on three sides and an isolated reef to seaward.'[21] In the morning *Penola* steamed into Stromness.

Penola remained at Stromness for seven weeks during which the crew, ably assisted by the Norwegian whalers, repaired and refitted the ship. It was hard work, often in very cold, damp conditions. Strong winds – known locally as the 'williwars' – funnelled along the fjords off the glaciers and snow-covered mountains blowing clouds of spume off the surface of the water. In the exposed dock where *Penola* was berthed this made for unpleasant working conditions.

The first task for the crew was to remove all the ballast, 100 tons of freezing cold, filthy pig iron, piece by piece, and the entire contents of the holds, including the coal. Ultimately, of course, it had to be replaced. Once *Penola* had been lifted out of the water, the main work could begin.

Ryder and his crew, helped by the Norwegians, worked hard, nine-and-a-half hours a day, seven days a week; by the end of September the refit was complete. The work consisted of the replacement of some worn or broken steel fittings on the masts, a complete overhaul of the engines and repairs to damage around the keel. On 2 October, after a brief trial of the engines, *Penola* set sail for the Falklands.

The return passage to the Falklands was, as Ryder put it, 'an interesting voyage'. It was 780 miles directly into the prevailing wind. It took *Penola* thirty days during which she sailed 2,536 miles. The outward, downwind passage had taken twelve days. The reason for the greatly increased length of the return passage was the need to work up to the Falkland Islands to the west against the prevailing wind. This entailed Ryder setting a course to the north on leaving Stromness. Indeed, the ship was carried so far to the east on this course that she did not regain the longitude of Stromness until the eighth day of the voyage. In the end she made her landfall in the Falklands from the north, having come round in a vast arc.

The return passage from South Georgia might have been epically circuitous but it was generally, being during the southern spring, a warmer, more pleasant trip than the outward passage. Early in the voyage Ryder reported that driving snow had whitened the masts and the rigging on the weather side and that 'the snow has to be shovelled out of the sails.' But as *Penola* sailed north so conditions improved. By 6 October the sea temperature had risen from the 31°F recorded at South Georgia to 43°F.

The voyage was not without incident. On the first day out it was discovered that some paraffin had leaked into the starboard freshwater tank. This reduced the water ration to 10 gallons a day. 'A most unwelcome discovery', as Ryder put it. On the same day Lisle, having reported some nasty fumes forward, was sent to investigate. 'He succeeded in producing a human turd wrapt in some newspaper from under the ladder but no trace of fire.' As no one owned up to the turd, 'it remains', Ryder remarked laconically, 'one of the mysteries of the Antarctic.'

Penola arrived back at Port Stanley on 1 November. Apart from the normal work of keeping the ship in trim, there was little for the crew to do other than enjoy the summer weather. The sensational news of the Abdication 'caused a certain amount of stir and speculation but that soon died away.' Brian Roberts – who had returned from South Georgia separately – and Lisle accompanied *Discovery II* on a short trip to the Straits of Magellan. Meanwhile Ryder was invited to stay with the Felton family, who owned a sheep station out in the country. 'Went riding most days, or shooting geese with a .22. It is fortunately the most interesting time of year & I was able to see them driving in flocks of thousands of sheep, hundreds of dogs and horses and clouds of dust.'

The Feltons were acquaintances from Ryder's earlier sojourns in the islands. They 'are a delightful family & I like them very much particularly the daughter Eileen who is a great sport.'[22] Interestingly, this letter (to his mother) is marked in Ryder's hand – at a much later date – 'Not for circulation'. Given its otherwise anodyne contents, it can only be the references to Eileen that caused him to mark the letter thus. We shall now never know what happened between Ryder and Eileen the farmer's daughter under the wide skies of the Falkland Islands.

The crew were still in Port Stanley for the Christmas festivities, but on 29 December *Penola* set sail, bound for Graham Land. Roberts had rejoined the ship for the passage south and Ryder had recruited another Falkland Islander, MacAtasney, to strengthen the crew. He brought the total of Falkland Islanders in the crew to four: 'We have found that the Islanders are very good hands.'

Almost at once, however, there was trouble on board. *Penola* was not far out of Port Stanley when Ryder realized that one of the watches was much weaker than the other. As the ship was about to enter the waters south of Cape Horn, some of the stormiest in the world, Ryder was determined, quite reasonably, that this should be rectified. Accordingly, he transferred Roberts on to the other watch in exchange for one of the Islanders. This upset Roberts as it disrupted his ornithological studies and he became very abusive. In the face of this attack on his authority as master of the ship Ryder had no option but to assert himself. Roberts was ordered below and told that the ship would return to Port Stanley in order to land him there. *Penola* then put about, continuing on a course back to the Falklands for eleven hours until Roberts recanted and apologized. The situation was aggravated by the fact that, as Ryder wrote years later, 'We had moreover given him every help and consideration' over the previous months. He had been excused all work on the ship in both South Georgia and the Falklands, allowing him complete freedom to pursue his scientific studies. In the end, it blew over and 'became a forgotten incident', but was another example of the difficulties that Ryder faced throughout the BGLE as skipper of an amateur crew.[23]

Now back on a southern course, *Penola* made for Deception Island, making slow but steady progress under sail, arriving on 22 January 1937. The remainder of the voyage down to the expedition's winter base at the Debenham Islands was delayed by poor weather. The ship left Deception Island on 25 January but was forced to return there to ride out a storm. *Penola* had made only about 8 miles progress in three days, thanks to thick fog in largely uncharted waters, infested with icebergs. Even for the most skilful navigator, in these circumstances potential disaster was only ever a few yards away. 'On one occasion', Ryder recorded in his diary:

we had been stopped for some hours with visibility not much over fifty yards. The fog suddenly lifted & disclosed the glistening whiteness of two large bergs not much over 200 yards away. We were in fact in the back wash off them. They looked rather nice but quite sinister.

Having returned to Deception Island, she set sail again on 31 January, reaching Port Lockroy on 3 February and Stella Creek – the expedition's first winter base – on 5 February. After a week spent at Stella Creek, *Penola* was summoned south to rendezvous with the shore party, sailing on 14 February. This was the 'most tiresome of all' voyages, inordinately delayed by adverse winds and poor weather; *Penola* did not arrive at the southern base until the evening of 23 February. It was more than eleven months since she had gone north to the Falklands. 'The shore party came aboard and everyone [was] full of news and chatter.'

The morning after this happy reunion, disaster almost befell the expedition:

> An unfortunate day. Weighed after examining the way in and proceeded between Barry Id and Brian and then sat on a rock for most of the day. We grounded very lightly being towed slowly by the *Stella* we were however unable to haul off till 7.00 pm in the evening. A most embarrassing position to strand being not above 200 feet from a high active glacier face. It fortunately did not calve and so all was well.

Looking back on the incident, Ryder considered that, had the glacier calved, 'I rather doubt if the ship would have survived.' The following morning, the *Penola* having been towed to safety, the glacier did calve.[24]

* * *

We have been following the fortunes of Ryder and *Penola* since they sailed north in March 1936, leaving the BGLE establishing its base in the Debenham Islands. Up to that point the expedition had not achieved as much as had been hoped, partly as a result of the failure to get further south for the first (1935) winter. We must now look at the achievements of the BGLE in the year that Ryder was away.

The story of the two long sledge journeys in September, October and November 1936 is an epic of endurance and courage but falls largely outside the scope of this book. They are described in great detail in John Rymill's *Southern Lights*, his history of the BGLE. Suffice it to say here that one team consisting of Colin Bertram, Alfred Stephenson and Launcelot Fleming penetrated the sound – later named King George VI Sound – between Alexander I Land and Graham Land. At the time this was by far the most southerly point reached by a sledging party in western Antarctica. During the 75-day journey, the three men, their dogs and sledges covered 600 miles, mapping 500 miles of coastline, 450 miles of which had never previously been seen by man.

The second team, consisting of Ted Bingham and Rymill himself, leaving the others at the northern end of King George VI Sound, set off to the east. The plan was to reach the eastern side of Graham Land overlooking the Weddell Sea. This entailed climbing up, with sledges and dogs, to a pass at 8,000ft before pushing on to the east. Their journey lasted seventy-two days.

The BGLE's scientists also carried out an extensive programme of research in meteorology, geology, glaciology and the biological sciences. It also succeeded in mapping much of the hitherto unmapped west coast of Graham Land. But it is on the discoveries of the two sledge journeys of late 1936 that the expedition's achievement rests. The discoveries made on these two journeys radically improved our knowledge of the topography of western Antarctica. Before the BGLE, Graham Land was thought to be an archipelago, whose islands were separated by channels running from the Weddell Sea in the east to the Bellinghausen Sea in the west. The BGLE conclusively proved that this was not the case: Graham Land is a peninsular of the Antarctic continent. Secondly, as a result of the discovery and mapping of King George VI Sound, Alexander I Land was established to be an island. Thirdly, the Sound itself, 15 miles wide, 250 miles long, flanked by mountains and filled with shelf ice was for the first time identified.[25]

* * *

Now that *Penola* had arrived at the southern base there was little left to do but pack up, load the ship and head for home, but even here the Antarctic weather intervened. On 1 March a storm began which blew for a week. The winds were so strong, blowing force 8 or 9, but gusting to 100mph at times, that it was impossible to continue with loading the ship. Indeed, for much of the time it was not even possible to negotiate the hundred yards between the ship and the base hut. It was an anxious period for Ryder, with the ever-present worry that the winds would drive *Penola* from her moorings, but they withstood the onslaught. Once the storm had calmed loading was rapidly completed. Ironically, departure was then delayed for a day by calm, still weather but early in the morning of 12 March the crew took in the warps, weighed anchor and set sail for South Georgia and home.

Before heading north Rymill and Ryder had agreed that the ship would make one final short voyage of exploration. So, on leaving the Debenham Islands, she stood out to the south-west with the intention of exploring the west coast of Alexander I Land, down as far as Charcot Island. *Penola* cruised off this coast for two days but pack ice and icebergs frustrated her attempts to push south. Nevertheless, she had got further down the coast of Alexander I Land (68° 36'S, 73° 41'W) than any previous ship. On 14 March, with time running short, Rymill decided that nothing more could be achieved so *Penola* turned north.

On the first full day of the voyage to South Georgia, 15 March, *Penola* managed an excellent 137 miles, entirely under sail. The ship did not, however, maintain this rate of progress. 'We had very variable weather', wrote Ryder later, 'Light winds, strong winds, heavy swell most of the time, head winds, and fair winds.'[26] While the crew worked the ship, the shore party was laid low by seasickness and, it seemed to Ryder, demoralization. This he put down to their living conditions ashore: 'They have paid such scant attention to points like tidiness, cleanliness, punctuality and good meals that they seem to have forgotten what these things look like.' As a result, the majority of the shore party 'largely remain in their bunks and are quite prepared to spend the voyage there. It would be interesting to see what attitude they would take if we all did the same.' Ryder's remarks reflected the gulf between his more disciplined, naval approach to the conduct of the expedition and Rymill's more laissez-aller attitude that had been present since *Penola* left England.

On 3 April *Penola* reached Grytviken, South Georgia, Ryder having made light of the island's difficult landfall. Two days later *Penola* was towed along the coast to Leith harbour. Here the shore party moved to the Salvesen transporter *Coronda*, while the crew began preparing the ship for the long voyage home. The shore party sailed for home in the *Coronda* on 17 April, their passages having been donated by Salvesen. By the end of April *Penola* was ready for sea. She finally set off for England on 3 May 1937.

The voyage home was, Ryder later recognized, 'probably typical for an old-fashioned sailing ship with all its frustrations.'[27] But with 'a well trained and keen crew' the *Penola* made good progress despite the variable winds. The further north she sailed, the warmer the weather and the more pleasant life on board became. At the end of June, by which time the *Penola* was in mid-Atlantic approaching the Azores, Ryder described the pleasures of life at sea to his mother:

[I] am writing this at 4.30 in the morning in my chart house Lisle is at the wheel we have the watch until breakfast … It is the hour of the day. The moon just paling before the advancing dawn but still throwing slanting shadows of the [masts] and sails across the decks. The settled sky with those little rosy flecks of cloud peculiar to the trade wind areas.

After stopping for several days at Horta in the Azores, *Penola* continued on her way once more on 19 July. By 2 August she was only 200 miles from Falmouth but, as had happened in *Tai-Mo-Shan* at the same point, in a flat calm. Unlike *Tai-Mo-Shan*, however, *Penola* could continue with her motors. But before doing so, Ryder took advantage of the calm to lower a dory into the water. He then rowed around taking photographs of the ship lying becalmed with every sail set. 'In the early morning haze and long oily swell, she certainly looked most attractive. The yellow sails pick up the sun readily, & give a good broad yellow reflection waving across the water.'

On 4 August the *Penola* made landfall on the Lizard at daybreak, before going into Falmouth to moor close to the *Cutty Sark*. As they approached Falmouth, Augustin Courtauld, himself a polar explorer, came out in his yacht *Duette* to meet *Penola*. On board to welcome the sailors home was a noisy crowd of well-wishers, friends and relations, including Ryder's parents and his sister Enid. After nearly three years and 26,936 miles *Penola*'s travels had come to an end.

Chapter 8

The Coming of War (1937–39)

Once *Penola* was safely berthed and the excitement of returning home after three years had receded, Ryder was overcome by weariness and a sense of anticlimax. 'I can recall', he wrote many years later, 'a wonderful feeling of satisfaction at having completed the voyage without loss of ship or life.' This sense of achievement was, however, overshadowed by the realization that no one in the wider world seemed to care what the BGLE had accomplished. 'It was all rather discouraging, one began to feel that we had wasted three years.' It was utterly irrelevant to the British public that miles of distant polar coastline could now be navigated in relative safety thanks to the BGLE's surveying. The fact that Graham Land was now indisputably established to be part of the Antarctic continent barely ruffled the surface of the British public's consciousness.[1] It was a far cry from the excitement and acclaim with which *Tai-Mo-Shan* had been greeted on her return to England three years previously. There were no private interviews with Admirals and Sea Lords this time.

The truth was that in the three years the explorers had been away the world had changed. The international situation was growing darker by the month. The fascist dictators were flexing their muscles in an ever more menacing way: Mussolini in Abyssinia in 1935 and Hitler in the Rhineland the following year. In Spain civil war had broken out. Britain had suffered a paroxysm of her own: the Abdication, peaceful to be sure but none the less traumatic for that. In such anxious times news of a successful polar exploration, however intrepid, created few waves.

Nor did the BGLE have the réclame of Scott's expeditions before the Great War. His grand object – to be the first man to reach the South Pole – had a heroic ambition that caught the public's imagination. Likewise, the death of Scott and his companions seemed to an adoring public to be a noble sacrifice on the altar of Progress, a failure but a glorious one. Filling lacunae in geographic knowledge, colouring in blank pages of the atlas, however important, lacked the eye-catching glamour of Scott and his peers. Similarly, the expedition survived the experience unscathed; the BGLE left no frozen corpses to be borne up to the explorers' Valhalla. Moreover, the world's indifference was at odds with the view that many polar explorers – and explorers in general – often have of themselves. As Ryder recognized, an occupational hazard of polar explorers 'is to become overburdened by a feeling of their own importance.'

On a mundane level, too, Ryder was brought smartly down to earth. Almost as soon as *Penola* was berthed and customs cleared most of the crew departed, leaving only James Martin, Hughie Millett and Lisle aboard. Ryder had to deal with the unfortunate MacAtasney, the cook, who, having contracted polio in the Azores, had to be taken from the ship to an isolation ward. In 1937 Falmouth's isolation ambulance was still horsedrawn so 'my first act back in my home country was to help round up the reluctant horse, which was grazing in a large field.' This was a far cry from navigating a ship through the perilous waters of Antarctica. Once the cook had been settled in hospital, the skeleton crew, together with Ryder's father, sailed *Penola* up the coast to Portsmouth where she was to be sold. She anchored off Spithead to await instructions. 'We waited most of the day', Ryder wrote forlornly, 'watching hopefully as various picket boats, harbour launches and tugs, etc., passed by ignoring our presence.' So much for the heroes returning in triumph.[2]

With *Penola* now paid off, it was time for Ryder to report to the Admiralty so, taking the ship's bell as a souvenir, he and Lisle set off for London. At the end of the *Tai-Mo-Shan* adventure Ryder had entertained quite serious thoughts of leaving the Navy. Now things were different. Nine months earlier he had told his father, 'At one time I had quite determined to leave the navy & go into some business but with all the rearmament I have swopped round.' He reported to the Admiralty with high hopes of being sent back to submarines which were, after all, his chosen speciality. The added attraction was that Philip Francis and George Salt were also both still serving in submarines.[3]

However, on arrival at the Admiralty Ryder was told that he must complete his time in 'big ships' – a standard part of a naval officer's training. He argued that 'big ship time' should properly be classified as 'general service' and what better form of 'general service' could there possibly be than three years under sail in *Penola*? 'This did not get me very far', Ryder wrote ruefully. So he was appointed to HMS *Warspite* as quarter deck officer and in command of 'Y' turret.[4] *Warspite*, then completing a major reconstruction and refit at Portsmouth, was earmarked to take over as Flagship of the Mediterranean Fleet.

This was, for a number of reasons, not what Ryder had had in mind. First, having spent nearly eight of his ten years in the Navy overseas, he 'was looking forward to a bit of old England'. On his return he had bought a sports car – presumably with the back pay that had accumulated while he was in the Antarctic; this would now have to be sold. His parents, too, were getting noticeably older nor had he seen much of them in recent years. Moreover, as he had told his father from the Falklands at the end of 1936, 'I think I shall make a good bid for getting married when I get home'.[5] Being sent to the Mediterranean for anything up to three years would put paid to that for the time being.

Secondly, he did not relish the appointment to *Warspite*: 'the last thing I wanted was to go to a battleship'. It would require, Ryder knew, major adjustment. 'For four years I had been in command having to make decisions and live by the weather. Now I was to be a watch-keeping officer on a Flagship.' The degree of independence (quite exceptional for a young officer) he had so enjoyed was about to come to an abrupt end. Ryder felt at the time that the Admiralty had decided that 'I needed a bit of smartening up and a bit of naval routine and discipline.' In fact, as he later conceded, 'they were really looking after my naval career.'[6]

The HMS *Warspite* to which Ryder was appointed was the seventh Royal Navy ship to bear that name in a line stretching back to the reign of Queen Elizabeth I. The incarnation that Ryder knew was one of the five *Queen Elizabeth* class battleships built just before the Great War, spawn of the naval arms race with Imperial Germany. Laid down in October 1912, *Warspite* was launched a year later and commissioned in March 1915. She was a huge vessel: 600 feet long – the length of two football pitches – and 90 feet across the beam, she displaced 32,500 tons. In 1914, the *Queen Elizabeth*s represented the *dernier cri* in battleship technology: oil-fired, mounting a new 15in gun, they could achieve a top speed of 25 knots. *Warspite* took part in the Battle of Jutland where she was badly damaged by shellfire. When Ryder joined the ship at the end of August 1937, she was coming to the end of a three-year reconstruction.[7]

Warspite was commanded by Captain Victor Crutchley, VC, DSC. Crutchley was an imposing figure. Tall and bearded – Ryder described him as 'a veritable Viking in appearance' – he was known by his subordinates in *Warspite*, somewhat unoriginally, as 'The Beard'. Crutchley had won his Victoria Cross for his great gallantry in a follow-up operation to the Zeebrugge Raid of April 1918. Brave and possessed of a commanding presence yet 'notably modest and reticent' Crutchley 'typified to many the ideal naval officer.' Yet despite her formidable commander the *Warspite* which Ryder joined was a troubled ship.[8]

Crutchley had taken up his command on 1 May 1937 by which time she had already started her programme of trials. During May and June the ship's company was brought up to strength with three drafts of ratings. On 28 June around 450 ratings who had been quartered at the RN Barracks, Portsmouth, were transferred to *Warspite*. On 29 June the ship was commissioned for service with her full complement. However, by this time there was an undercurrent of discontent on the lower deck. As many of the ratings came from Chatham, the prolonged posting at Portsmouth necessitated expensive travel home at weekends. Living conditions during *Warspite*'s trials had for many of the ratings been uncomfortable. Specifically, the fact that many of them were living in the naval barracks but working on the ship entailed a good deal of marching to and fro, often in poor weather. There was also a general feeling among the ship's company that she was being 'messed about'. None of these grievances was, of itself, particularly serious, but together they fermented an atmosphere of simmering resentment and low morale.

During the morning of 30 June a rumour began to circulate that weekend leave was to be curtailed prior to a supposed departure for the Mediterranean in the first week of July. Indeed, some leave was in fact curtailed over the weekend of 29/30 June, a move subsequently described by the Admiralty as 'ill-advised and unnecessary'. At about 2000 hours a small gathering assembled on the forecastlemen's mess deck, but as it was not noticed during 'Rounds' at 2100 hours presumably it temporarily dispersed. From around 2120 hours the meeting reconvened and grew until there were between seventy-five and a hundred men present. At around 2155 hours the meeting was brought to the attention of Captain Crutchley and Commander D.H. Everett, *Warspite*'s Executive Officer.

At 2210 an indeterminate order was passed for 'All men not turned in, fall in on the quarter-deck, any rig.' No one was sent to see that the order was carried out, but a large number of men, perhaps 150, went aft at once. When they reached the quarterdeck, however, they did not fall in in an orderly manner but massed on the starboard side of the ship. Meanwhile, Sergeant Greensmith of the Royal Marines, took charge of the detachment of Marines present, drawing them up away from the sailors. Commander Everett reported to the Captain who came aft and briefly addressed the men, reminding them that leave was a privilege and that as much would be given as was consistent with the work left to be done. Having delivered his speech, Crutchley left the quarterdeck. Everett then gave the command 'Ship's company, turn forward, dismiss!' As the men turned, several voices called out from the crowd 'Stand firm. We're not satisfied.' Fortunately Sergeant Greensmith acted promptly in ordering his men to clear the deck. The sailors did then depart and there was no more trouble.

There, for a while, the matter rested until leaks in the press about unrest in the *Warspite* and an anonymous letter prompted the Admiralty to investigate. Although scarcely a mutiny, this was nevertheless an act of ill-discipline – Ryder referred to it as a 'small refusal of duty' – a serious matter in any ship, let alone a flagship.[9] A Court of Enquiry found that 'neglect on the part of the Captain and the Commander was the primary cause of the incident of indiscipline.' It condemned the measures taken on the night of 30 June to maintain discipline as 'uncoordinated and totally inadequate.' Most damning of all was the Court's conclusion that 'a policy of concealment was deliberately adopted by the Captain on the night of 30 June and consistently maintained by all concerned until the convening of the Court of Enquiry.'

With these conclusions to hand, the Commander-in-Chief, Portsmouth, Admiral the Earl of Cork and Orrery recommended to the Admiralty that Captain Crutchley, Commander Everett and the First Lieutenant, Lieutenant Commander A.F.L. Evans, should be relieved of their appointments for 'the ineptitude shown in dealing with the insubordination' of 30 June. The Commander-in-Chief also recommended a number of other sentences including the dismissal or transfer of a number of ratings involved in the incident. The Admiralty acted on the Earl's advice, with the sole exception of deciding to spare Victor Crutchley the ignominy of being relieved of his command. The reason given for this reprieve was that the initial reports Crutchley received gave a false impression of the gravity of the episode.[10]

Such was *Warspite* that Ryder joined, not without misgivings, at the end of August 1937 as a replacement for the disgraced Evans. The need for a speedy appointment resulted in Ryder's entitlement to leave following his lengthy stint of foreign service being greatly curtailed. Meanwhile, the problems with *Warspite*'s steering gear kept her at Portsmouth until the end of 1937. The prolonged delay in leaving England allowed Ryder to attend the meeting of the Royal Geographical Society (RGS) on 1 November which formed a postscript to the BGLE and the voyage of *Penola*.

At the meeting John Rymill read a lengthy paper describing the activities and achievements of the BGLE. Once Rymill had read his paper – which Ryder considered 'rather heavy going' – and W.E. Hampton, the BGLE's second-in-command, had said a few words, Ryder got to his feet. 'I felt', he wrote years later, 'that something a bit more light-hearted was called for.' He was also determined to draw attention to the condition of *Penola*. 'I am afraid', he began, 'that I find it somewhat difficult to say anything very complimentary about the old ship ... As a sailing vessel she was not a good performer, and motoring was not exactly her strong suit either. She had one remarkable asset, in that she was entirely free from all forms of vermin.' Ryder then commented on the advantages and disadvantages of a largely amateur crew before paying tribute to James Martin, Hughie Millett and his brother Lisle. It was, he said, his very first speech in public and had been delivered without notes. His impression was that the speech had been well received by the audience.[11]

Once Ryder had sat down, a succession of notables spoke about the expedition and its achievements. Two of them went out of their way to praise Ryder's skill in handling *Penola*. The first was Sir Herbert Henniker-Heaton, who, as Governor of the Falkland Islands, had been all too aware of the problems confronting Ryder at Port Stanley. 'As regards the *Penola*, the wiseacres of the Falkland Islands were quite satisfied that if the ship ever got south she would never return.' The second was Admiral Sir William Goodenough, who had done so much to get Ryder appointed to *Penola* in the first place. Speaking of the anxieties that Ryder faced as captain, Sir William said:

when one thinks of the many thousands of miles covered under sail, the visits to uncharted waters, the bad holding ground and unsafe harbours, and many gales of wind, I think all will agree that it has been a fine display of reliance, of seamanship, and of determination.[12]

Sir William's opinion, as a recent past President of the RGS, was not to be dismissed lightly. However, Ryder's speech did not win universal approval; most notably, John Rymill took umbrage at what he had said about the crew and the ship. Rymill wrote to Ryder to tell him that he 'thought my speech in very bad taste'. How far Rymill was justified in this opinion is now difficult to say, since Ryder's extempore remarks were toned down for publication. Ryder – despite himself being a Fellow of the RGS – probably failed to adhere to the usual, rather academic courtesies that prevailed at such meetings, but Rymill's accusation seems unduly harsh.

Ryder was sad that their relationship had descended to this: 'From the outset I had liked and greatly admired John.' For his part Rymill had selected Ryder to join him on his long sledging journey in the first winter and they had worked well together reconnoitring the coast from the air. What spoiled their relationship was the trouble with *Penola* and Ryder's perfectly reasonable insistence on docking her to repair the engines. That this was thrashed out by telegram at long range between Port Stanley, London and Graham Land only increased the misunderstanding and acrimony. Ryder blamed himself: 'All that I seemed to have done was to fall into the same old controversy between the ship master and his owner or leader.'[13]

This was not quite the end of the story of the BGLE for Ryder. In 1939 he was awarded the RGS's Back Prize 'for his captaincy of *Penola* and his marine surveys' on the BGLE. The prize 'for the reward and encouragement of scientific geographers and discoverers' was worth £14 in 1939. In October the same year the King approved the award of the Polar Medal, in silver, to all members of the expedition, with a clasp inscribed 'Antarctic 1935–1937'.

In August 1939, with the world on the brink of war, Ryder was (as he put it) 'languishing' on *Warspite*, when he received a letter from Colin Bertram, the BGLE's biologist who had been part of *Penola*'s crew in the first year. Bertram was planning another expedition and wanted Ryder to command its ship. 'Quite frankly', he wrote, 'I should like to see you in command of a new expedition ship. You know the coast, you excel in handling a small ship & you have the real desire to know more about the country.'[14]

Coming from someone who had seen Ryder's handling of *Penola* at first hand, it was indeed a compliment. Ryder was, naturally, both flattered and interested: 'One thing I am quite sure of is that if I went I would have every confidence in you as a leader, and I feel quite sure that we would work very well together', he replied. Privately, he added that 'at least [Bertram] would start by knowing my shortcomings.' He did, however, enter a caveat: 'If we are in for a war my duty is with the fleet and I could not go. If we are in for a period of peace, may be I can serve my country better in the Antarctic.' The approach was a 'great encouragement' but he knew unquestioningly where his duty lay.[15] As it turned out, Ryder's reply was written less than a week before Britain declared war on Germany.

After spending the New Year of 1938 with his parents Ryder reported back to *Warspite*. On 5 January she finally departed for Malta, arriving on 14 January. Although Ryder was now back at sea, it was in very different circumstances. During the passage to Malta he told his mother that:

It seems very strange to me to be changing for dinner at sea & so on, which compares strangely with life in *Penola* & *Tai Mo Shan* when as like as not one didn't even undress to turn in.

The news of his brother Lisle's engagement to Enid Ralston-Patrick 'cheers me enormously' but failed to lift his sense of gloom entirely. 'I feel very despondent at leaving England', he told his mother. The prospect of two or more years in a battleship was a depressing prospect to a man of Ryder's adventurous spirit, but there might perhaps have been another reason for his gloom: a girl. 'I am glad you were able to meet Eve Naylor but I suppose when I return in 1940 she will scarcely remember my name even.'[16]

As *Warspite* forged through the wintery Bay of Biscay Ryder thought wistfully of *Penola*, 'reeling off the miles under a press of canvas homeward bound in the south-east trades.' Instead, he found himself 'back to 2½ years of spit and polish right under the Admiral's eye.' Once *Warspite* had arrived at Malta she was given an intense programme to keep the crew busy on the basis, Ryder supposed, that 'busy hands don't mutiny'. On 6 February, the Commander-in-Chief of the Mediterranean Fleet, Admiral Sir Dudley Pound came aboard his new flagship for the first time, 'not best pleased', according to Ryder, 'at having to hoist his flag in what had been a mutinous ship.'[17]

There is little point in tracing *Warspite*'s every move around the Mediterranean for the eighteen months that Ryder was with her. Precise details of her summer and winter cruises, of Fleet exercises and gunnery practice would quickly pall nor would it add much to Ryder's story. Nevertheless, his time on the *Warspite* was not, perhaps, quite as uniformly boring as Ryder had feared in advance. One of the consolations of being on a flagship was that, because of the Admiral's presence, the officers tended to be of a higher calibre than in a private (that is, ordinary) ship. 'This', commented Ryder, 'was an asset.' Commander Amery Parkes was Ryder's immediate superior, while the gunnery officer was Stephen Roskill, later a well-known naval historian. Roskill had been with Ryder in the *Ramillies* ten years earlier and the two would remain friends. As Ryder was in command of *Warspite*'s 'Y' Turret he came directly under his command. Roskill was an energetic and innovative officer who brought *Warspite*'s gunnery to a high pitch of efficiency and accuracy.

The other notable aspect of serving in a flagship was the presence of the Admiral himself. For indolent or inefficient officers this could, of course, be a positive disadvantage; in Ryder's case it seems to have worked to his advantage. Admiral Sir Dudley Pound, whose flagship *Warspite* was, already knew of Ryder. It was Pound who had, as Second Sea Lord, taken the train to Dartmouth to welcome *Tai-Mo-Shan* home three-and-a-half-years earlier. Now, as Commander-in-Chief he had an opportunity to watch Ryder in very different circumstances. Pound was known for his solicitousness in looking after the interests and nurturing the careers of his subordinates, a reputation that seems to be well-founded in Ryder's case. By May 1938 he wrote to Ryder's mother to reassure her about her son's progress. He 'found himself a bit "at sea" during the first month in *Warspite* [but] he very quickly picked up the threads and is doing very well.' The Admiral then offered some sage advice, 'What he has got to do at the present time is to get completely au fait with the "main line" of the Navy after his long absence away from it.'[18]

The other advantage of serving on the Flagship was that she tended to visit more salubrious parts of the Mediterranean than the lesser, private ships. Ryder recalled that when he had been in *Ramillies* as a midshipman 'we had usually been relegated to the fly-blown ports of North Africa, Bougie, Bizerta and the like …'. But *Warspite* spent much more time on the French and Italian Rivieras.

As Ryder had found in the *Ramillies* ten years earlier, the Mediterranean station offered young officers many opportunities to amuse themselves. Admiral Pound was a keen shot so much effort was diverted into providing him with his sport. In August 1938, with the Munich crisis unfolding, the *Warspite* was embarking on a cruise around the Aegean and the eastern Mediterranean, taking in Thaso, Mudros, Famagusta and a number of other stops. 'Most of these places', Ryder told his sister, 'are chosen so that the Commander-in-Chief can get his shooting.'

> The first day at Thaso I went shooting quail. One of a large party of officers with the Admiral. Organized very much on naval lines with the guns and beaters manoeuvred by flag signals. The Admiral is followed by an orderly with a bundle of different coloured flags for the purpose of manoeuvring the line of guns & beaters. Unfortunately there were practically no birds. The following day was little better.

There were other, less formal opportunities for shooting, too. The rock pigeons which lived in seaside cliff caves were a favourite target. The trick was while cruising around in a small motor boat at the foot of the cliffs to fire a Verey light into the cave and shoot the pigeons as they flew out. 'With the boat pitching they were extremely difficult, but again a splendid diversion.' When *Warspite* was at Alexandria there was snipe and duck shooting in the Nile delta to be had, too.[19]

Nor were Ryder and his fellow officers just there for the shooting. For the latter part of Ryder's time in *Warspite* the Fleet was based at Alexandria, its war station. 'I have been enjoying Alexandria quite a bit', he told his sister Enid in July 1939. We 'subsist on bathing parties, generally accompanied with bevies of Greek girls; some very attractive.' Ryder and three brother officers decided to give a party to repay the Greeks' generous hospitality. They organized

> a large scale moonlight picnic & chartered a 300 ton lighter which we had rigged up as Cleopatra's barge & garlanded with flowers etc. & were then towed around the fleet, passing close by the *Warspite* after dinner. When all the women shouted for the Admiral I thought we would get into serious trouble but nobody seemed to mind. We eventually returned on board in broad daylight with hampers of empty bottles, cushions etc. It was really a very successful party.[20]

It was evidently a memorable evening as Lieutenant Commander Fred Smith, who had served in *Warspite* with Ryder, when writing to congratulate him on his promotion in 1941, referred to Alexandria as 'the scene of your famous lighter picnic & orgy!'[21] Alexandria had other excitements to offer young, footloose and fancy-free naval officers. One night in September 1938 Ryder went ashore for the evening where he 'saw a cabaret – mostly women with very exotic figures dancing in that suggestive manner in which these people excel.' However tempted they were, discretion proved the better part of valour, 'we decided that we would not accept the suggestion until war has actually been declared.'[22]

Naturally the Mediterranean Fleet also offered opportunities for less fleshly, more vigorous, pursuits. There were regular Fleet regattas, for pulling and sailing races, chances to go walking ashore as well as less strenuous activities. In July 1938 the *Warspite* was at Navarino busy with the Fleet sailing races.

This is a lovely part of the world with its loneliness. Lovely white sandy beaches where one browns oneself in the sun. There are also some lovely old ruined castles, some washed by the sea, and others built into the crags of the hills. A very sketchable country.[23]

Isolated, romantic spots such as this never failed to touch Ryder's soul.

Ryder made two motorcycle excursions with Victor Clarke, a kindred spirit also serving in *Warspite*. 'Victor and I were both rather rebellious spirits,' Ryder recalled. On one occasion they took a motorcycle from the Mediterranean to Lake Geneva. This trip was billed as an intelligence-gathering exercise to report upon military activity on the French side of the Italian frontier. Ryder rode pillion on the luggage rack, an unforgettably uncomfortable experience as they bumped and bounced their way up the badly pot-holed, hair-pin mountain roads. Clarke and Ryder penetrated far up the mountain valleys, often staying in tiny, family-run auberges close to the frontier. 'It was quite a memorable trip.' On another occasion he and Clarke had an outing in Algeria while *Warspite* was at Bougie. They drove over the Atlas Mountains from the coast to Sidi bel Abbes, the headquarters of the French Foreign Legion. During the trip the two men 'quite seriously discussed' the possibility of joining the Legion. Perhaps not surprisingly, nothing came of it; indeed, with 'War clouds ... on the horizon ... we decided that we would be more likely to see action in *Warspite*.' So Red Ryder never became Beau Geste.

But for all the diversions that a posting to the Flagship of the Mediterranean Fleet offered, Ryder was, fundamentally, frustrated and ill at ease in a battleship. He was, and would remain throughout his life, a small-ship man. His letters of the time give full rein to his boredom and frustration. Thus in September 1938 he wrote to his sister Enid:

As you read this ... you will realize why I am unhappy these days and why at times I am in despair. I feel that the hour is practically at hand when we may be called on to defend our country, and then I think of myself shut away from all initiative and responsibility here carrying out duties which are performed in other parts of the ship by sub lieutenants. Treated with contempt by my seniors, and bored stiff with nothing to do, and unfortunately with no prospect of being shifted till the end of any possible hostilities.[24]

Ryder made several attempts to escape from the stifling routine of life in *Warspite*. His main hope was that he would be released for a naval staff course. This ambition was dependent on the say-so of Victor Crutchley, but 'the old rascal keeps putting it off'. He considered that Ryder was not suited for staff work; he was prepared, he told his frustrated Lieutenant, to recommend him for an independent command but not for staff work. But despite his frustrations, his career was still in the ascendant; on 1 June 1938 he was promoted Lieutenant Commander.

In February 1939, by which time Ryder had been in the Mediterranean for just over a year, he wrote to the Admiralty, drawing attention to the fact that his entitlement to leave had been greatly curtailed before joining *Warspite*. He informed their Lordships that he had suffered a bout of 'prolonged mental depression' from which he had now recovered. Ryder continued:

This has in the past been a common though not invariable experience with expeditions returning from Polar regions, and as in recent years there have been cases of suicide under these conditions ... I cannot but believe that it would be in the interests of the Service to make allowances for this should another occasion arise.

In the letter's formal, somewhat elliptical language Ryder is telling the Admiralty that he may again become mentally depressed, even suicidal, at some point in the future. This is an extraordinary letter for a serving officer in the 1930s to write, particularly one of Ryder's tough, uncomplaining nature and uncompromising view of duty. It is more of a howl of pained frustration than a reasoned argument for release. Indeed, years later he wrote across the top of the paper: 'I was pretty frustrated being stuck in the Mediterranean fleet flag ship – but I find it difficult to believe that I wrote this letter.'[25]

For all Ryder's obvious frustrations at his existence in *Warspite*, his eighteen months in the Mediterranean coincided with a period of increasing international tensions as the threat of war grew ever larger. Gradually, this imbued the ship's, and the fleet's, daily routine with added purpose. The Munich Crisis of August and September 1938 set the Mediterranean Fleet humming with the buzz of war. Coming on top of the *Anschluss* in the spring, it seemed to many, Ryder included, to confirm that only war could now stop Hitler. He told his sister, 'Personally I think the time has come when we ought to fight. The best we can hope to do is to put off the evil day and the present scheme of Chamberlain's is hardly "peace with honour".'[26]

The heightened diplomatic tension galvanized the Fleet, shaking it from the familiar patterns of its peacetime routines. 'We now have extra sentries', Ryder reported, 'one in the bow & one right aft and the officer of the watch armed with a revolver and ammunition. All suspicious craft approaching are flood lit by searchlight. Destroyers patrol off the entrance and during the day time we are busy fuzing shells and [with] ceaseless gun drill.' At Alexandria there was a palpable sense of excitement in the air as the Fleet moved on to a war footing. There are, Ryder recounted, 'Rumours of ships being sent hither and thither. Ships arriving after dark. Drawing money and provisions & sailing before day break.'[27]

On 8 October 1938, as the storms of Munich began to rumble more distantly, the clouds suddenly opened above Ryder's head. He was appointed, out of the blue, to his first independent command. The ship was HMS *Saltash*, a minesweeper. Ryder came alive, busying himself with all the tasks of a commanding officer, drawing the confidential books and signal manuals and making ready to go to sea. He took the *Saltash* to sea for the first time on 11 October. Two days later he proudly told his sister that 'I find that I have learned more useful information in the last few days than in a whole nine months in *Warspite*.'[28]

Ryder's command of the *Saltash* lasted only a fortnight but it was a great fillip for his morale. 'Minesweeping is tricky and interesting work as one has to manoeuvre the ships in the convoy at very close quarters for passing and sighting sweeps. The class of ship is not easy to handle although they are comparatively small.' He had thoroughly enjoyed his first taste of command: 'I am brown as a berry and feeling vastly better in every way'. '[T]he only snag', he concluded morosely, 'is having to return to *Warspite*.'[29]

At dawn on 7 April 1939 the Italians invaded Albania to gratify Mussolini's love of military adventure – the feebler and more insignificant the enemy the better – and to 'get even with Hitler over the German occupation of Prague'.[30] When Italian forces landed in Albania, *Warspite* was lying – or, as Churchill put it, 'lolling about' – at the Italian port of San Remo.[31] Ryder was on leave visiting his parents who were staying at Beaulieu on the French Riviera. It was clearly imperative that he rejoin his ship, indeed, Admiral Pound had decided to leave San Remo at once. To avoid trouble Ryder took a taxi from Beaulieu all the way along the coast to San Remo. Nearing the Italian frontier 'felt rather like going into enemy territory.' Then he remembered that his passport did not have a visa for Italy. 'I felt rather alone', he remembered, 'as the Fascist Police and Carabinieri closed in to examine my passport.' Fortunately, the lack of a visa went unnoticed.[32] He arrived back at San Remo just in time to rejoin *Warspite* before she sailed. As if to emphasize the potential danger of her situation, the captain darkened ship and ordered all hands to action stations as she steamed out to sea.

Once *Warspite* had returned to Alexandria, Ryder was offered the chance to become Air Defence Officer and second Gunnery Officer. He jumped at the opportunity. It was a much more interesting job as, with war now obviously imminent, countering the threat posed by the Italian air force was a high priority. 'It was no longer just peacetime practice'; there now seemed some purpose to the activity. Moreover, it was an open-air job and gave Ryder a certain amount of scope to use his initiative.[33]

Thus Ryder spent the last summer of peace. In August *Warspite* visited Istanbul as part of the diplomatic efforts aimed at preventing the Turks from joining the Axis powers. Indeed, so anxious were the British to secure Turkey's alliance that they signed an agreement giving the Turks a £25 million credit for war matériel and a transfer of £15 million of gold bullion from London.[34] The trip occasioned a good deal of revelry, with entertaining on both sides. *Warspite*'s officers were taken on a trip by steamer up the Bosphorus, returning by moonlight with female company thoughtfully provided by the Turks. In return, the British hosted a dance aboard *Warspite*. Unfortunately, the evening was not a great success as Atatürk's efforts to westernize the country had not yet, according to Ryder, modified traditional attitudes to dancing. 'Those over the age of about 25 could only rise to a kind of undulating movement akin to a modified belly dance.' After considering the problem, Ryder wrote, 'I decided that some strong drink was needed but "The Beard" stood watch dog by the bar. I was ordered to "get out and dance with some of those women over there".'[35]

This was the last important act of Ryder's peacetime service. The visit over, *Warspite* was not far out of the Dardanelles when the news arrived that Britain was at war. *Warspite* doused her lights and steamed for Alexandria. On 4 September, the day after Britain declared war on Germany Ryder wrote to his father,

> It has always been my hope and ambition that I may be called on to strike a blow in the defence of my country. Alas I am to be one of those stuck in the battleships of the fleet who never saw an enemy the whole war – just endless target practice – regattas etc.[36]

Little did Ryder know how wrong his fears would prove to be.

Chapter 9

HMS *Willamette Valley* (1939–40)

Within a fortnight of the outbreak of war Victor Crutchley in *Warspite* received a top-secret signal from the Admiralty. The signal asked whether Ryder would volunteer for service under Vice Admiral Gordon Campbell, VC. This laconic enquiry put Ryder into a high state of excitement as 'I needed no introduction to this officer.'[1]

Gordon Campbell had distinguished himself as an outstandingly courageous commander of Q-ships during the Great War. These vessels, apparently harmless merchantmen but in fact converted tramp steamers fitted with concealed guns, offered themselves as targets to U-boats with the object of luring them to destruction. Campbell, by remaining on board his ship after she had been torpedoed, waiting for the enemy to close, destroyed three of the eleven U-boats sunk in this way. He had been awarded the Victoria Cross for an action against a German submarine in February 1917, as well as the Distinguished Service Order and two Bars. During the 1930s, after retiring from the Navy, Campbell became a popular writer and lecturer, mostly on the subject of fighting at sea, including his own experiences in Q-ships. At the outbreak of war in 1939 he was brought out of retirement by the First Lord of the Admiralty, Winston Churchill, to oversee the commissioning of a new generation of Q-ships to replicate the tactics used so successfully during the Great War.[2]

This was not a invitation to be turned down. The chance to serve – albeit in an as yet unspecified capacity – under such a distinguished fighting sailor was the answer to Ryder's prayers after the longueurs of peacetime duty in *Warspite*. His war would not, as he had feared, now be spent in endless target practice and regattas. Having received the signal, Ryder at once packed and left *Warspite* on 18 September, hurrying up to Port Said where SS *Dunera*, a troopship, was departing for England. He made the ship only an hour or so before she sailed, later transferring to SS *Orion*.

Orion 'was a splendid ship, fitted out and victualled for a luxury cruise', in use as a troopship. As there was then only one other passenger on board, an RNR sub lieutenant, the two men were waited on by hundreds of stewards. 'We had', Ryder recalled, 'a sumptuous library to ourselves, a swimming pool and two tennis courts.' *Orion*, which could cruise at 24 knots, made a rapid passage home.[3]

Ryder immediately reported to Admiral Campbell. He briefed Ryder in detail about his new command, one of six or eight merchant vessels being fitted out for anti-submarine duties, the new generation of Q-ships. The Admiral stressed the need for absolute secrecy and also the need to ensure that the ship's camouflage was convincing down to the last detail. Ryder's new ship was HMS *Willamette Valley*, a 5,000-ton Cardiff tramp steamer. Built in 1928, she was capable of 10.5 knots. She was, in Ryder's opinion, the best of the new Q-ships as her single screw engine had, with full tanks, a cruising range of 24,000 miles at about 9.5 knots. On 29 September Ryder, now in the rank of acting Commander, took up his command at Chatham where *Willamette Valley* was being converted in the dockyards.

For the next two or three months Ryder lived in the naval barracks at Chatham while supervising the work on *Willamette Valley*. The main feature of the conversion was the fitting of her armament which consisted of four 4in guns on each side in addition to the normal Defensively Equipped Merchant Ship (DEMS) 4in gun on the 'bandstand' aft. She was also fitted with one 12-pounder gun and two torpedo tubes on each side, Asdic and depth charges. As the ship was flush-decked, all the concealed armaments were mounted in the 'tween decks. In order to open fire it was therefore necessary to drop the concealed gunports before training the guns on the enemy. The gunports were cut to a very exact fit to be as invisible as possible. They might, Ryder reckoned, be noticed by 'a very observant passer-by on the dockside', but from any distance they were indistinguishable from the rest of the hull. To ensure secrecy, the work was carried out with the ship swathed in tarpaulins.

For Ryder the most interesting aspect of his new command was deciding on possible disguises for the ship. Armed with a copy of *Jane's Merchant Ships* and other reference books Ryder spent his evenings devising various methods by which *Willamette Valley*'s appearance could be altered to make her resemble other ships. Disguising tricks included altering the shape and the location of ventilation cowls, the raising and lowering of the top masts and derricks and the removal of the aft 'bandstand' gun. As *Willamette Valley* had a distinctively squat funnel Ryder had a 10 foot extension made, thereby allowing him to alter the vessel's profile substantially at will. 'I had a most fascinating time planning these disguises', he recalled, 'and counted myself lucky in having such a free hand in specifying what I wanted.'[4]

If Ryder considered himself fortunate in the latitude he was allowed in the ship's conversion, he 'was even luckier when it came to officers.' Ryder had managed to secure the services of Michael Seymour as his First Lieutenant. Seymour, who had become a close friend of Ryder's during their time together in *Warspite*, was a 'first-class officer and a most attractive and amusing personality.'

Ryder was also joined in *Willamette Valley* by another old friend, the mildly maverick James Martin who had been first mate on *Penola*. He was eager to join Ryder's ship, but there was a snag: Martin was, formally, on the reserve of officers of the Guards Brigade. However, the War Office was very slow in calling him up so he wrote announcing that he was now serving as a lieutenant in the Royal Navy Volunteer Reserve (RNVR). The War Office was outraged but there was little it could do. He and Ryder had established an excellent working relationship during their three years together in the Antarctic. As a result, Ryder had every confidence in him: 'he was a first class seaman.' One of Martin's most important jobs was changing the ship's disguises, something that was done 'at sea, often in adverse weather conditions [and] invariably at night.'[5]

The remainder of the ship's company was made up of RNVE officers, reservists 'all feeling rather disgruntled at having been called up' and officers and ratings transferred to the Royal Navy from the Merchant Navy. The latter were known as T124X men, after the articles they signed on transfer. For the most part, these men 'entered into the spirit of the thing very well'. Once complete, the ship's company numbered ninety-three; none of them was a volunteer.[6]

One of the T124X officers, Lieutenant Commander Thompson, appointed to *Willamette Valley* as navigating officer, had in peacetime been with the merchant shipping Bank Line. His experience and advice was invaluable in helping Ryder to perfect his ship's disguise as an innocent merchantman. Admiral Campbell had emphasized the need to get the ship's cover story correct down to the last detail, but there were many traps for the unwary. For example, when *Willamette Valley* arrived in Southampton Water at the start of her commission, Ryder was about to lower the gangway to allow the pilot ashore. Thompson quickly whispered 'You never do that for a pilot, sir – only for the customs.' A small slip like that would have given the game away at once. As Ryder admitted, 'There was much to learn.'[7] On another occasion Ryder gave a pilot a packet of cigarettes which were marked 'For H.M. Ships only' which only emphasized how careful he had to be to preserve the disguise. Thompson was an expert at identifying other ships and their country or even port of origin, an invaluable asset in a Q-ship.

As a final touch to the ship's disguise she took aboard two pigs – passengers that would, of course, never be allowed to sully the scrubbed decks of one of the King's ships. As they spent most of their days outside the galley waiting for scraps, Ryder could see them from the bridge. One day they looked different; Ryder, focusing his binoculars, saw that some wag had painted 'Hitler' and 'Musso' on their flanks. There was one other unusual member of the ship's company: a parrot belonging to Leading Seaman Roberts. He was 'a splendid bird', Ryder remembered, 'that used to stand to attention for captain's rounds ... I used to look curiously into its red eyes wondering what it was thinking. Then when I had moved on to the next mess deck it shouted after me "fucking bastard".'[8]

Her conversion now complete and her crew assembled, *Willamette Valley* commissioned in the last week of February 1940. Admiral Campbell decided to come down to see the ship off. Arriving in plain clothes, he changed into full uniform below deck before addressing the ship's company.

The plan was that *Willamette Valley* would go round to Southampton to join a convoy down the Channel. To this end, during the night at Southend, she became Royal Fleet Auxiliary *Edgehill*. She had from now on three identities: HMS *Willamette Valley* for administrative purposes, RFA *Edgehill* for entering and leaving port, and whatever disguise she adopted while at sea. Ryder and his officers changed into standard Merchant Navy uniforms. Admiral Campbell, ever alert to security, questioned a pilot who had been on board about the ship. The pilot had, he said, noticed nothing untoward bar the fact that the officers seemed unusually well spoken for the Merchant Navy. The ship was officially cleared to carry secret boom defence equipment to Gibraltar. Five months after his dash home from Egypt and after months of careful planning, Ryder was ready to engage the enemy in a deadly game of bluff, requiring patience, cool nerve and unflinching courage.

The night before *Willamette Valley* joined the convoy, Michael Seymour and James Martin changed the ship's persona. She became SS *Aldington Court*. In the morning she weighed anchor as a convoy made its way out to sea from Southampton, joining its tail as a straggler. That night she slipped off on her own into the Atlantic.

'Looking back over the years', Ryder wrote later, 'I feel that some of my happiest days were when I was in command of my Q-ship. I felt I was at my best then.' He understood the job; he had Michael Seymour and James Martin as brothers-in-arms. His orders, too, were both 'broad and simple': 'Seek out and destroy the enemy.' This kind of freelance appointment gave Ryder enormous latitude. He could range around the North and the South Atlantic as well as the Southern and the Indian Ocean in search of the enemy. He could even venture into the Pacific if need be. Ryder felt he enjoyed the confidence of his commanding officer, Admiral Campbell (it was only later that Ryder discovered that the Admiral had in fact regarded him as his best captain), and the ship's company.[9] In 1986, three months before his death, Ryder received a letter from Con Blake who had served as a T124X radio officer in *Willamette Valley*. Blake told Ryder that he 'quite naturally and unconsciously set a wonderful example. With the responsibility you carried you never, ever, appeared ruffled or bad tempered!'[10]

For the first few days *Willamette Valley* cruised around in the Western Approaches. The difficulty which Ryder was to face for the next four months was neatly summed up in the log entry for 29 February 1940: 'Sighted the Norwegian ship *Ida Bakke* this morning. This is interesting in that it is only the second ship sighted in four days, although we have been sailing up and down the principal shipping routes of the world.' Locating an enemy submarine or surface raider would be akin to finding the proverbial needle in the haystack.[11] As Ryder later commented, 'it became apparent that the sea is a very large place and the chance of an intercept slim.'[12]

Having cruised in the Western Approaches for a few days without any contact with an enemy, Ryder set course for Bermuda via the Azores. Admiral Campbell had suggested investigating the islands which might well be used by enemy submarines and surface raiders for refuelling and shelter. *Willamette Valley* duly nosed around the islands for three days without seeing an enemy ship. Having failed to make any contact Ryder turned west towards Bermuda, where the ship arrived on 20 March after a slow passage against head winds and rough seas.

Once his ship was berthed in Bermuda, Ryder's main concern was – as it always was with his Q-ship in port – security. When *Willamette Valley* arrived there were two other Royal Fleet Auxiliaries in port. This was a worry to Ryder as 'There are only a limited number of ships in this service and they all know each other. Our bona fides were therefore suspect as soon as our approach was signalled.' The crew were allowed to go ashore each evening in uniform; their cover story was that they were a naval draft for Halifax. 'On the whole', Ryder concluded, '… secrecy was well preserved.' *Willamette Valley* spent eight days at Bermuda while the ship was painted black – 'quite the best colour as far as the gunports are concerned' – and the drinking water tanks resealed.

On 28 March she put to sea once more, intending to cruise down to the coast of Brazil where naval intelligence suggested that the oil routes might provide a tempting target for enemy surface raiders and submarines. Once clear of Bermuda the ship's identity was changed to pass her off as SS *Bolton Hall*, which Ryder had last seen entering the Thames estuary. This entailed repainting the funnel and altering her outline by removing Sampson posts, cowls and derricks. On 9 April the ship crossed the Equator, continuing to cruise in a south-westerly direction parallel to the coast of Brazil. Frustratingly, Ryder saw very few other ships and nothing that resembled the enemy. On 15 April, *Willamette Valley* altered course to make for Sierra Leone, where she arrived on 24 April.[13]

She had an unhappy time at Sierra Leone: 'By sheer mischance we had two cases of appendicitis, one broken rib and one cracked skull.' The threat of storms prevented the engines from being overhauled while the risk of malaria restricted shore leave, but the crew did receive a good batch of mail from home. On 1 May *Willamette Valley* left Sierra Leone following a large convoy towards Gibraltar but keeping astern and out of sight. She continued shadowing the convoy for a week until on 9 May Ryder received a signal reporting that a disguised raider had been sighted 500 miles or more to the north-west. 'This is unquestionably the most promising report we have had', thought Ryder, 'although the number of false alarms is inclined to make one sceptical.' This report was given added piquancy by a warning of an abandoned and burning schooner, possibly a victim of the raider. It was also reported that a German tanker, the *Rudolf Albrecht*, was in the Azores preparing to put to sea. Amending the ship's cover story by altering her sailing orders and bill of lading, Ryder changed course to the north-west.

By 12 May *Willamette Valley* had arrived in the area where the raider had been reported, but there was no sign of her. Given that the reports were now more than a fortnight old, Ryder concluded that the raider was probably already long gone. He decided instead to cruise around the Azores in the hope of encountering the German tanker that was reported to be putting to sea. This episode shows the difficulties and frustrations that faced Ryder. Out-of-date information, long distances and huge areas of sea made locating an enemy little more than a matter of chance.

On 14 May *Willamette Valley* passed the Azores island of San Miguel. Ryder could see a large vessel anchored off Ponta Dalgarda, which he tentatively identified as the *Germania*, an enemy tanker. This was the best chance that had so far presented itself for a stroke against the enemy. Seymour and Martin were both very keen to attempt it. Preparations were made to board the tanker by climbing up her cable, surprise the crew and set her adrift. In the end, after much thought, Ryder decided not to attempt the operation for fear of violating Portuguese neutrality – *Germania* was in Portuguese territorial waters – and because of residual doubts as to the ship's identity. 'I funked it.' 'Was I overcautious?', he wondered later. 'It would have been a great scoop, [but] I think perhaps I was wise.'[14]

On 20 May *Willamette Valley* arrived at Gibraltar. Ryder reported that the 'atmosphere is strained here on account of the Italian situation ... the civil population is being evacuated.' Indeed, after *Willamette Valley* had been in port for four days, Ryder received a secret message from the Commander-in-Chief ordering him to take his ship to sea as it was rumoured that the Italians were about to bomb the port. Ryder, having been refused permission to go into the Mediterranean, put out into the Atlantic to cruise up the coast of Portugal.[15] After a short and uneventful cruise, she returned to Gibraltar on 29 May.

The following day a dockyard tug, *Rollicker*, put her bow against *Willamette Valley*'s hull to push her clear of a channel to allow another vessel to pass. Unfortunately, the tug's bow pushed in the *Willamette Valley*'s aftmost gunport. The tugmaster was 'utterly mystified' and reported that she seemed a very odd ship. The gun port was 'badly buckled and jammed, and is inclined to show from the outside.' To repair the damage would require the construction of a new gunport which would inevitably reveal the *Willamette Valley*'s true nature. 'This is very undesirable as half of the dockyard workers live in Spain and news would very soon be back in Germany.' Ryder therefore decided to effect whatever repairs he could at sea. On 30 May the ship left Gibraltar once more. On the first night out of Gibraltar the crew worked hard at the damaged gunport so that it could be dropped 'if really required'. The hull was painted with a large patch of red lead about 15 feet forward of the damaged gunport 'to divert the eye.'[16]

Willamette Valley continued on a northerly course until she reached the north-west corner of Spain, at which point she turned to the south once again. On 4 June she passed some scattered debris in the water which Ryder supposed was the remains of a French ship which had been torpedoed in the area a week earlier. 'This is', Ryder noted despondently, 'the nearest we have been to war so far.' After fruitlessly chasing yet another report of an enemy submarine, Ryder received an order to return to Gibraltar. He arrived on 11 June, the same day as news reached him that Italy had entered the war.

So far Ryder had been criss-crossing the North and the South Atlantic, chasing rumours and unconfirmed sightings for more than three months. If he was despondent about his failure to close with the enemy, he received at Gibraltar a heartening letter from Admiral Campbell. 'What a splendid cruise you have made and [I] am sorry that nothing came your way; however, you are used to patience & success frequently follows it …' 'Your personal & official letters', the Admiral continued, 'have given me much confidence in you and I know you will do the right thing at the right time.'[17]

After a brief stay in harbour, Ryder and *Willamette Valley* soon put to sea again. Once away from prying eyes the ship's disguise was changed to make her resemble a Dutch vessel *Themisto*. At about this time Ryder received a signal directing him to work the 15th meridian up to the latitude of 50° N before making course for Halifax in Canada. Once these instructions had arrived Ryder decided to alter the ship's disguise yet again. The alterations give an interesting insight into the thinking of a Q-ship commander. Ryder felt that an armed ship would provide little incentive for a submarine to attack on the surface and, as almost all British ships were now armed, he therefore decided to assume the identity of a Greek vessel. Adopting Greek nationality would allow *Willamette Valley* to sail alone without a convoy – British ships invariably travelled in convoy – and to dispense with the DEMS gun. Balancing these advantages were three disadvantages: that the ship could not zig-zag; that it was restricted to the normal shipping lanes; and that in the event of its having to use the wireless in an emergency, there could be a problem.[18]

The ship's new disguise as *Ambea* of Piraeus was painted on to her during a night stop at sea in the form of two large, Greek ensigns, one on each side of the hull. Her name was painted on the bow and the stern, and on all the boats in the approved manner. Ryder decided that she would steam without lights at night and would continue to alter course after dark to shake off any shadowing enemies.

On 25 June Ryder intercepted a distress signal from SS *Yarraville* about 90 miles west of the Tagus. While *Willamette Valley* made for the given location, she signalled her position and intention *en clair* in the hope of drawing in the enemy. Reaching the *Yarraville*'s position there was nothing to be seen but oil and debris so *Willamette Valley* continued on her northern course. On 27 June Ryder radioed in code asking for permission to remain in the area for another week. As the ship was beyond the reach of aerial and surface patrols and, outwardly, unarmed he felt she offered a submarine a tempting target for a surface attack. Ryder's request was refused so the ship continued on her way to Halifax.

Shortly after dark on the evening of 28 June 1940 *Willamette Valley* was hit by first one then two more torpedoes. After the first torpedo hit, Ryder coolly carried out the planned drill, ordering the 'panic party' away in the hope of luring his attacker to the surface. The second torpedo started a fire in the engine room and the third, fired about forty minutes after the first, was the killer blow. *Willamette Valley* sank by the stern, rolling through 90° as she did so.

The story of Ryder's remarkable survival has already been told in the Prologue. There were, however, many other acts of courage, endurance and selfless devotion to duty from that terrible night. The first torpedo struck the ship on the port side just forward of the bridge. 'This could not', Ryder wrote in his report of the sinking, 'have happened at a more inopportune moment.' It was by then too dark to see whether the attacking submarine had come to the surface; moreover, the ship, silhouetted against the afterglow of the sunset on the western horizon, presented a fine target to the submarine.

As the main engine appeared to be undamaged, Ryder contemplated trying to escape by putting down a smokescreen but decided that the best course was to carry on with the normal drill. 'Our best hope' was that the submarine commander would surface and turn his searchlight on the ship thereby providing her concealed guns with an aiming point. This was an essential element of the ruse of Q-ship strategy. So the 'panic party' was embarked and sent away in two boats. The two boats had differing fortunes in the heavy sea and force 6 wind. The starboard boat, under Lieutenant Commander Thompson, was forced to return, against Ryder's shouted orders, about twenty minutes after it had left as it was shipping water badly. Its crew were ordered to hide for fear that the enemy would illuminate the ship. The port boat – on the weather side of the ship – managed to get away despite the dark night and the heavy sea. This was thanks largely to the actions of Midshipman Whittle who, despite not being the senior officer in the boat, appreciated the need to keep clear of *Willamette Valley*. Although the boat was damaged he reassured the crew, organized bailing and 'was largely responsible, in consequence, in saving the lives of 23 men.' This was, Ryder, wrote, 'a very credible performance' in a young officer.

The First Lieutenant, Michael Seymour, having inspected the ship, reported that there was little damage and no casualties, although one man was missing. The 'shock of the torpedo exploding was very great', but although it seemed to have caused little damage to the hull and engines, it had disabled the ship's telephone system, the Asdic and, probably, the radio. A distress signal was transmitted giving the ship's position; this was made four times but perhaps never got through. Although the ship's telephone system was out of action, Ryder, on the bridge, was able to establish contact with all positions by voice pipe. At this stage all hands remained at their action stations, waiting in case the enemy showed himself.

About five minutes after the panic party boat had returned – and three-quarters of an hour after the first attack – a second torpedo struck the ship on the starboard side in the engine room. This caused a 'tremendous flash which extended through most of the 'tween decks, plunged the ship into darkness and put the fire mains out of action.' A series of fires immediately broke out in the engine room, which Michael Seymour, hampered by the knocking out of the fire main, tackled by organizing a chain of men with buckets. This had some success in dousing the fires. At the same time in the forward section of the ship, James Martin was organizing his men to move ammunition away from the fire. Ryder on the bridge could hear Martin's orders through the voice pipe. Elsewhere, too, Ryder could hear through the voice pipes the desperate efforts being made to save the ship.

While the crew were struggling with the fires that were now blazing amidships and in the engine room, a third torpedo struck her under the stern. 'It was obvious to me', Ryder wrote, 'that this was final and I gave the order "All hands on deck".' Less than a minute after the explosion, the ship began to sink by the stern, heeling badly to port as she did so. *Willamette Valley* hung suspended in the water with her bows in the air for about half an hour before she sank altogether.

The courage and discipline shown by Ryder's men was exemplary. He did not give the order to abandon ship but 'the officers ... and many of the men must have realized all along that such an order would, in fact, never be given when engaged in an action of that type.' 'They were throughout therefore, faced with this fact in all they did. They nevertheless carried on, and, apart from the "panic party", the ship sank with all hands on board.'

After the second torpedo had struck, it must, Ryder wrote later, have been 'apparent to everyone that we were indeed in a desperate plight', yet everything was being done to save the ship until the last possible moment. 'With all lights extinguished, and the ship blazing amidships it is not difficult to visualise the conditions on the 'tween decks, and to realise the determination and self-sacrifice that was displayed.'

Once Ryder had given the order 'All hands on deck', the crew tried unsuccessfully to launch the two remaining small boats. One had been smashed by the explosion of the torpedo. The other, on the upper edge of the now steeply sloping deck, could not be launched. Ryder himself was thrown into the water from the bridge, grabbing a lifebuoy as he went.

Sub Lieutenant Pembery was also on deck when the third torpedo exploded under the stern. He was one of those who had tried to launch the remaining small boats but, unable to do so with the ship heeling over so far, Pembery jumped into the sea and swam clear of the sinking ship. There was a great deal of oil and wreckage floating in the water. Eventually he found an undamaged life raft floating upside down in the water and scrambled on to it. Pembery and eight ratings 'spent a most precarious night' on this raft. As the dawn came up he saw Whittle's lifeboat a hundred yards off and, abandoning the raft, the nine of them went aboard the lifeboat.

There were now twenty-four hands all told in the lifeboat, including Mr Pearson, the Chief Radio Officer, who had been picked out of the water, exhausted and covered in fuel oil, about half an hour after the ship had sunk. The boat had ample provisions and some water but, unfortunately, no compass. Pembery, being the senior officer, took command of the lifeboat. Although the boat had drifted some way from the scene of the sinking during the night, Pembery decided to remain hove to in the hope that a rescuer might appear. At midday the crew set sail to the north-east. Pembery realized that the little boat was 'well in the traffic routes of the Western Approaches' which gave him grounds for optimism that they might soon be spotted and rescued. Moreover, the heavy swell and strong winds of the previous evening were now moderating and the sun had come out. 'All in good spirits', Pembery reported on that first day, 'having benefitted by a strong sun which dried our wet clothing.'

For the first three days the little boat made good progress in fine, clear conditions in the general direction of the British Isles. On Sunday, the second day after the sinking, Pembery estimated that the boat had maintained a speed of around 5 knots all day. There were sufficient provisions on board so that all hands could have a small ration of food – a biscuit and some corned beef – and, most importantly, some water twice a day. The crew did all they could to keep each other's spirits up. Pembery reported later that Stoker Petty Officers Lockwood and Holland, Chief Petty Officer Symons and Stoker Loram all did much by their example to maintain cheerfulness and good morale in the boat during those trying days. Pembery's principal concern was the condition of Pearson whose face and eyes were badly blistered by immersion in oil and the effects of the sun and who was shivering continuously.

On the fourth day great excitement was caused by the appearance of a large aeroplane – 'probably R.A.F. Sunderland' thought Pembery – about 6 miles to their north. The crew fired some flares into the air but to no avail. Although the boat was not seen, the crew was greatly encouraged by signs that they were now within range of the patrolling seaplanes. That evening the weather took a turn for the worse with a heavy swell rolling in from the west. 'Dirty and most uncomfortable night', Pembery reported the following morning. On account of the rough weather he 'Kept all hands on stretchers and bottom boards, so all suffering from cramped positions and lack of sleep.'

By Wednesday, the fifth day adrift in the lifeboat, the crew's spirits were sinking. Food was getting short and the men were all now very thirsty. They had not seen an aircraft nor any smoke all day. Worse, the weather was now unpleasantly rough, with heavy seas and wind drenching them in spray, necessitating frequent bailing. The crew spent another wretched night 'rolling and tossing violently' but at 0530 sighted smoke. Pembery decided to make a bid to reach the ship, despite the poor conditions, and by hoisting a reefed mainsail in the lifeboat with all hands on the weather side to act as ballast, the little boat was soon bearing down on the ship. It was, it transpired, a large French trawler, *Donibone*. The British sailors went aboard at 0715, their ordeal finally over, after five-and-a-half days in an open boat. Their relief was immense: 'Thank God picked up at last', Pembery noted laconically in his makeshift log. He reported that 'We ... were rather disappointed to find it a French trawler, but I cannot speak too highly of the kindness which was shown to us.' The trawler's captain was persuaded to take the British sailors into Penzance where they arrived at 1130 on Friday 5 July.

The only other survivor from *Willamette Valley*, apart from Ryder himself, was Leading Seaman Roberts. Roberts had managed to swim clear of the ship as she was sinking before finding in the dark two hatch covers on which he was able to support himself. At about noon the following day – by which time he was completely alone in the middle of the ocean – he saw and was able to swim to an upturned life raft, possibly the same one that Sub Lieutenant Pembery had abandoned that morning. Roberts was, according to Ryder's wife who met him the following year, 'such a nice man, a typical sailor to look at, tall, broad, very blue eyes'.[19] With great effort he managed to right the raft and clamber into it. In it Roberts found two small water barrels, one empty but one full, which almost certainly saved his life. There was no food on the raft but he did find a piece of chewing gum and an abandoned jacket bearing the stripes of an engineer officer of the Royal Naval Reserve. This was all Roberts had to sustain him for seven days alone on the raft, adrift in the Atlantic. Eventually he was picked up by the SS *Perseus*, a British ship bound for Cape Town, suffering from severe sunburn to the face and arms. Despite this experience Roberts's faith in Ryder was such that as soon as he was able he volunteered to serve under him again.

Ryder himself survived, as we have seen, nearly four days on his tiny, makeshift raft without food or water. SS *Inverliffy*, the ship which rescued him, was sailing in convoy BHX 32. The ship which had spotted Ryder waving frantically in the water and had hooted her siren was the SS *British Chivalry*. Convoy BHX 32 was the last homewardbound convoy to be routed to the south of Ireland after the fall of France. As all subsequent convoys went round the north of Ireland, the chances of Ryder's being picked up had the sinking happened a few days later would have been greatly reduced.

Once on board *Inverliffy* Ryder was taken by his rescuers to the aft gun shelter where he was offered a swig from a bottle of rum which, his survival training in mind, he declined. 'Are you a seaman or a fireman?' the man asked, taking a deep swig from the bottle himself. Ryder, sticking to his cover story, replied that 'I was the Master of the packet when she sank.' 'Crikey', came the reply (or so Ryder relates), 'you won't tell the Old Man, will you?' Reassured he went off to tell Captain Alexander of his discovery and soon Ryder was helped up to the captain's cabin. Here his clothes were cut off him so that he was able to wash himself. He then set about gradually getting his body used to food and drink once more: 'Teaspoons of water, then some milk later on some thin bread and butter, then an egg.' Captain Alexander lent Ryder his bed and a pair of pyjamas but he could not sleep, despite his ordeal as 'I was in a turmoil of mind and my feet were beginning to hurt.'[20]

SS *Inverliffy* reached Plymouth on 5 July, the same day on which the main body of the survivors from *Willamette Valley* had been landed at Penzance. Once in Plymouth harbour Ryder was hoisted upside down out of *Inverliffy* on a stretcher by the inexperienced crew of a hospital launch. In this undignified fashion Ryder was carried up the same steps on which he had landed at the beginning of the war after his dash home from Egypt. On the quayside Ryder was loaded into an ambulance which set off for the hospital. Just as the vehicle arrived at the hospital gates, the air raid sirens started to sound whereupon Ryder was promptly – 'ungallantly but logically', as he later put it – abandoned as the ambulance crew ran for cover.

Ryder had suffered severe exposure during the four days he was in the water. Medically, his condition was diagnosed as erythema solaria to face, ankles and feet. Ryder, writing to his mother from hospital on the day he returned to England, characteristically played it down: 'I myself am in hospital here for a few days suffering from exposure. Swollen feet about sums it up so there is no need to worry.' He recovered under the eagle eye of Sister Finch, 'an attractive young woman who took her responsibilities very seriously or tried to.' Ryder was, as one might have expected, not a good patient and was soon ignoring Sister Finch's injunction to remain in bed in favour of sneaking off to the washroom to bathe his feet in soothing cold water.[21]

More mundanely, all his kit had gone to the bottom of the Atlantic with the ship. Having no clothes and no money he was forced to ask his mother if she 'could assemble something to get me home. Three pounds and some old clothes should do.' It was not until May 1941 that Ryder received compensation from the Admiralty for the loss of his kit. When the cheque for £151 did eventually arrive, it was £57 less than the amount Ryder had claimed.

If Ryder's feet were healing well, the mental scars inflicted by the sinking of *Willamette Valley* were causing him anguish. 'Mentally I am in great misery as I fear that all who sailed with me are lost', he wrote from hospital before he knew of the rescue of the men in the lifeboat. In time, as the full scale of the loss of life became apparent, Ryder had to come to terms with the fact that three-quarters of his ship's company had perished as well as two close friends, James Martin and Michael Seymour. It was, he confessed, 'a very sad and shattering experience.'[22] Of a ship's company of ninety, only twenty-six survived.

* * *

It transpires that *Willamette Valley* had been torpedoed by *U-51*, commanded by Kapitanleutnant Knorr, which then slipped away into the night without making any attempt to rescue the survivors of the stricken ship. *U-51* was herself sunk by the British in the Bay of Biscay on 20 August 1940.[23] Given the circumstances Ryder speculated whether the U-boat had realized that *Willamette Valley* was more than she seemed. Had the U-boat seen the crew lit up by the fire they were fighting after the second torpedo struck? This would, of course, give the lie to the idea that the ship had been abandoned and might have led the U-boat to question her *bona fides*. If the U-boat had realized *Willamette Valley*'s true purpose, this might have explained why three torpedoes were fired. That was more than would normally have been expended on an ordinary merchant ship.

In truth, the experiment with Q-ships at the beginning of the Second World War was not a great success. The tactic had worked well against U-boats during the Great War – as Admiral Campbell's record proved – but in 1939 and 1940 it was less effective. This was partly because in the early months – when *Willamette Valley* first went to sea – the new generation of Q-ships were intended to counter surface raiders. These enemy vessels, which varied vastly in size from pocket battleships to disguised merchantmen, were, according to Ryder, starting to appear on the high seas at about this time. 'We were rather like mobile mines trying to position ourselves in the path of one of these monsters', Ryder recalled, but finding them in the vast spaces of the Atlantic was difficult. In the early summer of 1940, the Admiralty decided that the Q-ships (or 'Freighters' as they were often known) should revert to hunting submarines. This change coincided with the replacement of Admiral Campbell by Rear Admiral Taylor not long before *Willamette Valley* was sunk. With this change, as Ryder put it, 'We were really making the age-old error of fighting this war with the previous war's weapons.' Indeed, after the sinking of *Willamette Valley*, the remaining Q-ships reverted to the less exciting role of Armed Merchant Cruisers. The U-boats would eventually be beaten after a long, costly battle by air power and destroyers, but not Q-ships.[24]

It was not, however, Ryder's fault that he was fighting today's war with yesterday's weapons. Admiral Campbell, as we have seen, had every confidence in Ryder's abilities as a fighting sailor. After his rescue the Admiral wrote congratulating him on his escape 'which was entirely due to your consummate courage and power of endurance – perfectly marvellous.' His captaincy of *Willamette Valley* throughout her commission had been exemplary. Rear Admiral Taylor recognized that her 'special service called for a high degree of patience, coolness, zeal and discipline' in her commander, officers and men. Taylor, annotating Ryder's confidential service record, added:

His fortitude & endurance is [*sic*] unbelievable & there are few men who would or could have survived close on 4 days hanging on to odd planks without food or water after the ship had received 3 hits from torpedoes.

Chapter 10

HMS *Fleetwood*, HMS *Prince Philippe*
and Marriage (1940–42)

After a fortnight in hospital Ryder's swollen feet had recovered sufficiently for him to be discharged. He spent a week convalescing at Charborough Park, near Wareham in Dorset, the home of the Drax family. Admiral Drax, who, as Commander-in-Chief, West Indies, had been Ryder's commanding officer and host in Bermuda, was away at sea but Lady Drax and her teenage daughters Elizabeth and Mary were there to dance attendance upon the recuperating hero. It was, he remembered, 'a carefree week'.

Ryder and Kathleen Drax had struck up a friendship in Bermuda, but Ryder's attentions were now drawn elsewhere. It was during his stay at Charborough that Ryder first became attracted to Elizabeth Drax. She was at least fifteen years younger than he, but evidently something sparked between the Admiral's daughter and the rising star of the Navy during that week in the Dorset countryside. By the end of the year Ryder was smitten. Writing to his mother from Scotland just after Christmas, he confessed 'I am feeling sad at having no word from Elizabeth Drax – very discouraged really. There is evidently no great enthusiasm on the part of her or her mother.'[1]

Ryder's stay at Charborough Park and his burgeoning infatuation with Elizabeth Drax were no doubt welcome distractions from his anguish at the loss of so many of *Willamette Valley*'s crew. Less than a year into the war Ryder had already lost two of his closest friends, James Martin and Michael Seymour. This loss was compounded by the news, received at about this time, of the death of his beloved eldest brother Lisle. Despite the six-year age gap they had always been close, brought together by a love of the sea and of sailing. It was in Lisle's boat *Edith* that Ryder had had his first taste of the sea. Later they had lived cheek-by-jowl for three years on *Penola*, sharing the joys and rigours of the Antarctic.

Lisle, following in the family tradition, had gone into the Army, being commissioned into the Royal Norfolk Regiment in 1922. Between 1927 and 1931 he had served in the Royal West Africa Frontier Force, during which time Midshipman Ryder visited him when *Ramillies* put in to Accra. He then returned to regimental duties before joining his brother on the BGLE in 1934. Back in England after three years in the Antarctic, in 1938 he married Enid Ralston-Patrick; their son Ralston was born in 1939.

Young Bobby with his *ayah*, India, around 1910. Note the elaborate 'pennyfarthing' pram. *Ryder family*

Colonel Charles Ryder and his three sons, around 1913. Bobby is on his father's knee; Ernle is standing on the chair and Lisle sitting on it. *Ryder family*

Cheltenham College, cricket XI, 1923. As a schoolboy and naval cadet Ryder was a proficient games player. He is sitting on the right-hand end of the middle row. Ernle is sitting cross-legged, to the left. *Copyright, Cheltenham College Archives*

The Ryder family, around 1926. Standing (I to r) are Enid, Margaret, Col. Ryder, and Ernle; sitting (I to r) are Lisle, Mrs Ryder, Violet and Bobby, holding the small dog. *Ryder family*

Midshipman Ryder served in HMS *Ramillies*, 1927–29. She was his first ship. *Ryder family*

Ryder's drawing of HMS *Vanessa* at sea. He served on the destroyer for three months in the Mediterranean, summer 1928. *Ryder family*

HMS *Olympus*. Ryder was responsible for navigating the submarine on her voyage from England to Hong Kong, April to June 1931. *Ryder family*

The crew of the *Tai-Mo-Shan*: (1 to r) Bertie Ommanney–Davis, Martyn Sherwood, Ryder, George Salt and Philip Francis. *Ryder family*

The silver screen: the crew of the *Tai-Mo-Shan* pose with Bette Davis, Hollywood, October 1933. *Ryder family*

The *Tai-Mo-Shan* approaching home under full sail, May 1934. *Ryder family*

30 May 1934: the *Tai-Mo-Shan* arrived at Dartmouth a day short of a year after leaving Hong Kong. The crew were greeted by hundreds of Navy Cadets in their boats, by their families and an array of senior officers. *Ryder family*

The *Tai-Mo-Shan* today: still in immaculate condition, 75 years on. *Jan McGready & Moya Bowler*

The *Tai-Mo-Shan* featured in the hugely-successful musical film *Mamma Mia*. Here Pierce Brosnan, who starred in the film with Meryl Streep, works a halyard on her foredeck during filming. *Ian Welsh*

British Graham Land Expedition, 1934–37: the *Penola* icebound during the first winter. *P. Stephenson & P. Rymill*

Camp during the sledging expedition into King George VI Sound, October 1936. *M. Bertram & P. Rymill*

Ryder took this photograph of the *Penola* under full sail from a rowing boat in a flat calm in the Western Approaches, south-west of the Lizard, August 1937. *Ryder family*

Members of the *Penola*'s crew working aloft during the voyage south. It was Ryder's responsibility to teach the largely amateur crew how to work the *Penola*'s antiquated rigging. *P. Rymill*

Lord remember me in this vast ocean

Ryder's impression of his miraculous survival following the sinking of HMS *Willamette Valley*, June 1940. *Ryder family*

Ryder's ink drawing of HMS *Fleetwood*, the frigate he commanded on convoy duty between August 1940 and January 1941. *Ryder family*

Ryder was appointed to the command of HMS *Prince Philippe* on 1 February 1941. Here she is at Penarth converting from a Belgian cross-Channel steamer to a Landing Ship Infantry, for raiding, Spring 1941. *Ryder family*

St. Peter's, Cranboume, Berkshire, 26 April 1941. The bridesmaid is Hilaré's elder sister, Prue. *Ryder family*

HMS *Campbeltown* showing the protective armour-plating added to the bridge for the raid on St Nazaire. *Ryder family*

Ryder's drawing of HMS *Campbeltown* ramming the lock gate at St Nazaire, 28 March 1942. Some of Ryder's drawings of the raid were later published in the *Illustrated London News*. *Ryder family*

Ryder's drawing of MGB 314's escape from St Nazaire down the estuary of the River Loire to the open sea, described by a war correspondent on board as 'a nightmare'. *Ryder family*

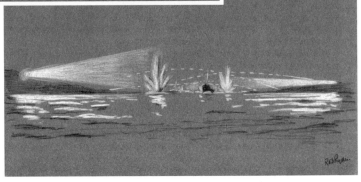

St Nazaire. Photograph taken on the morning after the raid showing the *Campbeltown*'s severely-damaged bows wedged into the lock gates. Within a few hours of this photograph being taken *Campbeltown*'s hidden charges had blown her to smithereens. *Ryder family*

Commander Robert Ryder RN around 1942. *Ryder family*

The son and heir: Ryder and Hilaré with Lisle, around 1944. *Ryder family*

Might of the father: Ryder holds Susan
aloft, around 1950. *Ryder family*

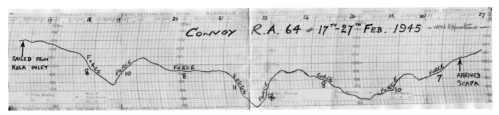

Barograph record of the storms encountered by HMS *Opportune* homeward bound with Convoy
RA64 from Russia, February 1945. Ryder later described it as 'terrible weather, the worst I have ever
known'. *Ryder family*

Ryder and Hilaré with his fellow Naval Attachés, Oslo, 1948. Standing on Ryder's left is the Russian
Attaché, Sokolov, and to Hilaré's left Bill Porter, the U.S. Naval Attache. *Ryder family*

GENERAL ELECTION

THURSDAY, 23rd FEB., 1950

ROBERT RYDER

Your Conservative Candidate

CENTRAL COMMITTEE ROOMS,
1, MERTON PARK PARADE,
KINGSTON ROAD,
S.W.19.

Telephone:— LIBERTY 3756

DISTRICT COMMITTEE ROOMS

ABBEY WARD—
HOPE MISSION,
87 HIGH STREET,
MERTON, S.W.19. LIBerty 3193.

BUSHEY MEAD WARD—
602 KINGSTON ROAD,
RAYNES PARK, S.W.20. LIBerty 3935.

CENTRAL WARD—
92 THE GREEN,
MORDEN, SURREY. LIBerty 5319.

MERTON PARK WARD—
6 CIRCLE GARDENS,
MERTON PARK, S.W.19. LIBerty 5114.

MORDEN WARD—
19 LICHFIELD AVENUE,
MORDEN, SURREY. MITcham 2720.

RAVENSBURY WARD—
27b The DRIVE,
MORDEN, SURREY. MITcham 3547.

RAYNES PARK WARD—
65 GRAND DRIVE,
RAYNES PARK, S.W.20. LIBerty 1348.

ST. HELIER WARD—
24 FARM ROAD,
MORDEN, SURREY. MITcham 1385.

WEST BARNES WARD—
43 ESTELLA AVENUE,
NEW MALDEN, SURREY. MALden 3864.

Published by: E. G. SORRIE, 1 Merton Park Parade, Kingston Road, S.W.19.
Printed by W. WILTON & SON, 56 Dundonald Road, Wimbledon, S.W.19.

A WORD FROM MRS. RYDER

I have told my husband that it is quite wrong to put us on the last page. "Women and Children first" should be the rule. But if I may be serious, may I assure you that above all things my husband is a family man and keeps in mind the simple fact that the home is the root and centre of our life. He counts on me to see that I give him a clear picture of how the policies of today affect us in the homes, and I want to help him. So together we are trying to visit every street. We very much hope to meet you in this way and hear your views.

May I just say that, whatever the outcome, my sincere hope is that the next five years may bring greater happiness and prosperity to you and your children.

Yours sincerely,

Hilary Ryder

"I hope to meet you personally, meanwhile here is my policy..."

THE ISSUE TODAY

What people want are **lower prices, more houses, lower rents,** and **work for all.** These are, I think, the basic needs.

If you will keep these in mind I will briefly outline first my case against the Socialists and then the Conservative alternative.

MY CASE AGAINST SOCIALISM

Vast sums of money have been spent by this Government to demonstrate the first period of Socialism as a paradise on earth. They have spent over **three times** the usual rate and have borrowed on an unprecedented scale. Our last assets abroad have been sold. They have devalued our money.

Today all that they can offer in the face of rising prices is a policy to stabilise wages and cuts in the housing programme.

You will note that, faced by these hard facts, they seek desperately to distract peoples attention by arguments over election expenses and provocative charges over unemployment.

And now, at this critical stage, the Socialists go to the country before the full effects of devaluation become apparent.

Significant too, is the fact, that in their manifesto you will see only a brief mention of the dollar crisis; no mention of Marshall Aid or what to do when it stops in 1952; no mention of Mr. Attlee's recent cuts and no word at all about taxation.

My main charge against the Socialists is, that they are far too rigidly bound to a policy of further Nationalisation without waiting to see if it really works. In my view they offer no adequate proposals for the economic difficulties which lie ahead.

CONSERVATIVE POLICY

Here are my views:—

COST OF LIVING. This is the first thing to tackle. On this all else depends. Here are some practical considerations.

High Taxation is forced on us by high Government expenditure. The tax on what you earn, the tax on what you buy and the tax on industry all put up the cost of living. A far more determined effort is therefore needed to cut out unnecessary expenditure and reduce taxation. This should be tackled on the following lines:—

Ministry of Supply, and Services Ministries and Board of Trade overlap. Ministry of Civil Aviation, Ministry of Transport and Air Ministry overlap. Ministries of Food and Agriculture should be combined. By amalgamation men and women could be released for more productive work in industry and considerable economy effected.

Excessive expenditure to be cut in the following:— Government Publicity, Government Entertainment, Government Hostels, travelling by Government Officials, the British Council, the Festival of Britain.

These reductions are in my view essential to restore prices. Economy in time may save disaster later. I look to expanding industry, and in particular, the restoration of London as world centre of finance and trade, to absorb those affected by a reduction in the Civil Service.

Nationalisation has raised the cost of living and has not brought contentment. I say stop all further measures till we know more about it. And in those industries already nationalised, reduce top-heavy organisations and introduce a more personal touch between management and worker.

Government buying of food, timber and other commodities is most inefficient. It necessitates heavy food subsidies which have to be met by purchase tax. This form of nationalisation must quickly be replaced by competitive trade.

TRADE AND UNEMPLOYMENT. These are closely related. In spite of base allegations by our opponents, the fact is that all parties support the 1944 White Paper on Full Employment. Unemployment has, of course, net yet arisen because there is still work for all, making good the war time arrears. The threat of unemployment arises if we cannot sell our goods to foreign countries and buy back raw materials needed to keep our factories going. There are two main considerations. Production and Cost.

POLLING DAY
THURSDAY 23RD FEB.

Production. Exhortation, Fines, Direction of Labour and a tax on increased earnings offer no way for getting good work from free people. I support the Conservative emphasis on incentives for good work and promotion by merit as a better way of stimulating production.

Cost. The high Cost of Living necessitates high wages. The high cost of coal raises the price of power and transport. Both these raise the cost of production. I say with emphasis, that every effort must be made to **reduce the cost of living.**

SOCIAL SERVICES. The Conservatives, Liberals, and Socialists have all helped to build up our Social Services during the last 50 years. The outline of what we have today was indeed published by Mr. Churchill's Coalition Government in 1944 in the White Papers on National Insurance and National Health. It is clear that these services fulfil a vital need in the homes of the people. I give my full support to these measures which the Conservative Party has done so much to bring forward. The danger today is that month by month as prices rise the benefits are worth less and less, and that the cost of the National Health Service is rising to a vast degree. The problem before us is how to place all these matters on a sound financial basis so that they will last. Once again I emphasise that the rising **cost of living** is the source of the trouble.

HOUSES. This is the most important of all Social Services. I am not at all satisfied that the Socialist Government has tackled this correctly or with the necessary drive. As first steps to providing more homes at cheaper rents, the importing of timber should be restored to competitive trade, and private builders should have an equal opportunity with the local councils to build homes for the people.

An opportunity for people to buy their homes on the instalment system must be brought within the reach of the ordinary working man.

TO SUM UP

I have said it is clear at my Adoption Meeting that I feel it would be wrong for me to regard myself merely as a mouthpiece of some party caucus. And indeed the Conservative party do not wish to be surrounded by yes men. The need today is for men who are prepared to think things out for themselves and speak from their heart and act according to their conscience. I hope from what I have written that you will see that I support the Conservative policy in a spirit of sincerity and conviction, it is I believe a courageous and practical policy to meet the difficult times which will face this country when Marshall Aid ends in 1952.

Yours sincerely,

Robert Ryder

Ryder's campaign leaflet for the General Election of 23 February 1950. He fought and won the new seat of Merton and Morden in south-west London for the Conservatives. *Ryder family*

The three candidates in the Merton and Morden constituency hand in their nomination papers at Morden Public Hall, 11 February 1950. Arthur Palmer (L), the Labour candidate, had won Wimbledon for the Socialists in the landslide victory of 1945. Roy Douglas, (centre), was the Liberal candidate; he lost his deposit. Ryder is on the right. *Ryder family*

Ryder on the campaign trail during the General Election of February 1950. *Ryder family*

Foresight. Ryder family

Millfleet. Ryder family

Watchdog of Wareham.
Ryder family

Hilaré in the early 1970s. *Ryder family*

Master and hound: Ryder and Brutus. *Ryder family*

Trolley Bus: Ryder with his
grandchildren, Oliver and Susannah
Bates, surmounted by Brutus, on
the terrace at Wolferton, early 1970s.
Ryder family

Ryder's medal set: Victoria Cross; 1939–45 Star, Atlantic Star; Defence Medal; 1939–45 War Medal;
Polar Medal; 1977 Silver Jubilee Medal; Legion d'Honneur; Croix de Guerre with palm. *Ryder family*

At the outbreak of war in 1939 Lisle, by now a major, was sent with his regiment to France as part of the British Expeditionary Force (BEF). The 2nd Battalion of the Norfolk Regiment landed in France on 21 September 1939 and spent the entire 'phoney' war there. As a result, when Hitler invaded France, it bore the brunt of the assault. As the British fell back on Calais and Dunkirk in the desperate days of May 1940, the Norfolks held a sector of the perimeter of the Dunkirk salient. On 27 May, after prolonged heavy fighting, the tattered remnants of the battalion laid down their arms. Lisle, who was by then in acting command of the battalion, was the only officer among the ninety men who surrendered to *Waffen SS* troops at Le Paradis. The *SS* then herded their prisoners into a nearby field and with two machine guns mowed them all down. There were, miraculously, two survivors from this barbarous act of mass murder, Privates Pooley and O'Callaghan. It was their evidence that condemned the German officer responsible to the gallows at the War Crimes Court after the war.[2]

When the battalion reassembled in England on 7 June it mustered just five officers and 134 men. Lisle was not among them and, as his fate was as yet unknown, he was reported missing. The massacre at Le Paradis did not become common knowledge until after the war, but as the months went by without Lisle's name appearing on any list as a prisoner-of-war so hope for him faded. On 29 December 1940 *The Times* reported him as 'killed in action' on 27 May and gave brief details of his career. His parents were only officially told of his death by the War Office in a letter dated 14 January 1941. Shortly after Lisle's death had been confirmed, Launcelot Fleming, who had come to know him well in the Antarctic, wrote an appreciation which also appeared in *The Times*.

It was no mean achievement for a first-rate soldier to be also a first-rate sailor, and I do not believe any other military officer has held so responsible a position in a sailing ship, certainly not in that of a Polar expedition. The Ryder brothers and [James] Martin ... were a wonderful team to educate an amateur crew in seamanship.[3]

However, this was the summer of 1940, the darkest and most dangerous hour in Britain's history, her fate hanging in the balance as the Royal Air Force fought the *Luftwaffe* over southern England. In a memorandum dated 4 July 1940, Winston Churchill reminded all those who occupied positions of responsibility in government or the armed services that it was their duty 'to maintain a spirit of alert and confident energy' and 'set an example of steadiness and resolution'.[4] This was, Ryder wrote, typical of 'the "Backs to the Wall" spirit which was at this time animating us all.' With the nation straining every sinew to resist the German onslaught men such as Ryder were urgently needed. He was passed fit for duty on 10 August, and appointed to the command of HMS *Fleetwood* on 16 August. Although he had been passed fit for duty his feet were still sore enough to prevent him putting on proper shoes so he joined his new command in bedroom slippers.

Ryder took command at Sheerness in the Thames estuary one evening after midnight. HMS *Fleetwood* was a frigate, but, as an early example of the class, suffered from unreliable equipment, notably her radar, but the ship was well officered and otherwise in good shape. The First Lieutenant, George Hutchinson, had originally been a term senior to Ryder but had left the Navy. He had been in the ship since the start of the war, seeing action during the Norwegian campaign so he had a close knowledge of her. This was just as well as Ryder had been thrown in at the deep end. On his arrival Hutchinson informed him that *Fleetwood* was due to sail at 0300 that morning in command of a convoy to Methil in the Firth of Forth. Ryder had no experience in convoy work, which involved a good deal of manoeuvring, forming up the convoy, stationing the escorts and opening the boom gates. In addition the Thames estuary was heavily mined and littered with dangerous wrecks. The East coast convoys at the time were frequently attacked by dive bombers, by submarines and by E-boats.

Ryder got an early taste of what he could expect. The convoy had not gone far when two enemy aeroplanes attempted to dive bomb the convoy. Fortunately, they missed. *Fleetwood* opened fire on the planes as they swooped away flattening out at sea level – 'like a pigeon out of the trees' – but missed as the pilots, cunningly, managed to get the Mid-Barrow Lightship between themselves and *Fleetwood*'s guns. In general, though, air attacks were only sporadic nor did the German E-boats attack any of the convoys that Ryder escorted. The notorious North Sea fogs were often a greater worry than the enemy. After shepherding around six convoys between the Thames and the Firth of Forth, *Fleetwood* was transferred to Methil.[5]

Fleetwood's duties now consisted of escorting the ships from the Forth round the top of Scotland to rendezvous with the ships from Liverpool before taking them out into the Atlantic. Once the convoys had reached the meridian of 25° W – by which stage it was hoped that they would be through the U-boat zone – the escorts would rendezvous with an incoming convoy. Two examples will give a flavour of the anxieties of escort work. At dusk on 16 September 1940 *Fleetwood* – with Ryder commanding the escort – and the corvette *Bluebell* rendezvoused with convoy HX 71 out in the North Atlantic. At 1530 the following afternoon, *Treganna*, the leading ship in the convoy's starboard column was torpedoed; she 'sank at once'. Despite great efforts by the escorts, only four survivors were rescued. By 20 September the convoy had reached the Moray Firth on Scotland's east coast, where, at 1545 a good contact was obtained on *Fleetwood*'s Asdic, suggesting the presence of a submarine. A depth charge was dropped. As the crew waited with anticipation for signs of an enemy, the explosion succeeded only in blowing up a shoal of whitebait.[6]

On 30 September Convoy OA 222 left Methil at 0830 bound for the Atlantic. Once more Ryder was in command of the escorting ships. Later that day *Fleetwood* obtained a good Asdic contact. A pattern of depth charges were dropped and this time it seemed to have scored a hit as 'considerable quantities of diesel fuel came to the surface.' On 3 October Ryder reported that 'Yesterday was probably a good example of a convoy being stampeded by a porpoise.' The phosphorescent wake of a porpoise was mistaken at night by the crew of one of the merchantmen for the wake created by a submarine's periscope. One of the ships in the convoy then reported that another vessel had been torpedoed, which resulted in a good deal of confusion, panic and wasted time.[7]

At the end of October *Fleetwood* was transferred to coastal convoys on the east coast of Scotland. This was, Ryder noted, 'a relatively light duty' with only about four days at sea at a time, with the bonus of being able to take refuge in Scapa Flow while awaiting the inbound convoy.[8]

For Ryder personally his spell in command of *Fleetwood* was a time of mixed fortunes. While he was stationed at Rosyth, a busy naval base, there were friends with whom he could while away the hours, notably Launcelot Fleming. Scapa Flow was less congenial. There were other periods too when he felt less happy. He had told his father from the Falklands as early as 1936 that he wanted to get married. Ryder had spent about eight of the preceding ten years aboard – three of them in the Antarctic – which had curtailed his opportunities for finding a wife. At the age of thirty-two perhaps the joys of bachelorhood were starting to fade. Even solitude, normally something Ryder relished, was losing its attraction. As he told his mother in October 1940:

> I feel lonely these days. I have in fact spent the whole of today by myself & went for a long walk but rather wished I had someone with me. I wish very much really that I was married & had a home even a temporary one – but how can one get married unless one gets some leave.[9]

Ryder's loneliness in Scotland was exacerbated, one suspects, by two emotional entanglements. The first was the backwash of his relationship with Frances Woods, to whom he had been engaged at the time he took his Q-ship to sea in February 1940. Almost nothing is known about their relationship beyond the fact that Ryder decided, while adrift in the Atlantic after *Willamette Valley* had been torpedoed, that should he survive he would break off the engagement. Clinging to his pieces of wreckage for nearly four days, he had much time to take stock of his life. Frances Woods, he evidently decided, was not the girl for him. His decision was not well received *chez* Woods. A month or so after taking command of *Fleetwood* he told his mother:

> I got a letter from Mrs Woods enclosing the photos of myself which I gave to Frances & asking for hers to be sent back. A stupid business to my mind. I don't know where hers are. One was sunk & the others I haven't opened yet. It's funny what a lot of trouble people go to to make themselves objectionable.[10]

Three weeks later he complained again, this time to his father, that he was getting 'objectionable letters' from Frances's mother. However, he received a friendly

Christmas card from Frances herself. 'A sudden change, perhaps she is getting over her sorrows', Ryder wrote. 'I hope so. I will send back a little reply, carefully worded so as not to give any encouragement.'[11] And, in Ryder's defence, it is only fair to add that he always felt a certain residual guilt as Frances never married.

At the same time he was pining for Elizabeth Drax. 'I wish Elizabeth were up this end of the country then it would be different.' Perversely, Ryder was getting unwanted letters from Frances and her mother, but the billets doux from Elizabeth Drax, for which he longed, never appeared. In the New Year Ryder received

> a telegram of congratulation [on his promotion] from Lady Drax, which was really nice of her. I feel that these are encouraging symptoms but I should be happier if I [had] a bit more encouragement from Elizabeth herself.[12]

The promotion in question was to the rank of Commander, gazetted on New Year's Eve 1940. He could now sport a third stripe on his sleeve and, for the first time, gilt oak leaves on the peak of his cap. Just as importantly, his pay increased sharply from about £35 to about £55 a month. Ryder considered himself lucky to be promoted at the 'early' age of thirty-two, but it may have been, partly, a recognition of his service in command of *Willamette Valley* and of his survival after her sinking.

* * *

With Ryder's promotion he was now too senior an officer for *Fleetwood* so on 16 January 1941 he relinquished his command. 'I was sorry to leave *Fleetwood*', he wrote later. 'I felt safe in her; she was small with a shallow draft, and had a good ship's company and seemed to be a happy ship.'[13] However, his superior officer, Captain Kerr, recorded an equivocal verdict on Ryder. 'Has amazing pwrs. of endurance', Kerr noted in Ryder's confidential service record. 'Not brilliant & inclined to be stubborn, ex[cellent] C.O. in war as he is v. cool & unperturbed.' Having relinquished command of *Fleetwood* he went south for two weeks' leave before taking up his next appointment.

History does not relate precisely when Ryder first met Hilaré Green-Wilkinson, but, it seems, they had been introduced by his sister Enid Campbell who lived at Winkfield close to Hilaré's parents. She and Hilaré did war work together in a Voluntary Aid Detachment (VAD) and, despite an age difference of more than twenty years, warmed to each other. Katherine Penley, who knew Hilaré well at this time, says that Enid thought she would be 'just the thing' for her brother after his broken engagement. So Enid played Cupid for the somewhat reserved, diffident Ryder. Perhaps they were introduced in the summer of 1940 after Ryder had been rescued from the sea, but if they had been Hilaré did not make much of an impression on him. If his letters home are to be believed, he had eyes only for Elizabeth Drax, at least until the end of his time in *Fleetwood*. So perhaps Ryder and Hilaré did not meet – or at least start to take one another seriously – until he came south in January 1941. John Green-Wilkinson, Hilaré's brother, says that they met at a dance at The Pantiles, a night club in Bagshot. 'They just clicked', says Katharine Penley. Family legend has it that Ryder pretended his feet were still too sore from the effects of his prolonged immersion in the Atlantic to permit him to dance. This was a great disappointment to Hilaré, who loved dancing, but she nevertheless sat out with him.[14]

Whenever it was that Ryder and Hilaré met, they now began a typical, whirlwind wartime courtship. From the beginning of February Ryder was stationed at Penarth in South Wales while Hilaré was living with her parents at Lovel Hill, near Windsor. Ryder's duties conspired with the restrictions and inconveniences of wartime travel to ensure that the couple saw each other only infrequently. All thoughts of Elizabeth Drax were now banished. By 14 March Ryder was sufficiently confident to propose to her during a visit to Windsor. Although Hilaré, who was suffering from measles at the time, was covered in spots and running a high temperature, Ryder nevertheless seized the moment. He gave her six months to make up her mind: 'You will have a good chance while you are convalescing of deciding whether you want to marry me or not.' Three days later he wrote to her, now every inch the ardent suitor.

> I love you dearly Hilaré and admire you tremendously and I really am frightfully keen to marry you. If you say "no" I will be miserable as I know it would be no use asking you again.

Before signing off Ryder added a plea: 'God bless you, and please don't keep me in suspense too long will you.'[15]

He need not have worried; Hilaré had no doubt. From her sickbed and despite her measles, on receiving Ryder's letter of 17 March, she wrote at once accepting him.

> I thought I must write and tell you that I love you and am feeling so terribly happy about it. I really think I must have always but I knew for certain late on Sunday night when my temperature was 105°!

She had thought that she would wait to tell him when they next saw each other, 'but when I got your letter this morning it struck me how unfair it was not to tell you at once.'[16] This put Ryder out of his misery. 'It was indeed', he wrote, 'a great joy getting your letter and I am in consequence all bubbling over with happiness.'[17]

So who was the girl who so captivated Ryder? Constance Hilaré Myfanwy – she disliked the name Constance so always used Hilaré – was the third daughter and fourth child of the Reverend Lumley Green-Wilkinson and his wife Myfanwy. They had six children in all, four daughters and two sons, one of whom, Oliver, later became Archbishop of Central Africa. Ryder himself described Hilaré's parents as 'respectable rather than dashing', an unfairly (if only mildly) disparaging description of a middle-aged clergyman and his wife.[18] Hilaré had been born on 15 May 1918 – so was twenty-two at the time of her engagement – at Ascot where her father was serving as Rector. She had, it seems, a happy childhood, as part of a large, well-heeled and well-connected clerical family, living in various rambling but comfortable vicarages. During a tour to Italy in 1928 the family had an audience with Pope Pius XI. In 1921, her father became Vicar of Bournemouth and in 1930 the family moved to Lovel Hill, an imposing house in Windsor Forest. Katherine Penley remembered the Green-Wilkinson children from this time in their 'delightful house ... [with] delightful parents, too.'[19]

By the age of twenty-two, Hilaré had blossomed into a talented, confident, beautiful young woman. The portrait photograph of her taken for the frontispiece of *Country Life* a year after her marriage shows Hilaré as attractive, poised and thoughtful. She had, by all accounts, wonderful, long blonde hair: one of Ryder's brothers-in-law told her 'If you cut your hair off it would be a crime.'[20] She had been dispatched to a finishing school in Paris to broaden her horizons. Here she had acquired a veneer of Parisian sophistication as well as a decent command of French. But most of all, it seems, it was her character that Ryder found so beguiling. Her brother John described her as 'sociable and lively', an ideal foil for the rather more reserved Ryder. He thought she was 'so well suited to me and so unselfish', as well as 'very practical & helpful'.[21]

Once the happy news had been announced, letters started arriving from friends and relations. Neil Campbell, Enid's husband, told Hilaré that 'I really & always have felt that Bob may some day God willing be a great man, & you I feel sure are just the girl to help him.'[22] Admiral Goodenough wrote to Hilaré to assure her that 'I am one of Bob's warmest admirers & supporters ...' The Archbishop of Canterbury, Cosmo Lang, was a family friend as Hilaré's father had served as his chaplain during much of his time as Archbishop. Lang wrote to Hilaré on receiving the news:

> I need not tell you how excited & delighted I was. I know nothing of this Commander of yours except that he is a very lucky man and what your father has told me of his war adventures.[23]

Ryder was, naturally, pleased that his parents approved of his choice of bride. As he told Hilaré, 'My mother I know admires you greatly,' adding jokingly that 'my father won't mind as long as it doesn't interfere with any of his bridge commitments.' But the most heartfelt endorsement of all came from Enid Ryder, Lisle's widow,

> In fact I don't think I can wish you any greater happiness than my married life, short as it was, to Lisle. The Ryder boys make grand husbands, & one feels so

darned safe with them … You are marrying into such a true family, & one who will never let you down.

That was praise indeed.[24]

'I hate the idea of a long and protracted engagement',[25] Ryder told his fiancée shortly after they had become engaged and indeed very soon the preparations for the wedding were under way. A sapphire and diamond engagement ring was purchased; the banns of marriage were read; the church booked and caterers engaged. One choice did worry Ryder: whom he could ask to be his best man? The problem was that of his two brothers, Lisle was dead and Ernle in India; of his close friends, Michael Seymour and James Martin had perished in *Willamette Valley*, while of his shipmates from *Tai-Mo-Shan* George Salt had gone down with his submarine in the Adriatic the previous autumn and Philip Francis was away at sea. He contemplated asking Admiral Gordon Campbell to stand in but decided against it. He even wondered, half-seriously, whether a suitable candidate could be rented from Harrods. In the end he asked Lieutenant Commander Anthony Vyvyan Thomas, known as 'Johnnie', a submariner and navigation expert, who had been invalided out of the Navy at the beginning of the war with chronic asthma. Although Thomas and Ryder barely knew each other at the time of the wedding, this was the start of a friendship which endured for the rest of their lives.[26] Ryder, meanwhile, was keeping his fingers crossed that he would not be ordered away by the Admiralty at the eleventh hour.

Robert Ryder and Hilaré Green-Wilkinson were married at St Peter's, Cranbourne, near Lovel Hill on 26 April 1941 by Cosmo Lang, Archbishop of Canterbury, assisted by the bride's father. St Peter's is a modest church built entirely of rag flint without a tower or steeple. Its interior is equally unassuming apart from an elaborate, painted wooden altar piece. The bride, who wore a gown of white crepe, with full bodice and skirt, and a lace veil held in place by a floral headdress, was given away by her uncle, Brigadier Louis Green-Wilkinson. Her elder sister Prue was the only bridesmaid.[27] Ryder wore uniform. Most appropriately, one of the hymns chosen for the service was 'Lead us, Heavenly Father, lead us/O'er the world's tempestuous sea'.

Afterwards a reception was held at Lovel Hill at which 'Most excellent food' was provided by the caterers, the wedding guests drank white wine, cup and champagne. The only serious concession to wartime austerity was the wedding cake itself, as Hilaré had warned Ryder. 'You can't get ones with icing-sugar so don't get excited when you see it; the outside is all paper. Rather a good imitation though.'[28] Once the reception was over the Ryders, now man and wife, left for Cheltenham where they spent their wedding night in a hotel.

The wedding had gone perfectly. Lumley Green-Wilkinson summed it up to Hilaré the very next day.

Bob too was a model, he looked as though he was enjoying it, and I never saw him distrait when talking to anyone & some must have been bores. He won universal praise ... As for you, darling, you were just a perfect bride.

A friend of the family, Reggie Boyle, struck an an appropriately optimistic note.

I hope [Hilaré] has unlimited happiness before her – she will have anxious days no doubt, but they will pass, and there is no possible opinion but that she has picked a good one – a man of great strength of character.

* * *

The spring of 1941 was no time for a prolonged honeymoon. Indeed, as Ryder had to return to his ship, he and Hilaré drove back to Penarth from Cheltenham after only one night. Their first marital home were lodgings at Holms Farm at Dinas Powis, a village within walking distance of the docks at Penarth where Ryder's ship was being converted. The house was on a farm surrounded by 'cows, pigs, sheep, hens, ducks, and Guinea fowl' and, a bonanza in times of rationing, there were 'Plenty of eggs & cream so far ... [which are] completely wasted on Hilaré who doesn't like either.'[29]

Ryder had been at Penarth since he joined his new ship there on 1 February. On leaving *Fleetwood* he had been appointed to the command of HMS *Prince Philippe*, a Belgian cross-Channel motor vessel intended for the Ostend–Dover route. She had been spirited out of Antwerp docks in a nearly-completed state just before the German army occupied the city. At Penarth *Prince Philippe* was fitting out for landing raiding parties on the coasts of occupied Europe. In early March 1941 there had been a successful raid by British Commandos at Lofoten off the Norwegian coast and other, similar operations were planned. She was 'a fast, attractive-looking vessel' with a maximum cruising speed of 23½ knots, ideal, it was hoped, for this kind of work.

She did, however, have two peculiarities. She had no watertight compartments, only a number of watertight bulkheads, making her more vulnerable to sinking should her hull be damaged. Her other oddity was that she had no wheel: steering was by means of two press buttons, one red, one green. Ryder requested that a proper wheel be installed but was told to use what he had been given. At Penarth *Prince Philippe* was being equipped for her new role with the installation of a new type of gravity-operated davit, four sets on each side. These were for hoisting out the 'Eureka' landing craft for putting Commandos ashore. She was also fitted with anti–aircraft guns, while the ship's accommodation was extensively reconfigured.[30] For Ryder, who was fascinated by the technicalities of shipbuilding (witness *Tai–Mo–Shan*), this was absorbing work. 'I have had quite an interesting day looking round my ship; & poring over the prints and plans of the decks etc. deciding where to fit people in. It's rather intriguing ...'[31]

Less satisfactory were the officers Ryder had been allocated. They were entirely drawn from the Merchant Navy – under the T124X arrangements – and the Royal Naval Reserve (RNR) and were, according to Ryder, 'very indifferent officers.' They were also inexperienced, as Hilaré explained to her father. 'There is such a terrific amount to organize and most of the officers being RNR and new to the job [Ryder] not only has to tell them what to do but how to do it.' Two incidents illustrate their shortcomings in Ryder's eyes. As *Prince Philippe* was putting to sea for the first time from Penarth for her trials, Ryder was informed that there was an unknown woman still on board. It seems that she was the landlady of one of the T124X engineering officers who had failed to pay his rent. She had installed herself in his cabin awaiting payment. This was not the sort of behaviour to be expected of an officer. Much worse was the engineer officer who deliberately sabotaged a dynamo.[32]

The seven weeks that Ryder and Hilaré spent at Dinas Powis in May and June 1941 were an idyllic introduction to married life. There was, for sure, much for Ryder to do in commissioning his ship, but at the day's end 'I come bounding home to be with my Hilaré.' She felt the same, telling her sister Prue that '… really and truly we are both quite drunk with happiness and laugh so much'. There was much to enjoy in their new surroundings, too. Hilaré warmed to Penarth, 'a typical sea-side town, … like Swanage, with all the right sort of ice-cream and bucket & spade shops along the front.'[33]

For Ryder it was period of great happiness, filled with the joys of spring. At the end of May, he and Hilaré went walking in one of the nearby bluebell woods.

It has been a great joy to me seeing the spring & summer come the first time I have been able to do so for very many years … The rooks, the farm yard noises, the buds and blossom. The green leaves and the daisies and the buttercups in the fields. All the simple things which at one time I thought never to see again and made more precious by having Hilaré with me to help me enjoy them.[34]

On 14 June *Prince Philippe* was commissioned and put to sea for her trials. Ryder now had to learn to handle her and, although not without one or two alarms, he quickly did so. During her maiden voyage along the coast to Milford Haven the electric steering gear – the green and red buttons – failed, leaving the ship going round in undignified circles. Fortunately, she was well out to sea at the time and so clear of all hazards. Once the defect had been temporarily repaired Ryder steered 'a very wobbly course' into Milford Haven.

From there *Prince Philippe* sailed to Dartmouth to collect her Eureka landing craft. On 23 June the ship, having loaded her Eurekas, left Dartmouth bound for Scotland. As she made her way out to sea, picking up speed to 21 knots, two enemy fighters appeared on the port quarter. The Messerschmitt 109s dived out of the sun down to 150 feet raking the ship with machine gun and cannon fire before pulling up and away. A 100lb bomb was dropped, too, but mercifully exploded in the water 50 feet astern. Astonishingly no one was injured, despite the fact that an entire bucket full of bullets was swept up from the deck. One of the senior petty officers got a bullet through the crotch of his trousers but survived intact. A water tank was punctured and two landing craft holed but, on the whole, *Prince Philippe* had escaped lightly from what could have been a nasty incident.[35]

Prince Philippe sailed to Inveraray on the west coast of Scotland to report to the Combined Operations Training Centre. For a fortnight the crew practised hoisting and lowering the Eurekas, landing in difficult places and making rendezvous at night and so on. Ryder was anxious to work his ship up to a high state of efficiency, as he could all too easily imagine 'having to get the "hell out it", after some raid and the need to recover our Landing Craft while under way'. After relentless practice, the ship was able to perform this complicated manoeuvre at 10 knots in the dark. 'I could feel morale beginning to build up', Ryder remembered.[36]

Once the training was over *Prince Philippe* was ordered to Falmouth to take part in an operation. However, as she was steaming south, the order was – as so often in war – countermanded and the ship diverted to the Clyde where she remained for five days. On 13 July *Prince Philippe* sailed to Liverpool, where she picked up the attachments for the ship's collision mat. *Prince Philippe* then left Liverpool to return to the Clyde.

In the early hours of 15 July 1941 the ship ran into thick fog in the North Channel, the strait between south-west Scotland and Northern Ireland. At 0245 *Prince Philippe* was off Corsewall Point near Stranraer when, from the bridge, Ryder heard a ship's fog horn boom out through the fog on the starboard bow. As visibility was very poor, he immediately ordered the engines to be stopped. Then, with all eyes on the bridge straining into the murk, the ship drifted slowly through the fog. The fog horn seemed to suggest that the other ship was passing *Prince Philippe* on a parallel and opposite course. At 0251, thinking that the other ship, unseen and unseeing, was slipping astern, Ryder rang down for 'slow ahead'. For a minute-and-a-half *Prince Philippe* nosed nervously through the fog. At that moment Ryder saw a white light – indicating one or other side of the other vessel – dimly through the fog. It was perhaps 200 yards away. Twenty seconds later, he saw both the other ship's white lights: she was coming straight towards *Prince Philippe*. Realizing that a collision was now inevitable, Ryder ordered 'hard a starboard and full ahead' in the hope of swinging his stern away from the other ship. It was too late. At 0253 SS *Empire Wave* crashed into *Prince Philippe* just abaft the funnel on the starboard side.

The impact of *Empire Wave*'s bow caused massive damage to *Prince Philippe*'s hull which was cut nearly half way through and badly buckled. The ship began making water fast so that Ryder ordered all hands on deck at once and a signal was put out requesting assistance. *Empire Wave* was asked to keep her engines moving slowly ahead while the damage to *Prince Philippe* was assessed. Once the full extent of the damage became apparent Ryder ordered all boats to be lowered and all hands to muster on the port side of the ship. He then ordered all the crew bar a small party to take to the boats. After about twenty minutes *Empire Wave* was asked to back off, whereupon Ryder tried his port engine. As this was functioning Ryder, having decided to beach *Prince Philippe* at Lamlash on the island of Arran, set off slowly on a northerly course, still in thick fog. After an hour, however, the steering gear compass and the echo sounder failed so the engine was stopped. It was 0438. Two minutes later the sound of a steam ship's engines were heard on the starboard bow. About three minutes later *Prince Philippe*, by now practically stationary, collided slowly with MV *Lowick*.

Lowick was not seriously damaged, but *Prince Philippe* was now beginning to founder. She was filling with water and her generators were out of action. It was no longer possible to use the engines. Ryder therefore transferred the only casualty, Sub Lieutenant Moncur RNR, together with the confidential books and other valuable stores to *Lowick*. The remaining crew then attempted to fit the collision mat but it was found to be too small to cover the gash in the ship's hull. *Prince Philippe* remained stationary in thick fog until mid-morning when, at 1030, the Navy tug *Salvonia* arrived and took her in tow. Ryder ordered the tug to tow his ship to Carlingford Lough in Northern Ireland in order to beach her there. However, under tow *Prince Philippe* gradually listed more and more to port before finally laying over on her port side, at which point Ryder and Leading Seaman Roberts – who had so bravely survived the sinking of *Willamette Valley* – finally abandoned the ship, the last to do so. Three minutes later, at 1150, she sank.[37]

Prince Philippe had been lost but fortunately there was only one casualty, Sub Lieutenant Moncur, who died of the injuries he received in the accident. The rest of the crew all made it to safety. For Ryder the loss of his ship had been a worrying and distressing experience. As Hilaré explained to her father:

> It really is too tragic for words. You can imagine what Bob feels like after all the work and planning he has done for the past months. She was proving such a success, the men were all working well at last and he was tremendously proud of her.

Even in this dark hour Ryder was cheered by the attitude of his men. Despite the loss of the ship everyone seemed very cheerful. Hilaré went to the hotel in Greenock where the ship's officers and their kit were gathered. 'One thing pleased Bob tremendously', she noted. 'His officers & Petty Officers came to him in a body and asked to serve under him again.'[38]

Very soon, too, the wheels of officialdom began to grind into action. Shortly after landing Ryder spent three hours with the Chief of Staff at Greenock. On 18 July a Court of Enquiry sat to investigate the loss of *Prince Philippe*, the hearing lasting all day. Ryder received the verdict of the Court in a letter dated 20 October 1941. Ryder, it said, was held 'to blame for not ensuring that boat and collision-mat drills had been sufficiently exercised and also for not ensuring that a better organization existed for the immediate investigation and report of damage.' As a consequence he was awarded a mark of Their Lordships' displeasure.[39] These findings were, in the circumstances, harsh and provoked a vigorous rebuttal from Ryder. For example, as the attachments for the collision mat had come aboard (through no fault of his) only hours before *Prince Philippe* left Liverpool on her final voyage, it seemed grossly unfair to blame Ryder for failing to practise drills. But the Admiralty was unmoved; the mark of displeasure remained on his record. On the other hand, Ryder was relieved that he had not been found guilty of the much more serious offence of hazarding his ship. Nor had he been blamed for the collision itself.

* * *

As Ryder had now been sunk twice in a year the Admiralty decided to give him a shore job, 'a rest cure' as he put it. He was appointed Naval Liaison Officer to General Alexander's staff at Southern Command HQ in the Palladian splendour of Wilton House. He took up the appointment in August 1941. After the rigours and responsibilities of command at sea it was a leisurely posting involving staff work and touring Southern Command's extensive coastline. The greatest joy of the secondment was that he and Hilaré were able to set up house together. In September they moved into the Manor House at Wilton, a gracious, stone building in attractive gardens.

Chapter 11

The Raid on St Nazaire, Operation *Chariot*: Hatching the Plot (February and March 1942)

On 25 February 1942 Ryder received a signal at Wilton ordering him to attend a meeting at Combined Operations HQ (COHQ) in London at 1500 the following day. Although keen to get back to sea after six months ashore, knowing that Combined Operations were 'rather resented' by the other services he 'viewed this ... with some misgiving as I had no wish to be a "go between".' He travelled to London in the expectation that he had been summoned to yet another 'ordinary low-power meeting'. However, once he arrived at Richmond Terrace he was swiftly disabused of this notion. Slipping into the meeting about fifteen minutes late, he was 'confronted with a formidable array of senior officers, a good deal of gold lace about, and I went a bit pink in the face and sat down at the back of the room.'

Having had a copy of the agenda thrust into his hand, Ryder surveyed the scene. Lord Louis Mountbatten, the Chief of Combined Operations (CCO), in the chair, was explaining the plan for some operation to Admiral of the Fleet Sir Charles Forbes, the Commander-in-Chief, Plymouth. Listening with rapt attention to Mountbatten's exposition were two other admirals and all the Combined Operations top brass, including Captain John Hughes-Hallett, RN. Also listening carefully was Lieutenant Colonel Charles Newman. On the table was a detailed model of a dockyard. Ryder had not been in the room very long when Mountbatten said:

'We now come to item five ... Commander Ryder has been appointed to command the Naval Forces under the C-in-C Plymouth.' Mountbatten looked up. 'Is that all right, Ryder?'

'Yes sir', Ryder replied. 'I really didn't think there was much else I could say in front of that lot', he remembered years later. The discussion moved on but after the meeting Ryder was introduced to Charles Newman. He drew Newman aside and asked him 'Where the Hell is this place?' 'Oh, didn't they tell you?', Newman laughed, 'Well, it's St Nazaire.'[1]

Ryder was, naturally, very flattered to have been chosen to command the operation: 'at a stroke my morale which had been languishing since the loss of

Prince Philippe soared into top gear.' This was, he wrote later, 'something I fully understood and knew just how to tackle.' It almost seemed as if he had been destined for the job. 'I felt that all I had done previously led up to this. I knew what I wanted. I could picture the whole action and had complete confidence in my ability to lead this force.'

If to Ryder it seemed as if his entire naval career had steered him with predestined inexorability to this moment, the real reason was perhaps rather more pedestrian, even haphazard. Long after the war he met Admiral Townsend who had, in 1942, been serving in the Second Sea Lord's Office and had therefore been responsible for Ryder's appointment. Naturally, Ryder asked him why he had been selected. 'Oh, that is quite easy to explain', Townsend replied. 'You were the only Commander available.'

Standing against Townsend's breezy explanation of bare necessity for Ryder's selection to lead the operation are two pieces of evidence. The first is an anecdote related in C.E. Lucas Phillips's *The Greatest Raid of All* (1958). John Hughes-Hallett telephoned the Second Sea Lord's Office at the Admiralty to ask for a naval officer to command the raid.

> 'I want an able Commander for a special job', said Hughes-Hallett. 'He must be a really first–class man.'
>
> 'I'll see what can be done', came the reply, 'but, as you can well imagine, the best men are pretty well booked up. Is it really necessary to have a specially able chap?'
>
> 'You can count on a VC for him, if that's a guide', replied Hughes-Hallett.
>
> 'Oh, well, if you can guarantee a VC ...'
>
> 'Obviously there's no guarantee, but that's the size of the job.'[2]

The second came to light during Ryder's time as Naval Attaché in Oslo after the war when A.V. Alexander, who had been First Lord of the Admiralty at the time of St Nazaire, visited Norway. Alexander talked, Hilaré told her father, 'in a very interesting but rather conceited way about his time at the Admiralty.'

> He mentioned, among other things, that it was Dudley Pound who urged him to send Bob to St Nazaire. We knew Pound was a great supporter of Bob's but it was interesting to know he had recommended him, and with high praise so it seems.[3]

So perhaps there was more than the random chances of availability to Ryder's appointment. Maybe the powers-that-be at the Admiralty, right up to the First Sea Lord himself, Sir Dudley Pound, considered Ryder the right man, fitted by his experience, for the difficult task that lay ahead.

Raiding has a long and honourable history in the annals of British arms, stretching back to the Elizabethan Age. Sir Francis Drake's raids against the Spanish in the

West Indies and at Cadiz – the famous 'singeing of the King of Spain's Beard' – were the start of a tradition of seaborne assaults that persisted into the twentieth century. In the Second World War Drake's rich mantle was assumed by the rather unromantically named Directorate of Combined Operations (DCO), created by Winston Churchill in the perilous days of June 1940. Even as the defeated British Army was escaping from Dunkirk, Churchill was urging the Chiefs of Staff not to retreat entirely into a defensive shell. 'We ought to organize raiding forces and keep the Germans guessing at what point along the hundreds of miles of coast under their control we should strike them next.'[4]

Indeed, once the Western Front had disappeared with the fall of France, raiding became the only means of striking direct at the enemy. The first Director of Combined Operations was a Royal Marine, Lieutenant General A.G.B. Bourne, who was succeeded a month later by Admiral of the Fleet Lord Keyes. Keyes had a distinguished record as a fighting sailor in the Great War, most notably in leading the raid on Zeebrugge in April 1918, and several weighty blows were struck against the enemy during his time at the DCO. The raid on the Lofoten Islands off Norway in March 1941 and the *coup de main* at Spitzbergen in August together with some smaller raids in the Mediterranean theatre were the most successful operations during Keyes's tenure. In October 1941 Keyes was replaced as DCO by Lord Louis Mountbatten.

By the beginning of January 1942 the focus of British naval strategists in northern waters was the threat posed by the *Tirpitz*. This German battleship, sister ship to *Bismarck* and identical to her in almost every respect, had been working up in the Baltic, immune from attack. But the 'Ultra' decrypts revealed to the Admiralty in the early days of January that *Tirpitz*, now operational, was preparing to leave the safety of the Baltic. She left Gdynia on 11 January and, after calling at Wilhelmshaven, arrived at Trondheimsfjord in Norway five days later.

Once *Tirpitz* had arrived in Norway, she came into play as a major piece on the chess board of naval strategy. Even if she remained securely berthed in her distant fjord, she posed a vital and immediate threat to Allied shipping, the threat of the so-called 'fleet in being'. What were her intentions? So long as she remained in Norway the Admiralty would have to retain a powerful fleet at Scapa Flow in order to forestall any attempt by *Tirpitz* to escape into the Atlantic. The consequences of a battleship of her power and speed getting among the slow-moving merchantmen of the Atlantic convoys were too dreadful to contemplate.

Churchill told the Chiefs of Staff on 25 January 1942 that, 'The destruction or even the crippling of this ship is the greatest event at sea at the present time. No other target is comparable to it.'[5] The problem was that, so long as *Tirpitz* remained in the Norwegian fjords, she was almost immune to attack. However, there was another way in which her threat could be diminished, which lay on the west coast of France, far from the Norwegian waters that sheltered *Tirpitz*. It was the mighty dry dock at St Nazaire.

The Forme Ecluse Louis-Joubert, to give the immense dry dock its full title and style, had been completed in the early 1930s to house the liner *Normandie*; 385yd long and 55yd wide the dock could accommodate a ship of more than 85,000 tons. The gates (or 'caissons' – pronounced to rhyme with 'racoons') at each end of the dock were massive sliding, steel constructions measuring 167ft long, 54ft high and 35ft thick, with compartments that could be flooded to withstand the pressure of water when the dock was dry.[6] This was the only dry dock on the western coast of occupied Europe large enough to accommodate *Tirpitz*. By a strange quirk of history, the dock's gates had formed part of the German reparation payments to France under the Treaty of Versailles.

If the use of the *Normandie* dock could be denied to the Germans, they would perhaps have second thoughts about allowing *Tirpitz* to steal out into the Atlantic. It was to the safety of St Nazaire that her sister ship *Bismarck* had been making when she was finally sunk by the Royal Navy in May 1941. Likewise, were *Tirpitz* to venture into Atlantic waters she would need St Nazaire as a refuge for repairs and refitting, but destroy the giant dry-dock and the threat posed by *Tirpitz* would be greatly diminished. Without St Nazaire as a bolthole, it would be foolhardy to risk the ship in the Atlantic.

The day after his memorandum to the Chiefs of Staff Churchill discussed the problem of *Tirpitz* with the First Sea Lord, Sir Dudley Pound. With the Prime Minister's words ringing in his ears, Pound ordered that Mountbatten be told to look at how the dry dock at St Nazaire might be neutralized. This was not the first time that staff at Combined Operations had looked at this, but previous proposals had never got beyond the initial planning stage. It was, it seemed, too difficult a target, too inaccessible and too well defended.

However, Mountbatten, always politically astute, already had a solution up his sleeve. His naval planners at DCO, headed by Captain John Hughes-Hallett, had as recently as 21 January drawn up a list of raiding targets in occupied Europe, among them St Nazaire. On 23 January Hughes-Hallett discussed the list with Mountbatten who asked him to prepare outline plans for the operations. This he did. The solution he and Commander David Luce devised was brilliantly original and, at a stroke, made possible an operation that had previously seemed impossible.[7]

'It has frequently been asserted', Hughes-Hallett wrote, 'that St Nazaire was chosen because of its great lock – the only place the *Tirpitz* could be docked on the Atlantic coast. In fact this is not so.'

St Nazaire's attraction to the DCO planners as a raiding target lay originally more in the fact that it was the most distant target on the French coast that could be reached by a raiding force with only one period of daylight during the voyage. But there was another attraction to St Nazaire, too, because 'although one of the most heavily defended ports in Europe, a glance at the Chart revealed a fatal defect in the siting of the defending batteries.'

The port of St Nazaire lies about 6 miles up the River Loire from the sea. The main dredged approach channel, the Charpentiers channel, ran close to the shore along the northern side of the estuary and was covered by several heavy coastal defence batteries, smaller calibre guns and searchlights. To the south and seaward of this channel was a vast area of shoal water which became mud flats at low tide. However, as the range of the tide at the mouth of the Loire was very great, Hughes-Hallett felt that it might be possible for a vessel drawing no more than 12 feet to cross the shoals during the high spring tides. 'If this was so, it would be possible for the raiders to pass over the shoal water and enter the deep water channel very close to St Nazaire itself, and run the gauntlet of only one of the batteries.'

Once the Admiralty's splendidly-named Superintendent of Tides – if only he had been around in King Canute's time – had confirmed that Hughes-Hallett's hypothesis was sound, he and Luce set about drawing up a plan of attack.[8]

Their plan, which took only an hour to draw up, posited the destruction of the dry dock as the principal goal of the operation. Previous plans had incorporated operations against St Nazaire's submarine pens and other maritime installations. This concentration on the dry dock, it was hoped, would ensure the immediate and wholehearted support of the Admiralty. Politically, it was a masterstroke since, as we have seen, at that precise moment the problem posed by *Tirpitz* loomed large in the Admiralty's thinking. If Hughes-Hallett and Luce wanted permission for their raid, this was the way to go about securing it.

The core of Hughes-Hallett's plan was the use of an expendable ship, packed with explosive, which would cross the shoal water before ramming the outer gate of the great dock. The Commandos and demolition squads would disembark and, once the ship had exploded, attack various dockyard installations. A torpedo boat would then enter the flooded dock to fire her charges at the inner gate. Meanwhile an accompanying flotilla of motor launches (MLs) would come alongside in the dock to take off the Commandos before returning to England.[9] While details of the plan were altered as it evolved, the use of the expendable ship, the 'floating bomb', remained its essential characteristic. Once drafted the plan was explained to Mountbatten on 6 February, he approved it before, in turn, presenting it to the Admiralty.[10] On 25 February Hughes-Hallett's outline plan was approved by the Chiefs of Staff. Operation *Chariot* was now live.[11]

Time and tide wait for no man: the planned attack could be carried out only during the high spring tides expected over about three days at the end of March. So, with only a month to go before the operation had to be carried out or abandoned, there was a vast amount to be done. The first step was to summon the naval commander, hence the signal to Ryder on the day that the Chiefs of Staff approved the plan. Newman, leading the Commandos, had been summoned from Scotland to COHQ two days previously.

However, by the time Ryder arrived at Richmond Terrace for the meeting on 26 February, the Admiralty had not allocated an expendable ship for use in the raid. Given the importance that the Admiralty attached to preventing *Tirpitz* sallying forth into the Atlantic and the resourceful originality of Hughes-Hallett's plan, this was simply perverse. At the Chiefs of Staff meeting the previous day, Sir Dudley Pound had been asked to consider whether a suitable British ship could be made available.

With the question of the expendable ship still unresolved, Ryder and Newman decided to formulate a plan for carrying out the attack using only light forces, that is MLs and other coastal craft. This, they felt, would circumvent the Admiralty's evident reluctance to provide an expendable ship for the operation. Hughes-Hallett, however, would not countenance this fundamental change in his original plan. So they decided to force the Admiralty's hand. Unless a suitable ship were allocated before 3 March, they insisted, there would be insufficient time to prepare fully for the operation. The ultimatum was passed to the Admiralty, where it had its desired effect. On 2 March Sir Dudley Pound told the Chiefs of Staff that a British ship had been provided.[12] The ship in question was an elderly American destroyer, HMS *Campbeltown*, one of fifty obsolete ships given to Britain in exchange for the use of naval bases in the West Indies. Launched in 1919, she had served in the American Navy as USS *Buchanan* but by 1942 she was in her dotage. That afternoon Ryder and Newman went to Portsmouth to inspect the ship. She was flush-decked, 95m long and almost 10m across the beam, displacing around 1,200 tons. At full steam she could achieve 35 knots, but at slow speeds was awkwardly cumbersome.[13] Ryder, having seen *Campbeltown* for the first time, described her as 'very unmanoeuvrable and about as obsolete as possible'.

From the moment Ryder learned of his appointment he worked flat out: 'The task was formidable', he wrote later. Unlike Newman, whose Commando was already a well-oiled, well-trained unit, Ryder had to start from scratch; 'I was single-handed.' 'No staff – no office – no car, not even a telephone and no ships; everything including the collection of the force and its training had to be achieved in less than four weeks.'

His first problem was to get himself relieved of his responsibilities at Wilton. After the meeting at Richmond Terrace Ryder returned to Wiltshire where he was granted leave, although he had to return later to hand over to his successor and to help Hilaré pack up the house. 'It was for me most exasperating not to have been relieved earlier of my previous appointment.'

Ryder and Newman were accompanied on their first visit to *Campbeltown* by Constructor Commander Merrington, an old friend of Ryder's from their time together in *Warspite* before the war. This was an unexpected bonus for Ryder. 'I had a friend at Court … in the … complicated relations between the Admiralty and their dockyards.' Having looked over the ship, they returned to London where they drew up a list of the alterations to be made to the ship. 'To give some idea', Ryder wrote later, 'of the speed at which we were working this most important task which comprised a complete list of alterations and defects, was completed in less than an hour.'

The alterations to *Campbeltown* concentrated on lightening her so that she could pass over the shoals in the mouth of the Loire. All her armament was removed and replaced with eight twin Oerlikons. The bridge was fitted with bullet-proof plating and armoured shields were installed on the decks for the Commandos to shelter behind during the run-in to St Nazaire. As *Campbeltown* had four funnels it was decided to remove two of them and cut the tops of the remaining two at an angle in order to alter her profile. It was hoped that in poor light this would make her look more like a German destroyer. Merrington advised that the work should be carried out in the dockyard at Devonport and that the old destroyer should be moved there at once.

Once the question of *Campbeltown*'s modifications had been settled, Ryder travelled to Plymouth to report to Admiral Forbes. In London, Ryder had experienced obstruction and difficulty at every turn, 'no one seemed interested in getting me what I wanted.' 'All I could find was an antagonistic atmosphere between the Admiralty and Combined Ops. and time was vital.' Once in Plymouth, however, Ryder found a completely different situation. In answer to Ryder's plea for help, Forbes replied simply, 'I'm here to get you what you want', and, Ryder recorded gratefully, 'he was as good as his word.' As Forbes said, it is 'Not much use being a Commander-in-Chief if you can't get what you need.' He deputed his senior staff officer, Commander McCrum, to ensure that Ryder got what he wanted. For example, Ryder and Newman both wanted to have a mobile headquarters ship, separate from *Campbeltown*: 'I can only say that when I had suggested this at COHQ Hughes-Hallet was most impatient about it', but McCrum secured the use of MGB 314.[14]

Once Ryder was established in Plymouth he set about, with the help of Admiral Forbes and Commander McCrum, gathering the staff he would need for planning the operation. Lieutenant Bill Green, RN, a specialist navigator, was appointed as navigation officer (he also served as Ryder's chief of staff) while Lieutenant Nigel Tibbits, RN, an explosives expert, was given the responsibility of working out how best to convert *Campbeltown* into a floating bomb. 'Tibbits and Green, of course, both played a splendid part in the operation and I was very lucky to have them', Ryder reflected. The Canadian Sub Lieutenant O'Rourke, RCNVR joined as signals officer and Lieutenant Verity, RNVR as beach master.

Campbeltown arrived at Devonport on 7 March, rather later than Ryder had hoped following his request that she should sail 'as soon as possible'. Once at Devonport, however, the work to modify the destroyer began in earnest. Ryder was delighted to find that Mr Grant, whom he had known years before in Hong Kong, was in charge of the work on *Campbeltown*: 'we could not have a better man to superintend this work.'

There remained the question of who would take command of the ancient *Campbeltown* on her last and most glorious voyage. Her captain when she arrived at Devonport was Lord Teynham, who happened to be a cousin of Hilaré's. Despite the fact that he had left the Navy as a Lieutenant quite a few years earlier, Ryder was happy to have him on the raid. Admiral Forbes, however, understandably insisted that an active service destroyer officer be appointed for this vital and technically demanding task. So it was that Lieutenant Commander Sam Beattie took command of *Campbeltown*. 'I was overjoyed at the idea of getting Beattie whom I knew well', Ryder wrote. The two men had joined the Navy in the same

Special Entry in January 1926 so had done much of their training together. 'I could wish for no one better,' Ryder wrote.

On 10 March, two days before the forces were due to begin assembling, Admiral Forbes convened a meeting at his headquarters in Plymouth with Ryder and Newman. The two explosives experts, Nigel Tibbits and his Army counterpart Captain Pritchard, attended to explain their plans for demolishing *Campbeltown*. Also present were Ryder's navigator and signals officer, Green and O'Rourke, Lieutenant Commander W.L. Stephens, RNVR, commanding officer of 20th ML Flotilla and Senior Officer of the whole ML force and Lieutenant Commander Woods, RNVR, commanding officer of 28th ML Flotilla. The company was completed by Lieutenant Dunstan Curtis, RNVR and Sub Lieutenant Wynn, RNVR, the commanding officers, respectively, of the headquarters gunboat MGB 314, and MTB 74.

With all the important naval personnel present, the meeting, having formally accepted Tibbits's demolition scheme, discussed the route that the force would take to St Nazaire. The main concern was to avoid being spotted by enemy reconnaissance planes. 'We were told that the only regular one was the Paris Zenit which passed over the Scilly Isles at 0800 each morning. Our time of sailing was to be after that time therefore.'

The meeting also discussed the training programme. The principal training exercise was a mock attack on Devonport harbour, planned for the night of 21 March, codenamed Exercise *Vivid*. No attempt was made to keep the exercise secret, indeed it was 'laid on in the most open-handed manner possible' and advertized as a test of Devonport's defences. The Commandos were to be landed from the MLs only as it was felt prudent to keep *Campbeltown* out of the picture. As Ryder and Beattie had decided that ramming a lock gate at full steam was not a manoeuvre which could realistically be practised, the old destroyer would sit out *Vivid*.

With plans now advancing and work on *Campbeltown* in full swing at Devonport, Ryder departed to Falmouth, where his little fleet would assemble before sailing for St Nazaire. On 12 March he established his headquarters in the conservatory of the Tregwynt Hotel (now the Membley Hall Hotel), which had been requisitioned by the Navy for the use of the Senior Officer at Falmouth. The hotel was on the seafront from where it commanded a magnificent, sweeping view of the Cornish coast. High on the bare, windswept headland to the east was the defiantly solid, circular bastion of Pendennis Castle.

The following day *Princess Josephine Charlotte*, the troopship carrying Newman's No.2 Commando, arrived from Scotland. On 13 March the MLs started arriving at Falmouth. Hughes-Hallett's original plan had specified eight MLs carrying the Commandos to accompany *Campbeltown*. By the time the force assembled at Falmouth it had expanded to incorporate sixteen MLs, four more to transport the additional troops needed for fighting and demolition and another four to act as a 'spearhead' for the approach formation. The latter, which were equipped with torpedoes, had been specifically requested by Ryder to give the flotilla extra firepower during the run-in up the Loire in the event of unforeseen emergencies.

The 'B' Class Fairmile MLs were the workhorses of the Navy's Coastal Forces, ideally suited for service in the Channel, chasing off the enemy's small craft, hunting submarines, rescuing ditched airmen, escorting merchant ships and so on. The MLs were 112ft long and 19.5ft across with a pair of 650hp American Hall-Scott marine engines, which gave a maximum speed of around 18 knots. They were not, however, at all well adapted for an assault upon a heavily-defended port. They were 'very handy and seaworthy', but their hulls were constructed 'of two thin skins of mahogany, with a lining of calico between, so that they would not resist even a rifle bullet'. The MLs were equipped with some light armour around the bridge and a few splinter-mats, but that was the sum total of the protection offered to their crews and the Commandos on board. To make matters worse, each ML had, in order to increase its range for the raid, two extra 500 gallon petrol tanks fitted on deck. The extra tanks greatly increased the MLs' already high risk of fire. With the exception of the torpedo-carrying boats, all the MLs had had two Oerlikon cannons installed, one fore and one aft, in lieu of their original armament.[15] Ryder's verdict was that the MLs 'were really ... unsuited for such a hot action as in the event transpired but such was the state of the country at that time that this was the best that could be done.'

With Ryder now installed in his makeshift headquarters and the specially-adapted MLs arriving by the hour, there was a pressing need to concoct a convincing cover story. Ryder therefore invented, and placed himself in command of, the 10th Anti-Submarine Striking Force. 'I let it be known with all due secrecy' that the new arrivals were to conduct long-range, anti-submarine sweeps into the Atlantic to the south and west of the Isles of Scilly. This explained both the MLs' additional fuel tanks and their upgraded guns. Ryder had been conscious of the importance of absolute secrecy in Operation *Chariot* from the start. For example when he, Newman and Merrington first visited *Campbeltown* at Portsmouth, Ryder would not allow Newman to go on board. 'Charles,' he said, 'I can't possibly let anyone in khaki go on board that ship!'[16]

Ryder put considerable thought into embellishing the cover story. He made some signals creating the impression that the 10th Anti-Submarine Striking Force was working up at Falmouth before transferring overseas. One such signal read:

M.L.s wishing to land their dinghies to make room for additional twin Lewis gun mounting may do so. They are, however, to arrange with S.N.O. to have them sent to F.O.I.C. Greenock and have them labelled 'For transhipment'.

Another one ordered that

Senior Officer M.L.s is to arrange for the supply of two suits of tropical rig for crews of all M.L.s. These are to be drawn before the force sails for the Clyde on 2nd April.

'The drawing of Sun helmets,' Ryder wrote later, 'was initiated on this occasion for the first time.' Claiming, most uncharacteristically, a first for himself, he did concede that 'It later became rather hackneyed in some war films.' Much of Ryder's energies were spent during the first days at Falmouth covering for the greatly increased level of activity, so noticeable in a small port. For all his efforts, he had little reassurance.

My fellow conspirators seldom met me without some tale of appalling disclosures, and, of course, one never knew how successful one's efforts had really been. All one did know for certainty was that if the enemy found out about our plans, we would receive a very hot reception.

Inextricably intertwined with the question of security was the dilemma of when to tell the Commandos and sailors what was afoot. For the first few days after the Commandos and the MLs arrived in Falmouth, neither group had any idea that there was any connection between them at all. The Commandos saw a few MLs pottering about; the ML crews noticed the *Princess Josephine Charlotte* moored at the quay but thought little of it. Newman wanted to suspend all leave from 15 March so that he could brief his men, but it was felt that such an early suspension of leave would give rise to gossip in the town. In the end, Ryder and Newman decided to wait until after *Vivid* to suspend leave, as the men would inevitably begin to speculate at that point.

Once Ryder had established and embellished his cover story, he could turn his attention to training his force. In this respect there was a very marked difference between the naval elements and Newman's Commandos. The Commandos had been honed to a high pitch of skill and efficiency by exhaustive training in Scotland. Their morale was high, they were all volunteers, young, keen and very fit. A good minority of them had seen action during the Norwegian campaign and the demolition teams had trained intensively and in detail for their particular tasks. They also had, in the form of Charles Newman, an inspiring leader.

Newman, a building engineer by profession, was a married man of thirty-seven at the time of the raid, of medium height and solid build, a pipe permanently clenched between his teeth. Known universally as 'Colonel Charles', he commanded the loyalty and affection of all his men, officers and other ranks alike. One of his officers described him as 'convivial, gregarious, a non-intellectual, ringside, rugger-playing hearty, who also played jazz and music-hall on the piano.'[17] Another remembered him resembling 'a battered old elephant', adding that Newman was 'an unruffled chap, like an uncle really.'[18] Beneath this somewhat bluff exterior, however, lay deep reserves of steely determination and courage.

The naval element of the raiding force could not have been more different. Assembled on an ad hoc basis from Coastal Forces, the officers and crews of the MLs were inexperienced. Indeed, the eight MLs of the newly-formed 28th Flotilla had never been to sea together, while the MLs of 20th Flotilla had been accustomed only to manoeuvring in twos or fours. The only vessel that had seen action was the gunboat, MGB 314, commanded by Dunstan Curtis, which had had a brush with an enemy patrol boat while running agents in and out of France. Lieutenant Bill Tillie, commanding ML 268, had by a curious coincidence served under Ryder in *Willamette Valley* from which he was one of the few to escape with his life. Most of the officers were 'Wavy Navy', that is, Royal Navy Volunteer Reserve, and the ratings 'hostilities only' men, not all of whom were volunteers.

Once the MLs had assembled at Falmouth Ryder set about working them up to a reasonable pitch of efficiency. 'At the first opportunity I took Woods's flotilla [28th] to sea and, in fact, we had as far as possible M.L.s to sea every day and night'. Even when the MLs were not at sea 'they were made to shift berth in the narrow waters of Falmouth Harbour on the darkest of nights.' Once Lieutenant Commander Stephens arrived Ryder put him in command of all the MLs and 'he put them through the most rigorous training, altering course wildly without signal to try and shake off those who were not keeping their wits about them.' Back in harbour Stephens would make the crews berth, cast off and berth again repeatedly until they were inch perfect.

On 16 March Ryder planned to take the MLs on a thirty-six hour sweep out into the Atlantic with the Commandos on board. Unfortunately, as the flotilla rounded the Lizard the wind freshened, with gales and rough seas forecast. Despite Stephens's assurances that the MLs would stand up to the weather, Ryder decided to make for shelter. 'Although I funked the Atlantic at night in our present state of training, we maintained a steady twelve knots to the Scilly Isles.' This, he noted sadistically, 'was a splendid sea sick test'. Having sheltered overnight in the Scillies, the flotilla spent the whole of the next day manoeuvring by signal until it ran into thick fog. Then it was able to practise its close, night-time (or bad weather) formation. The exercise greatly eased Ryder's worries about the MLs: 'I returned much impressed with the seaworthiness and reliability of these M.L.s'.

On 18 March Newman briefed his officers about the impending operation. Thirty-nine of them listened behind the locked doors of the *Princess Josephine Charlotte*'s wardroom to Newman describe the plan as 'the sauciest thing since Drake'. Newman explained the attack, on an as yet unnamed port on the coast of France, with the help of a map drawn on a blackboard and the model brought from COHQ. The following day the men were told the details of the attack. Newman made it clear to the assembled company – the Commandos only, not the sailors – that anyone who felt uncomfortable about taking part would be allowed to stand down without reproach, an offer that spoke volumes of the dangers of the operation.[19] Not a single man did so.

MGB 314, the gunboat which was to serve as Ryder and Newman's headquarters, also arrived in Falmouth on 18 March as did the four extra MLs armed with torpedoes. MGB 314 was a Fairmile 'C' Class gunboat. She was slightly shorter and narrower than the B-Class Fairmiles and, like them, wooden hulled. She was powered by three Hall-Scott engines which could speed her along at 23 knots with a maximum of 26 knots. Her armament consisted of a Vickers 2-pounder pom-pom on the foredeck and a Rolls-Royce 2-pounder cannon aft. Amidships she had, twin half-inch machine guns mounted in power-operated turrets; and on the bridge there were .303 machine guns.[20] Her principal drawback from Ryder's point of view was her lack of range: her petrol tanks did not contain sufficient fuel to get her to St Nazaire, let alone back again. 'We were,' Ryder wrote, 'in two minds as to whether to take her or not.' However, he was keen to have a headquarters ship and with no alternative in the offing, decided that, if necessary, she should be towed there and back.

The dress rehearsal for the raid on St Nazaire, Exercise *Vivid*, took place on the night of 21 March. Taking the form of a full-scale attack on Devonport dockyard, it was, wrote Ryder, 'very satisfactory from the defenders' point of view and gave us much food for thought.' The value of the exercise was enhanced by the fact that the North Yard at Devonport bore a remarkable resemblance to St Nazaire. Ryder and Newman led the force in on MGB 314, as would happen during the raid proper. 'Frankly,' Ryder wrote,

we found it difficult. The dazzling effect of the searchlights not only confused us but made us feel most uncomfortably conspicuous, and finally although we led the force to the right place in the dockyard more by luck than anything else, a large liner was berthed just where we didn't expect her and half the M.L.s overshot the mark.

'Altogether there was a good deal of confusion', Ryder later admitted; it was all much more difficult than had been supposed. To add to Ryder's discomfiture, Admiral Forbes, who had watched the exercise, 'was most scornful of our efforts.' He was, however, able to reassure Forbes that 'we had learned more by our failures than we should have, had all gone well.'

Once the MLs had returned to Falmouth from *Vivid* on 23 March, the preparations for Operation *Chariot* entered their final phase. Ryder had decided that this was the moment when the ML crews should be told of their target. Hitherto Ryder and his staff had gone to great lengths to ensure that the ML flotillas appeared to be engaged in normal coastal operations. But now that the crews were in on the secret, full security was imposed. All MLs were ordered to refuel, take on water and anchor out in the Carrick Roads, beyond the port. Shore leave was stopped.

One lesson that *Vivid* had brought home sharply was that the MLs' existing camouflage, a scheme of pale blues, greens and white designed to help them blend in with the sea mists, had to be changed. By searchlight at night these colours made the little boats stand out with alarming clarity against the dark water, presenting an easy target to enemy gunners. So once the MLs were anchored off Falmouth the crews busied themselves repainting the hulls in 'Plymouth Pink', the drab shade of mauve used by all other Royal Navy ships serving in the Channel.[21]

As the *Chariot* force was due to sail on 27 March, Ryder now had only three days to perfect his plans. 'The 24th and 25th were busy days for me', he wrote later, 'and full of suspense.' During these days Ryder issued and went over his detailed orders with the eighteen commanding officers of the naval force, illustrating his points with the plans, photographs and model of St Nazaire. Ryder's orders set out the sailing formations, the order of attack and instructions for reforming on the route home. While explaining his detailed orders to the ML commanders, Ryder 'emphasized that I relied more than ever on the initiative and enterprise of each commanding officer and instructed them to brief their coxswains, guns' crews and officers in the same manner.'

Hughes-Hallett and Luce's original plan had been greatly expanded – there were now sixteen MLs, instead of the original eight, MGB 314 as headquarters ship and MTB 74 – but its key characteristic, the expendable, exploding ship remained. What had changed were the arrangements for exploding the destroyer once she had rammed the dock. The original proposal envisaged that the ship would be blown up with the Commandos still ashore, taking cover. Given the size of the explosion required to wreck the dry dock's colossal gates, both Ryder and Newman felt that this placed their men at too great a risk. According to Hughes-Hallett, it was Admiral Forbes who insisted that the explosion be delayed until the troops and sailors had withdrawn.[22]

On the other hand, the early proposals for a delayed explosion failed to convince Ryder. He was worried that should the charge not explode or the fuses be shot away, he would be giving the enemy a destroyer, albeit an elderly and, presumably, badly damaged one. It was decided therefore to scuttle *Campbeltown* before exploding the charge with underwater fuses. This would also have the advantage of placing the explosion as close as possible to the bottom of the lock gate where it would cause the maximum damage. The technical issues were resolved by Nigel Tibbits, the explosives expert. He proposed that the 'bomb' should consist of twenty-four depth charges, divided into four groups of six, totalling 7,200 lb of explosive. As Tibbits wrote in his secret appreciation, 'The explosion of three tons of Amatol is devastating.' He devised a complicated system of fuses to ensure that the charge could not fail to go off, including provision for the insertion of long-delay fuses into the charge as *Campbeltown* came into the river.

Tibbits also resolved the problem of where in *Campbeltown* to mount the explosive charge. The problem was that no one knew how far back the ship would be buckled by the impact with the lock gate. Tibbits proposed that the charges be mounted on top of one of the fuel tanks on the centre line of the ship, just abaft the steel column supporting the ship's forward gun. 'Here', wrote Tibbits, 'it should be unaffected by buckling, etc. of the ship.' The charge was set in concrete partly to protect it and partly to deceive any inquisitive Germans who might inspect the ship after she had been scuttled. Tibbits's scheme laid Ryder and Newman's fears to rest: 'we felt', Ryder wrote, 'that [it] covered us against a whole multitude of circumstances which we could not foresee.'[23]

Captain Hughes-Hallett's original plan specified that a diversionary air raid should take place over St Nazaire as the attacking force steamed up the River Loire. As outlined to the Chiefs of Staff, 'An essential feature of the plan is that a heavy air raid should be carried out on the dock area during the last phase of the approach and throughout the operation.' As Hughes-Hallett remarked, 'The idea was an old and very debatable one'. Clearly the object was to force 'the coast defence gunners [to] take cover and [keep] the eyes of the German look-outs on the sky'. However, as Hughes-Hallett pointed out, 'it could equally be argued that an air raid – especially if ineffective – may have the opposite effect of alerting the guns' crews and look-outs.'

But there was a Cabinet ruling in force against the blind bombing of French towns which could only be waived on the authority of the Prime Minister himself. Without this permission bomber crews would not be allowed to release their bombs where cloud obscured the target.[24] This was to prove a controversial aspect of the St Nazaire operation.

Campbeltown arrived at Falmouth on 24 March. She was a curious sight now that her modifications were complete. The two funnels, one taller than the other, cut at a rakish angle, gave her, as intended, more than a passing resemblance to a German *Möwe* Class destroyer. Her bridge was now enclosed with bullet-proof plating and her ship's guns replaced by Oerlikons on 'bandstands'. 'We couldn't help smiling when we saw her appearance', Ryder remembered. Once she had anchored in the roadstead beyond the harbour, Ryder went aboard to welcome Beattie. He took with him the German naval ensign that he had, in great secrecy, procured as part of *Campbeltown*'s disguise. Since the completion of her modifications, Beattie had been busy mastering the quirks of his new and unusual ship. 'She had been lightened', he recalled,

> so much to get over the various sandbanks that she wouldn't handle like an ordinary destroyer at normal speeds. I discovered however that at roughly 17 knots and above she would handle like an ordinary destroyer and this set the speed at which I determined to ram because if I had to do any manoeuvres just before hitting the dock I didn't want to have to think about the turning circle.[25]

Earlier in the day the two *Hunt* Class destroyers, *Atherstone* and *Tynedale*, allocated to escort the flotilla, had also arrived. Ryder transferred his headquarters to *Atherstone*. Now, with a staff to help him and gunners, signalmen and mechanics at his beck and call Ryder threw himself into a frenzy of activity. 'In my opinion more was done to put our force in order in these last two days than we could have hoped to do in two weeks without these resources.'

One of the most pressing issues for Ryder was a shortage of ammunition. Incredible as it may seem for a force about to undertake so dangerous and important an operation, the *Chariot* flotilla was woefully short of ammunition. The guns in *Campbeltown* had their correct quota, about 1,800 rounds per gun, but for the MLs 'our supply was pathetic'. Ryder's efforts to secure extra supplies were mostly unsuccessful. Lieutenant Commander Jenks of *Atherstone* 'most nobly' offered Ryder half of his ammunition, and with that and other small additions each ML had around 800 rounds. 'How many of our countrymen', Ryder wondered bitterly, 'realised that we were setting out to make a frontal attack on one of the most heavily defended enemy bases with only half our allowance of ammunition?'

By 25 March Cornwall and the Western Approaches had enjoyed five days of fine, sunny spring weather, with calm seas. There was a 'real feel of summer in the air', Ryder told Hilaré.[26] Good weather was an overriding requirement for *Chariot* and the anticipated conditions had arrived on cue. Ryder knew that in early spring 'spells of up to ten days of easterly winds are common in the approaches to the Channel'. This warm, sunny weather heats up the land to create a haze. These were the ideal conditions in which to make the passage to St Nazaire, nor was Ryder anxious to risk a break in the weather. So having ascertained that Newman and his men were ready, Ryder asked Commander McCrum if the sailing time could be brought forward by twenty-four hours. Permission was duly granted for *Chariot* to leave Falmouth the following day, 26 March. *Campbeltown* would have to take her chance with the tide over the shoals not being at its highest.

'I imagine', Ryder wrote, 'the Commanders of such expeditions always get last minute shocks.' Nor was he any exception. The first, and most alarming, was the revelation on the evening of 25 March – now the eve of departure – that a squadron of four German torpedo boats/destroyers had moored in the harbour at St Nazaire. Part of the 5th Torpedo Boat Destroyer Flotilla, their presence had been revealed by aerial reconnaissance photographs taken that very morning. At this late stage there was little that could be done about this unwanted development, although McCrum promised Ryder that he would ask for two extra destroyers to be sent to cover the flotilla's return to England. In the meantime he and Newman would have to trust to luck.[27]

At 1345, fifteen minutes before sailing, Lieutenant Commander Woods, commanding officer of the MLs in the port column, fell ill and had to be left behind. 'This was', Ryder recalled, 'a great blow.' Woods had been one of Ryder's principal collaborators; they had mulled over the difficulties and examined the plans and the model in minute detail. They had even used a torch behind the model to simulate the effect of the searchlights. Ryder evidently had great faith in him: 'If Woods led his column to the right landing place', he wrote, 'all would be well.'

It was a warm, sunny, typically English spring afternoon, perfect for a picnic in the meadows or a walk on the hills. On a day such as this even the war could seem far away. At 1400 on 26 March 1942 the sixteen MLs slipped quietly away from Falmouth into the calm seas of the Channel, the fighter escort circling overhead. The three destroyers, *Campbeltown* with her deadly cargo and the two escorts, *Atherstone* and *Tynedale*, followed the MLs out to sea. They were bound for St Nazaire.

Chapter 12

Operation *Chariot*: the Raid on St Nazaire (26–8 March 1942)

As Ryder's little fleet steamed towards the open sea it took up its daylight sailing formation, Cruising Order No.1. Devised by Ryder to resemble an anti-submarine sweep in keeping with his cover story and to put inquisitive observers off the scent, the formation was shaped like a broad, flat arrowhead. In the centre was *Atherstone*, serving as the headquarters ship with Ryder, Newman and their small staffs on board. Bobbing on a tow rope in her wake was MGB 314. Spread out in echelon on either beam about 200 yards apart were the MLs, eight to port, eight to starboard. In the open spaces astern of the MLs were *Campbeltown* with MTB 74 in tow and *Tynedale*.[1] Once clear of land, Ryder set a course to the south-west.

Once the flotilla had taken up its cruising stations, Ryder had to make good the loss of Lieutenant Commander Woods, the commander of the port column of MLs. Shuffling his officers he promoted Lieutenant Platt, RNR, the next most senior officer, to command of the port column, drafting in the 'spare' commanding officer, Lieutenant Horlock, to take over Platt's ML. This was far from being an ideal arrangement as it meant that two MLs were going into action without the commanding officer under whom they had trained. But Ryder had little choice.

Despite the limited training that Ryder had been able to organize, 'the day we sailed was the first time the whole force had been in company.' He spent much of his time on that first afternoon at sea signalling to the MLs to keep closed up in station: 'I must have made about fifty signals to this effect.' While Ryder was anxiously shepherding his flock from *Atherstone*'s bridge, others were able to relax in the warm sunshine. Charles Newman, also on *Atherstone*'s bridge, remembered the scene vividly.

> The thrill of the voyage was upon one – the study of the navigational course with the Navy, the continuous look-out for enemy aircraft, the preparation of one's own personal kit to land in and the deciphering and reading of W/T messages from the C-in-C brought nightfall upon us in no time.

In MGB 314, being towed along by *Atherstone*, Dunstan Curtis and his men 'sat about gossiping as though it were a pleasure party, helping ourselves to the raisins that I always had in saucers on the bridge.'[2]

On *Campbeltown* the eighty or so Commandos under the watchful eye of Major Bill Copland, Newman's second-in-command, mingled easily with the ship's crew. 'There was little to do', Copland remembered, 'all our preparations had been made ... and it only remained to arrange our tours of duty for AA defence, rehearse "Action Stations" and wait.' Newman had ordered that no khaki uniforms should be seen on deck of any of the flotilla's vessels, so the Commandos borrowed 'motley naval kit'. Nevertheless, at one point during the afternoon Newman felt moved to make the signal: 'Too many obvious soldiers on deck in all boats.' Copland remembered that once someone had realized that this was *Campbeltown*'s last voyage, the men began breaking open the ship's supplies. All sorts of goodies began to appear, he remembered, butter, bacon, eggs, bottles of sherry and so on.[3]

Newman had briefed his Commandos about the operation and its intended target a week or so before they sailed. The naval ratings, however, had been left in the dark; when the flotilla steamed out of Falmouth none of them knew whither they were bound. Once at sea the officers let their men into the secret: St Nazaire was the target. Many of them had long suspected that something big was afoot; the fiction of the anti-submarine sweep had not convinced everyone, particularly the older hands. Beattie mustered *Campbeltown*'s reduced ship's company on the quarter-deck where he broke the news to them.

As Beattie spoke to his men on *Campbeltown*'s quarter-deck, immediately astern of her the crew of MTB 74 were hard at work as their boat was towed along by the destroyer. MTB 74 was commanded by Sub Lieutenant Micky Wynn, RNVR, a young, eccentric Welsh aristocrat. The chief intelligence officer at COHQ, the splendidly-titled Wing Commander the Maquis of Casa Maury, described Wynn as 'mad as a hatter but he has a very useful toy.'[4]

The 'toy' was MTB 74, a specially-modified version of the Vosper 70-foot motor torpedo boat, an 'eccentric craft', one Charioteer called her, in many ways ideally suited to her commanding officer. Modified to attack the German battlecruisers *Scharnhorst*, *Gneisenau* and *Prinz Eugen* holed up in the French port of Brest, her torpedo tubes had been resited on her fo'c'sle. The idea was that the torpedoes – known as 'Wynn's Weapons' – their motors removed and replaced with extra explosive, could be fired at very short range into the enemy ships at anchor over their torpedo nets. In order to have any hope of getting into a position from which such an attack could be launched, MTB 74 would need great speed. To this end she was fitted with three V12 1,250hp supercharged Packard engines which could sustain 35 knots but reach 40 if required. For slow manoeuvring at up to 6 knots, she had two auxiliary engines.[5] The trouble with this arrangement was that, as MTB 74 was incapable of any speed in between these extremes, sailing in company with other vessels was not her forte. She also used a great deal of petrol. For these reasons, if she were to be taken on the raid, she would have to be towed there and back.

Once *Scharnhorst* and her squadron had escaped from Brest in mid-February, Wynn and MTB 74 were at a loose end but he managed to get himself and his boat incorporated in the plan for Operation *Chariot*. She was included by name in Hughes-Hallett's outline plan approved by the Chiefs of Staff on 25 February. She 'is specially fitted out for an operation of this sort', he noted. Hughes-Hallett hoped that she could be used either to attack the inner lock gate, other subsidiary targets or, in extremis, to take over the main attack should *Campbeltown* come to grief.

Ryder, however, was not so keen on this outlandish addition to his force. When MTB 74 arrived at Falmouth he noted that she carried

every form of insurmountable defect and [was] painted in such a dazzling style that even the cows in the fields paused in their endless task of converting grass into milk and looked down on her in astonishment as she passed.

When MTB 74 returned to Falmouth after *Vivid* with a defective engine, it looked as if her fate was sealed. Wynn, however, had other ideas and managed to procure a replacement engine. The crew, supervised by his chief mechanic Bill Lovegrove, worked round the clock to install the new engine. Wynn was able to report his boat ready for sea to Ryder on the morning of departure, although in fact the crew were still fine-tuning the new engine as the MTB was towed towards St Nazaire.[6]

At 1911 on the evening of 26 March Ryder altered course to steer almost due south. As dusk fell, the solitary Hurricane which had kept watch over the flotilla as it sailed south swooped low over the ships before turning for home. To Ryder, watching the fighter disappearing northwards into the gloom, 'it was the last visible link with the homeland we had left six hours before.' 'Much lay ahead', he added, 'and even the least imaginative of the company present, alone with his thoughts, must have speculated as to his future.'[7] Once darkness had fallen, the destroyers raised the German ensign in case they should run into fishing trawlers during the night.

The following day, 27 March, dawned 'bright and clear'; rather to Ryder's disappointment the 'visibility was extreme' when some haze or low cloud would have been welcome. At 0700 Ryder changed course so that the flotilla was now heading towards the coast of France. Five minutes later, just as the flotilla was shaking out into its day-time formation – the arrowhead anti-submarine sweep – a sharp-eyed officer in *Tynedale* noticed a suspicious object on the port beam, around 7 miles away. Fearing that it was an enemy submarine, Ryder at once ordered *Tynedale* to investigate while *Atherstone* cast off MGB 314 before joining the pursuit. As *Tynedale* – still flying the Nazi ensign – closed it became apparent that the object was indeed a submarine, surfaced and stationary. She was *U-593*, commanded by *Kapitanleutnant* Gerd Keibling, on her way to St Nazaire for repairs.[8] When the destroyer was about 5 miles away, the submarine fired a recognition signal; *Tynedale*'s reply – a pure guess – appeared to satisfy her commander as she remained on the surface until about 0745.

At this point *Tynedale* was about 5,000 yards from the submarine when her commanding officer, Lieutenant Commander Tweedie, decided to attack. Hauling down the German flag he ran up the White Ensign before opening fire but missed the submarine which at once crash-dived. *Tynedale* continued at speed to where the submarine had last been seen; here, thirteen minutes later, she dropped a pattern of depth-charges. When the shock forced the submarine to the surface *Tynedale*, this time at close range, opened fire on her once more. Almost immediately, the submarine dived again. As the U-boat disappeared for the second time, *Atherstone* joined *Tynedale* and Ryder ordered the two destroyers to search for the submarine. They criss-crossed the sea where the submarine had last been seen but failed to make contact. *Tynedale*'s Asdic had been damaged so after two hours Ryder abandoned the hunt. His worry was that the submarine had sighted his flotilla and raised the alarm.

> With any luck the submarine had only seen the destroyers and so after hunting him and keeping him down for two hours, we retired at high speed in a South Westerly direction, rejoining our forces by an indirect route. Should the submarine then pass a report he would, with luck, mistake us for two destroyers on passage for Gibraltar.

It was fortunate indeed that Ryder took this precaution as the submarine had in fact seen the MLs as well as the destroyers. Moreover, at 1347 – several hours after the destroyers had disengaged – she had signalled their presence to the German Group Command West: '0620 [0720 BST] three destroyers, ten MTBs, 46° 52′ N, 5° 48′ W, Course West.' This signal was received at Group Command West at 1420 where it was taken to show that the British squadron was making for Gibraltar, as Ryder had hoped.[9] It was a lucky escape. Two French trawlers had witnessed the action between the destroyers and *U-593*, but 'they legged it at such a rate that I felt confident they had not sighted our force', Ryder recalled.

U-593's signal had a further unintended consequence. It was Keibling's opinion that the British squadron he had sighted had been on its way out to sea after a night's minelaying along the French coast. It was this that prompted him to signal that the British ships were steering a westerly course, that is, away from St Nazaire, not towards it. As a direct result of *U-593*'s signal, the four ships of the 5th Torpedo Boat Destroyer Flotilla, whose unwelcome presence in the harbour at St Nazaire had been spotted two days previously, were ordered to patrol off the coast that very night. Thus, unwittingly, *U-593* contributed to removing a major hazard from Ryder's path.

By the time the destroyers rejoined the main body of the flotilla it had lost any pretence of an orderly formation.

> The morning's excitement had fitted everyone's imagination and Asdic reports of submarines to the right and to the left were being busily investigated by an

ever-straggling line of MLs. I refused to be stampeded by shoals of fish and as we came up we acted as 'Whipper in' and ordered them to rejoin.

By 1100 order had been restored and, much to Ryder's relief, after the clear, bright start, the sky had clouded over. If the reconnaissance aircraft were sent out following the submarine's signal, the low cloud would hamper their search for Ryder's little fleet. Furthermore, as they had made such good progress so far, Ryder was able to order the boats to reduce speed to a 'very moderate' 8 knots. This, by reducing the vessels' bow waves and wakes, greatly diminished the chances of the flotilla being spotted from the air.

No sooner had the flotilla assumed its cruising formation once more than a large fleet of fishing trawlers hove into view. This was a problem that Ryder had anticipated and discussed with his commanding officers before sailing. 'Most of the advice I received', he remembered, ' … was either to sink them on sight or some measures which I considered too barbarous.' Being 'far from convinced' that the Germans would have agents in the fishing trawlers, Ryder, before leaving Falmouth, issued the following order, 'Spanish trawlers and neutrals sighted are to be boarded by *Tynedale* and sent in with a prize crew. In the case of the French fishing vessels, the crews are to be taken off and the vessels sunk.'

At first Ryder ordered the destroyers to steer in such a way that the MLs were hidden from the trawlers: 'Eventually, however, we were cornered and had to act.' Two trawlers were well apart from the others so Ryder sent *Tynedale* to investigate the one on the port beam, while MGB 314 was ordered to slip her tow and board the trawler on the starboard side. The trawlers, *Le Slack* and *Nungressor et Coli*, were boarded, the crews taken off and all the ships' papers, charts, sailing instructions, and so on removed. The two trawlers were then sunk by gunfire. Once the trawlers' captains had been interrogated, Ryder was 'reassured about the other trawlers and I decided to sink no more.' Indeed, the trawler skippers seemed remarkably friendly and understanding in the circumstances: '*C'est la guerre*, seemed to cover their sentiments', Ryder remembered. It fact it was a difficult decision for Ryder to take. Although the trawler skippers had told him that there were no wireless sets nor German agents aboard any of the fishing boats, if they were in cahoots with the enemy they would hardly have admitted it to Ryder. On the other hand, there were too many boats to sink, too many crew to take off, nor did he have the time in hand to deal with the entire fishing fleet. Ryder had to make a quick decision; he chose the path of least resistance – the humane course – but was fortunate that the trawlers did not betray his purpose.

Once the flotilla was clear of the fishing fleet, it continued on an easterly course for the coast of France. 'The afternoon was uneventful', Ryder recalled, 'and I even managed some sleep.' The flotilla's course across the Bay of Biscay had been planned in 'the somewhat pious hope' that the Germans would be hoodwinked into thinking that its destination was La Rochelle. At 1704 Ryder received a signal confirming the presence of the enemy motor torpedo boats off St Nazaire and warning of the possibility that the flotilla might encounter them. Two hours later he was informed that reinforcements in the shape of two destroyers, *Cleveland* and *Brocklesby*, had been dispatched at full speed from England. Ryder was not impressed. 'The existence of this superior enemy force on the West Coast of France had been reported weeks before and we ourselves had reported their presence at St Nazaire the day before sailing.' Ryder had pressed for the extra ships to be dispatched in time, but 'Eventually, when they were bound to arrive too late, they were sent.' As he caustically noted, this demonstrated clearly 'the futility of sending reinforcements too late.'

Ryder was still as alert as ever as he kept watch over his force from *Atherstone*'s bridge. During the afternoon he signalled to Bill Tillie in ML 268 to 'Go round MLs telling them all by hailer to reduce Aldis signalling.' He did not want unnecessary lamp signals to catch the enemy's eye. Likewise as dusk approached, he signalled to the whole force: 'Glass on wheelhouses most conspicuous at night. Must be covered with paint, paper or grease on outside.' Ryder was glad to be busy: 'the weight of responsibility outweighed all fears for one's safety', he wrote years later.

> A Commander is lucky in this respect compared to, say, a junior rating who has little to divert his thoughts as he goes into action.

Nevertheless as evening came without any signs that the enemy had discovered them, 'our spirits rose'. 'It seemed incredible', he wrote, 'that we could really steam here in broad daylight without being spotted.'

As darkness fell Ryder stopped the force so that he and Newman could transfer as planned to MGB 314 for the run-in to St Nazaire. Ryder was accompanied onto the gunboat by Lieutenant Green, the navigator, and Sub Lieutenant O'Rourke, the signals officer; Newman, by his adjutant, Captain Day, Captain Terry, the intelligence officer, and Gordon Holman, the press correspondent. Also transferring to MGB 314 with Ryder was Leading Signalman Pike. He had been specifically recruited for *Chariot* as not only was he bilingual but could send and receive Morse code messages in German. As Ryder laconically put it, 'This opened up possibilities.' During the outward voyage he composed 'a signal calculated to confuse the enemy and cause delay in their opening fire'. By way of additional insurance 'we hunted out the signal in the International Signal Book for forces being fired on by their own side'. As the MGB pulled away from the destroyer, *Atherstone*'s company gave her a cheer. At the same time Wynn's MTB 74 slipped her tow from *Campbeltown* to take up her station at the rear of the flotilla.

At this precarious moment one of the boats in the port column, ML 341 commanded by Lieutenant Douglas Briault, fell behind; one of her engines had broken down. Platt, the stand-in commander of the port column, came alongside to ask Ryder for permission to reduce speed while the ML's crew tried to repair the fault. He got short shrift,

This had been foreseen and spare M.L.s were stationed astern for such an eventuality and I am afraid that I rather curtly told him to act in accordance with his instructions. Anyhow, we couldn't at that time afford to reduce speed.

Unfortunately for Briault, the miscreant engine was not repaired until 2220 by which time it was far too late to catch up with the flotilla.

At 2000 Ryder altered course to the north-east. The flotilla was now heading straight for the mouth of the Loire; there was about 75 miles to go. At the same time, the force took up its prearranged order of battle, the formation for the attack itself. MGB 314, with Ryder and Newman on the bridge, was at the head of the column. Two-and-a-half cables (about a quarter of a mile) behind the MGB was *Campbeltown*. On either side of her, stretching astern away into the dark, were the two columns of MLs. At the head of each column was a torpedo-carrying ML: on the port side Lieutenant Irwin in ML 270; on the starboard side, Lieutenant Boyd's ML 160. Bringing up the rear was Wynn's MTB 74. The two escorting destroyers glided off into the dark to take up their positions a mile out on either side of the main body of Ryder's flotilla. Now cloaked in darkness, the flotilla increased speed to 15 knots.[10]

The move to the gunboat was another turn of the ratchet. Even the normally cool and unruffled Newman recorded that at that moment 'One felt very much nearer the fighting and one's nerves instinctively became just that little bit tighter.' Gordon Holman, the war correspondent attached to the MGB, recalled the move vividly, 'We had been going along very easily and rather giving the impression of a sweeping party, but this was all changed as night fell.' With this the clouds broke, so that the moon lit up the sea. It was, Holman wrote, 'a good deal too bright to please us, and we were thankful when a damp, cold sea-mist came up to take the sharp edges off everything.'[11]

For the next two hours the flotilla steamed north-eastwards towards the mouth of the River Loire. The next, and final, reference point on the planned route was the rendezvous with the submarine, HMS *Sturgeon*, in a pre-arranged position just 40 miles from the estuary. The idea was that *Sturgeon* would act as a direction-finding beacon for the flotilla, enabling it to locate accurately the mouth of the Loire. Her commanding officer, Lieutenant Commander Mervyn Wingfield, RN, had taken great care to fix his position accurately. He brought his ship to the surface, with only its conning tower above the waves, and, at the appointed hour, began flashing the letter 'M' in Morse code, into the night to the south-west.

However, Bill Green, the navigator, 'was pretty sure of our position, [because] although we had been unable to get star sights, he had had frequent glimpses of the sun and the calm weather greatly helped.' At 2200 the watching eyes on the MGB's bridge saw, dead ahead, *Sturgeon*'s signal flashing in the dark. Green had succeeded triumphantly in bringing the flotilla all the way from England to precisely the correct spot. He modestly admitted many years later that 'it was an enormous relief to me to see the submarine dead ahead.'

As the flotilla passed *Sturgeon* greetings were shouted between the ships in the dark. 'Hello, Mervyn', shouted Jenks through a loud-hailer from *Atherstone*, 'are you in the right place?' 'Yes', the reply came back, 'within a hundred yards but don't make so much noise.' Corran Purdon, a twenty-year-old subaltern at the time of the raid, vividly recalls the encounter with *Sturgeon*.

It made you really feel that Britain ruled the waves. In spite of the German Navy and the German *Luftwaffe* and so on here was this British submarine with a very British captain waving and shouting British messages to us.[12]

Once the flotilla had passed, *Sturgeon*, her job done, slipped quietly beneath the waves and away. At the same time *Atherstone* and *Tynedale* peeled off from the flotilla. They were going no nearer the French coast but waiting out at sea to cover the MLs as they made their way home. Now Ryder's little fleet, *Campbeltown*, the fifteen MLs, MGB 314 and MTB 74, was on its own. Ahead lay 40 miles of dark sea; beyond that the perilous shoals of the Loire estuary, a coast line bristling with enemy guns and the port of St Nazaire itself.

The flotilla steamed on through the night towards the coast of France. The weather had, from Ryder's point of view, improved; there was now a good covering of cloud and it was raining. If this was a welcome development for the sailors it was less so for the airmen who were flying down from England to mount the diversionary raid on St Nazaire. From the start this had been an integral element of the plan, although as the RAF's enthusiasm for the task steadily diminished so the number of bombers that its high command was prepared to commit decreased. Nevertheless, a force of thirty-five Whitleys and twenty-five Wellingtons took off from England at about 2200 that night bound for St Nazaire.[13]

The first wave of bombers arrived over St Nazaire at about 2330, running into heavy flak. The drone of their engines carried down to the men on *Campbeltown* and the MLs far below, an encouraging sign that all was going according to plan. However, all was not well. Flying in one of the bombers in the hope of being able watch the operation unfold was Captain John Hughes-Hallett. When the bombers, he wrote, 'arrived over St Nazaire the whole area was hidden by a great thunderstorm, while remaining almost as light as day in the full moon above the thunderclouds.'

The cloud cover was down to around 6,000 foot, but as the pilots were prohibited from flying below that height it was impossible to see the targets below. We have already seen that there was a strict proscription against the blind bombing of French towns which only the Prime Minister was able to relax. In this instance, according to Hughes-Hallett, Churchill had in fact granted an exemption to the ban, but by 'a tragic misunderstanding the Prime Minister's instructions never reached the Bombers'. 'With great gallantry', Hughes-Hallett recalled, the bombers remained for sixty-five minutes in the area, frequently diving into the clouds to escape German fighters, and in the hope of seeing the ground. But no bombs were dropped and the only result of the air raid was the loss of a number of bombers and the alerting of the German Garrison and gunners.[14]

At 2320 *Kapitan sur Zee* Merke, the commander of St Nazaire's aerial defences, was alerted to the impending arrival of the British bombers. Soon his batteries were illuminating the night sky with their searchlights and the flak guns firing shell and tracer into the clouds. But the longer the bombers remained overhead and the fewer the bombs that fell, the more suspicious Merke became. At about midnight, he remarked to one of his staff that 'some devilry is afoot'. He then signalled to all army command posts that 'the conduct of the enemy is inexplicable and indicated suspicion of parachute landings.'[15]

Far below the Commandos and sailors now approaching the estuary of the Loire were blissfully unaware of events above the clouds. From about midnight, Ryder recalled,

gun flashes were seen in the distance to the north–east and at about 0030 … it was obvious that considerable air activity was in progress as gun flashes extended over a wide arc with considerable flak.

As the flotilla steamed ever closer to the estuary, Ryder and Newman's men busied themselves with the final preparations. On *Campbeltown* Nigel Tibbits inserted the long-delay fuses into the explosive charge concealed in the forward part of the ship. From now on she was a floating mine, primed to explode. Elsewhere on the destroyer at around midnight Copland called his officers together for a final conference. It was, Copland remembered, a 'calm, confident, cheerful gathering' at which 'the atmosphere, outwardly at all events, far from seeming electric, was quite ordinary'. At the end of the conference 'I gave the order "Action Stations, please Gentlemen"', Copland recalled, 'and we left the wardroom for our allocated stations.'[16]

At 0030 the MGB passed the buoy that marked the beginning of the shoal waters of the estuary. The flotilla was now about 12 miles from its target, with sixty minutes to run until zero hour. As the flotilla approached the estuary the MGB had been ranging around on either side of *Campbeltown* taking soundings and checking the distances to the shore to help in navigating through the shoals. A few minutes later the flotilla passed the wreck of *Lancastria*, the cruise liner sunk by bombing while evacuating British troops in June 1940. The *Lancastria*'s gaunt remains looming up on the port beam were a stark reminder of the dangers of these shallow coastal waters.

For fifteen minutes or so, the ships ploughed on into the mouth of the river. At 0045, when 'we could dimly discern the northern shore', Ryder altered course slightly to compensate for a strong northerly set and ordered *Campbeltown* to reduce speed to 11 knots. As her stern rode lower in the water at speed, it was expected that this would enable her to pass without grounding over the mudflats that lay so close under the surface. In fact, *Campbeltown* did ground twice. For the men on the destroyer, their nerves already taut, these were anxious moments. The ship stranding on the mudflats under the guns of the German batteries was too awful a prospect to contemplate. As Michael Burn remarked, 'We'd have been a laughing stock of the entire world; the Germans needn't even have fired at us, they could have just left us there.' Bob Montgomery, the tall, spare, young demolitions expert, remembers looking over *Campbeltown*'s side at the churning water and offering up fervent prayers that the ship was not stranded. Corran Purdon, whose demolition party was stationed below for the run-in, 'felt it thrashing over the mud; we thought "Oh my God, I hope we're not stuck".' Contact with the mud reduced the destroyer's speed to about 5 knots until she was able to pull herself clear. Ryder, on the bridge of the MGB, was in blissful ignorance of this drama. 'I knew nothing of this until much later, thank goodness.'[17]

Even so close to the target the rest of Ryder's little fleet was still unable to keep proper station. 'Looking astern', he recalled,

I could only count about half the force but I hoped that this reduction [in speed] would enable them to catch up. I cursed the blighters for not keeping closer up, but there was little else that could be done as it was much too dangerous to signal now.

At about this moment, Ryder saw through the gloom on the port beam 'the dim shape of a patrol vessel or guard ship in the deep water channel.' The vessel appeared not to notice the intruders but it later emerged that its lookouts did in fact see the flotilla but, having no wireless, could not alert the batteries on the shore.

Just after 0100 the flotilla passed the Le Vert beacon to the north without seeing it. At this point, the British ships, by approaching St Nazaire over the shoals, were at least a mile further from the nearest German battery on the northern shore than they would have been had they used the dredged channel. This was the chink Hughes-Hallett had spotted in St Nazaire's defences, which his plan was designed to exploit. Had Ryder's ships been in the dredged channel under the northern shore of the estuary they would have been seen at once. More than a mile further out in the estuary, however, in the dark and in an unexpected position they escaped detection for much longer. As the ships passed the Le Vert beacon, they were 5 miles from the harbour itself; there was half-an-hour to run.[18]

As *Campbeltown* and the MLs continued up the estuary towards St Nazaire, it seemed incredible that they could remain undetected. Surely the enemy could hear the throb of the engines of the seventeen small craft and the destroyer. 'It was indeed very exciting at this stage', Ryder remembered, 'and our feelings were very buoyant but suppressed.' By this time the men on the boats could smell the countryside and even make out hedges and trees on the northern shore.

At 0120 the MGB passed a quarter of a mile to starboard – that is out into the estuary – of the disused tower of Les Morées. The tower was about 2 miles from the harbour, leaving Ryder's flotilla a twelve-minute run into the target. Once the flotilla had reached Les Morées it was past the heavy batteries, but had entered the narrows where it was barely a mile from the flak batteries on the north shore of the estuary. It was astonishing that the force had got so close without being spotted. It could not last. 'At this moment', Ryder recalled,

> we had evidently been detected in some way, probably the beat of so many engines had been heard by some coast watchers as one searchlight away on our port quarter from near No.3 Heavy Coastal Battery was suddenly switched on down the Charpentiers Channel. The warning had evidently been given as this was a signal for all the searchlights on both banks of the estuary to be switched on.

It was 0122; their cover was well and truly blown.

> From that moment the entire force was floodlit. Each boat with her silvery white bow and stern wave was clearly visible with the *Campbeltown* astern of us rising up above all the others. The glare of a disturbed enemy was upon us.

With the entire force now brightly illuminated, Ryder had to gain his ships time: 'all we could do was bluff the enemy.' They were now within 2 miles of the harbour and its dry dock. With every minute that the enemy could be hoodwinked into not opening fire Ryder's ships would steam closer to their target. In ten or eleven minutes they would be there. At his shoulder on the MGB's bridge was his secret weapon, the bilingual Signalman Pike.

As the searchlights lit up the flotilla, two German signal posts flashed messages to the MGB, one from the harbour area dead ahead – in fact, from the guard ship *Speerbrecher* moored off the East Jetty – and one on her port beam. With two signals to contend with at the same time, Pike had to act quickly. On Ryder's instructions he flashed in reply to the harbour's challenge a bogus call sign – provided by Naval Intelligence – and told them in German 'to wait'. Pike then turned to reply to the signal on the port beam, 'informing them that we were "proceeding up harbour in accordance with previous instructions".' While Pike was replying to the enemy signals one of the light batteries on the north shore opened fire on the flotilla. Ryder had, in briefing his officers, 'laid great stress ... on the importance of not opening fire too hastily and, at this moment, everyone nobly held their fire.'

Amazingly, the bluff worked. All firing stopped at once while several of the searchlights were switched off. 'It was really very exciting seeing the enemy actually acknowledging our signal word by word', Ryder wrote. However, *Speerbrecher* flashed another message towards the flotilla to which Pike began to reply by making the signal 'Wait'. As he was doing this, the flotilla was again fired on, although in a desultory fashion 'with obvious hesitation'. Ryder's ploy had sown the seeds of doubt in the defenders' minds. Pike then made to *Speerbrecher* the enemy signal for 'a vessel considering herself to be fired upon by friendly forces'. 'Who the enemy imagined we were, I don't know, but the fire stopped and we gained a few precious minutes.'[19] Ryder later reckoned that the bogus signals had gained the flotilla four vital minutes, in which time it travelled about two-thirds of a mile further up the river towards St Nazaire.

A minute or two later, at about 0128, the bluff came to an end. The Germans opened fire on the flotilla from all directions: suddenly the air was thick with coloured tracer. Ryder had one last trick up his sleeve, 'the trump card of the day', a Verey pistol loaded with a star-burst German recognition signal. He fired the pistol into the air, but 'instead of sailing majestically up into the heavens it flopped over the side into the sea.'[20] Unknown to Ryder, it was a cartridge designed to be fired down from an aeroplane.

Campbeltown struck her German ensign and ran up the White Ensign while the MLs broke out their White Ensigns astern as the whole flotilla opened fire with every weapon they had. The *Campbeltown*'s eight Oerlikons and machine guns, and her forward 12-pounder all blazed away. The MLs, too, opened up with their Oerlikons, two to each boat while the Commandos joined in enthusiastically with their Bren guns. Ryder, on the MGB's bridge at the head of the flotilla, had a grandstand view of the action.

> It is difficult to describe the full fury of the attack that was let loose on each side. Owing to the air attack, the enemy had every gun large and small fully manned and the night became one mass of red and green tracer.

Now, with only a mile to go, *Campbeltown* had regained the deep water of the dredged channel and so was able to increase her speed to nearly 20 knots for the final approach. In the MGB Ryder was heading close past the bows of *Speerbrecher*, the guard ship. With her 'light camouflage paint and high structure [she] stood out clear in the searchlights and was easily the most conspicuous ship in the river.' As a result, she took a terrible pasting. She fired a single burst at the MGB, whose gunlayer, Able Seaman Savage, 'instantly scored a direct hit on the gun position and plastered the ship from end to end.' Looking back as the MGB surged past the hapless *Speerbrecher*, Ryder could see that the Germans were shooting at their own boat. As *Campbeltown* and the MLs went past her, they too raked her with fire.

Now *Campbeltown* was bearing down on her target, the massive caisson of the dry dock. She had now reached 20 knots. Every enemy gun, large or small, that could be brought to bear on the destroyer was firing at her, some at point-blank range. She was being hit continuously, inflicting terrible casualties among the crew and the Commandos. In the armour-plated wheelhouse Beattie coolly waited as his ship surged towards the great lock gate. At the vital moment a searchlight lit up the lighthouse at the end of the Old Mole, giving Beattie an aiming point. With about 200 yards to go Beattie saw the giant caisson for the first time, an 'indistinct black line' in the shadows created by the blinding beams of the searchlights that criss-crossed the harbour. Lining *Campbeltown* up with the great lock gate, Beattie gave the order to ram. The destroyer checked slightly as she tore through the torpedo nets before smashing into the lock gate. Her bows were buckled back 36 feet by the force of the impact. *Campbeltown*'s fo'c'sle, which had ridden up over the caisson, projected a foot out over the inner face of the gate. It was 0134; Beattie was four minutes late.[21]

Ryder, on the bridge of the MGB still at the head of the flotilla, blinded by the glare of the searchlights, saw none of the last seconds of *Campbeltown*'s voyage. As *Campbeltown* made her final approach past the Old Mole the MGB peeled off to starboard to give her a clear run to the lock gate. 'The next we saw of her', Ryder recalled, 'was the moment of her striking the lock gate.'

> There was a grinding crash, and a flash of some minor explosion on her fo'c'sle and she came to rest. We were unable to see the soldiers scrambling ashore but we could see that she remained fast in the gate with all her guns firing hard up the lock.

But get ashore the soldiers did. Once *Campbeltown* had ploughed into the caisson Bill Copland started to order his men off the ship. 'Looking at her', he recalled,

> it looked as though every gun in the world was firing shot of one sort or another into her poor battered sides in the glare of what seemed like six searchlights. And [disembarking] looked impossible, which of course it wasn't.

Once those of his Commandos who could do so had disembarked, Copland went round the destroyer to check that everyone had left the ship. He got 'a bit frightened' remembering the tons of explosive hidden below decks and, thinking that they might go up 'a bit quickly', left the ship.[22] Meanwhile, once Beattie had given the order to abandon ship, two engine room artificers opened the seacocks and other valves that would flood *Campbeltown*. Once the scuttling charges had been fired, it would require an immense effort to remove the destroyer from the caisson. The bomb was firmly in place next to the front face of the lock gates. Thanks to Beattie's cool skill and seamanship and the courage and resolution of *Campbeltown*'s crew, the first part of the plan had been triumphantly achieved.

Once *Campbeltown* had rammed the lock gate Curtis brought the MGB round in a circle behind her stern towards the Old Entrance. Newman, now that he could see his men scrambling ashore over *Campbeltown*'s bows, was desperately anxious to join them. As the MGB skirted round *Campbeltown* a battery of Bofors guns on the opposite bank of the river opened fire on her 'with unpleasant accuracy'. 'I think', Ryder recalled, 'they could see us clearly silhouetted' against the searchlights. Curtis nosed the MGB into the Old Entrance, bringing her alongside a pier on the downstream side used in more peaceful times by the ferry. Here Newman and his small headquarters staff jumped ashore. The MGB then turned in the confined space of the Old Entrance and berthed on the upstream side to take off the surviving members of *Campbeltown*'s crew, some of them very badly wounded.

As Ryder climbed the steps to the quayside a grenade landed between the gunboat and the jetty, exploding close to him. Several men on her crowded deck were wounded. For a moment 'a sinister burning smell' convinced Ryder that the MGB was on fire but it soon cleared.

He now set off to satisfy himself that *Campbeltown* was firmly wedged in position in the lock gate and sinking. Accompanied by Pike, armed with a broken bayonet and now Ryder's self-appointed body guard, he hurried along the quay. They were stopped and challenged by a crouching figure with a tommy gun, a British Commando, to whom Ryder gave the pass word – which happened to be his own name – before continuing on his way. Reaching the smashed caisson, Ryder hailed *Campbeltown*'s forlorn, smoking, bullet-riddled, corpse-strewn deck but there was no reply.

> I stepped forward and hailed again but was greeted by a burst of fire which I imagined came from one of the ships in the dock. It struck the masonry of a small hut close by me. I dodged behind the hut and watched *Campbeltown* for what seemed a to be a good five minutes.

To his relief, Ryder saw a series of small explosions along her port side and heard others from the starboard side – presumably the scuttling charges. He could see that she was firmly held by the bow and was now settling by the stern. Deciding that all had gone according to plan, he turned to retrace his steps to the MGB. As he did so, the winding house, mined by the Commandos, exploded, raining Ryder and Pike with debris. A minute later, the pump house exploded too, and shortly afterwards the winding house at the far end of the dry dock blew up in its turn. The Commandos had been going about their business with deadly efficiency.

Ryder returned to the MGB where he found Micky Wynn and MTB 74 awaiting orders. Knowing that *Campbeltown* was secure against the lock gate, he ordered Wynn to fire his torpedoes against the lock gates of the Old Entrance before setting off down river for the sea and home.[23]

Out in the river, however, things were not going so well. The two columns of MLs followed *Campbeltown* in as she lined herself up to ram the lock gate. In the maelstrom of artillery and gun fire, the wooden-skinned, highly inflammable little craft stood little chance. The six MLs of the starboard column were detailed to land their Commandos at the Old Entrance, adjacent to the dry dock. The first to be hit was ML 192, commanded by Billy Stephens, at the head of the column. 'This was', as Stephens explained with masterful understatement, 'a somewhat delicate position to be in because everything which failed to hit the *Campbeltown* was liable to hit us and we started to get our pasting very early on and it was quite tough.'[24]

As the MLs passed the heavily-fortified Old Mole they came under ferocious fire. Several shells hit ML 192 at close range, wrecking her steering gear and engines; she then burst into flames as she sheered off out of control towards the quays. None of the other MLs in the starboard column fared much better. Immediately astern of Stephens's vessel was ML 262, commanded by Lieutenant Ted Burt. He managed under fire to land his Commandos as planned in the Old Entrance but they were forced to re-embark. Burt then left the Old Entrance and sped off down river, still under heavy fire. Passing the Old Mole he stopped to help the crippled ML 457 commanded by Lieutenant Tom Collier. Collier implored him to press on down river but by now the enemy had got Burt's ML in his sights and she was hit by three shells in quick succession, reducing her to a burning wreck. The next motor boat in the column, ML 267, commanded by Lieutenant Beart, followed Burt's ML into the Old Entrance. Like Burt, he landed his Commandos only for them to re-embark but came under heavy fire which soon reduced his ML to a wreck. Beart himself was killed.

Astern of Beart in the starboard column was ML 268, commanded by Lieutenant Bill Tillie. Tillie's vessel came under accurate, sustained fire as it turned into the Old Entrance and was soon ablaze. A minute or two later the ML blew up 'spreading far and wide a fountain of blazing petrol.' Tillie himself survived but almost all of the rest of the crew were killed. Only two of the seventeen Commandos on board escaped; the rest were drowned or perished in the pools of burning petrol on the surface of the water. The fifth boat in the starboard column was one of the torpedo boats, ML 156, commanded by Lieutenant Leslie Fenton, a film actor. Unable to land his Commandos, his boat badly damaged and himself, his second-in-command and the senior Commando officer all seriously wounded, Fenton decided that he had no option but to withdraw. After an agonizingly slow, fighting passage down the river ML 156 reached the sea.

The only one of the MLs in the starboard column to land its troops successfully was ML 177, the sixth in line, commanded by Lieutenant Mark Rodier. Ignoring the destruction all about him, the burning wrecks of the MLs in front of him and the withering fire from the Old Mole, Rodier coolly took his boat into the Old Entrance where his Commandos jumped ashore. He came alongside at about 0140, six minutes after *Campbeltown* had rammed. In this short time, almost the entire starboard column of MLs had been destroyed or crippled. Rodier was then ordered by Ryder to go alongside *Campbeltown* in order to take off some survivors. All her officers including Beattie, the First Lieutenant Gough and Nigel Tibbits came aboard and a number of other ratings. Rodier, his ML still substantially undamaged, then set off down river for the sea. It was 0157.[25]

The MLs in the port column were detailed to land their parties of Commandos at the Old Mole. This was a heavily defended jetty that protruded into the estuary about 400 yards downstream from the Old Entrance. While the partly enclosed

Old Entrance with its high quays did offer the MLs a modicum of protection – especially since the quaysides were not in enemy hands – the Old Mole was desperately exposed. It offered vessels coming alongside no protection whatever from enemy fire and was, moreover, itself in enemy hands. These difficulties were compounded by the fact that the quayside was 25 feet above the level of the MLs' decks at high tide. The MLs of the port column were attempting to land troops at the Old Mole at exactly the same moment as their sister ships of the starboard column were broaching the Old Entrance. Their attempts lasted no longer – and fared little better – and were finished within fifteen minutes of *Campbeltown*'s ramming the lock gate.

ML 447, commanded by Lieutenant Platt, was at the head of the port column. His troops consisted of Captain Birney's assault party, whose job it was to knock out the dangerous and heavily fortified pillbox on the mole itself. The ML was hit and set ablaze while attempting to land its Commandos. The survivors were heroically rescued by Tom Boyd's ML 160 and carried to safety and, ultimately, England. Tom Collier in ML 457 did succeed in landing his Commandos at the Old Mole, the only ML from the port column to do so. Having landed the troops, the ML pushed off but was hit almost at once, whereupon she burst into flames before exploding. Of the four remaining MLs in the port column only one, ML 307, got close enough to the Old Mole to land her Commandos but was forced to retire before she did so. The other three MLs withdrew without attempting to land their Commandos. All four made it to the open sea. ML 270, the torpedo boat leading the port column, also withdrew from the river having been damaged by gunfire. She too reached the sea.[26]

With MGB 314 berthed in the Old Entrance, Ryder would have witnessed the destruction of Tillie's ML. But he had little idea of the fate of the rest of the MLs of the starboard column and none of the boats of the port column. Once the MGB had taken on board the remaining survivors from *Campbeltown* and watched as Wynn fired his torpedoes at the lock gate in the Old Entrance, it was time to see what was happening at the Old Mole. As Curtis manoeuvred the gunboat out of the Old Entrance into the river, it was approaching 0230; the flotilla had been in the harbour for an hour. The hellish scene that greeted Ryder as the MGB emerged into the river took his breath away. The Old Mole was obviously in still enemy hands. 'Up and down the river there seemed to be about seven or eight blazing MLs'; the very water itself seemed to be on fire as the pools of floating petrol burned; smoke drifted across the river from the burning wrecks and the air was alive with gunfire. Curtis relates that 'It was the only time that I ever saw [Ryder] momentarily at a loss.'[27]

Nor was the MGB herself undamaged: the 2-pounder aft gun was out of action as were both the .5in twin machine guns. Crucially also her wireless gear had been shot away so Ryder was unable to communicate with the rest of his force. Able Seaman Savage, completely exposed to the enemy in the MGB's bows, engaged the pillbox on the jetty. Savage, aiming the 2-pounder with great accuracy, silenced the pillbox by firing his shells in through its narrow embrasures. 'The pillbox came to life again and in what was a personal duel Savage ... silenced it for a second time.'

'Matters were without doubt getting out of hand now.' The Old Mole was firmly in enemy hands nor did Ryder have the troops on the MGB to storm the position, even if he could get in to land them. He decided to return to the Old Entrance to make contact with Newman. However, the gunboat arrived to find a fierce battle going on across the Old Entrance. 'We were unable to join in this battle as we were unable to see which was our own side.'

> Somebody, presumably, one of our own side, climbed back on board *Campbeltown* and poured a fierce fire from one of the Oerlikon Guns into the general confusion. He was shot and fell from his gun.

'There seemed to be little that we could do here', Ryder noted. This was putting it mildly; the MGB was in a desperate position. 'We were', he recalled vividly,

> floodlit by the blazing building close by, and lying stopped. Being the only ship left, we were attracting the individual attention of all hostile positions that could see us. Most of the tracer from close range passed low over our heads but we must have also been clearly silhouetted to the Bofors Batteries on the south bank as they again opened an unpleasantly accurate fire. We could see it coming straight at us, an unpleasant feeling. But they seemed to be shooting short and it mostly struck the water and ricochetted over our heads.

Ryder told Curtis to light and drop a smoke flare in the water astern of the MGB to give her some cover. As it sparked and fizzed into life, Ryder, Curtis and Bill Green, the navigator, held a hurried council of war, crouching on the bridge. The MGB was being hit repeatedly. All her guns bar the 2-pounder in the bows manned by the gallant Savage were out of action. The MGB had perhaps forty extra men on board, many badly wounded, making it difficult to move about the boat. The decks were slippery with blood. Her own crew had been reduced to just three unwounded men. Nor was there any prospect of taking off Commandos; both embarkation points, the Old Entrance and the Old Mole, were held by the enemy. The MGB was being fired on from all angles; it was only a matter of time before she was hit badly and set on fire. There was nothing more she could do: they decided that the gunboat must leave at once.

Ryder was loath to abandon Newman and his Commandos but there was no alternative. As he recalled many years later:

> This was an agonizing decision to make. We'd been working closely with the Commandos and Charles Newman ... and to leave them behind was very sad but we were faced with the fact that the only two possible places for a withdrawal were firmly in enemy hands.[28]

'The run down the estuary was a nightmare experience', remembered Gordon Holman, the war correspondent. 'There were guns and searchlights all the way. The heavy batteries at the mouth were thirsting for our blood, having missed us altogether on the way in.' With the 'sparking and spluttering of the phosphorus contents' of the smoke flare drawing the enemy's fire, the MGB departed down river at full speed. It was now 0250, an hour and sixteen minutes since *Campbeltown* had rammed the lock gate. Passing *Speerbrecher* they noticed with grim satisfaction that the Germans were still firing on their own ship; she was on fire amidships and lower in the water than she had been. As the gunboat sped down the estuary, Holman takes up the story.

> Getting up to a speed of about twenty knots, the M.G.B. ran the gauntlet of fire from both banks. Searchlights held the little vessel in giant beams of light, fresh positions switching on as we came within their radius. Behind us we left a long tail of smoke, purposely made, which helped us because the enemy's gunners often fired into it thinking that we were screening other vessels. The little vessel, which had been first in and was now attempting to be last out, was ahead of the smoke and picked out as clear as day in the glare of the searchlight.[29]

After passing Les Morées Tower, the heavy coastal batteries began to fire on the MGB. Oddly, while the tracer from the flak batteries invariably passed behind the gunboat, the shells from the heavier coastal guns fell mostly ahead of her. 'Great plumes of water rose up ahead of us', wrote Ryder, 'leaving a column of thin misty vapour which must have helped to conceal us.' As the MGB forged down the estuary, the searchlights gradually lost her in the dark, first from the north bank and then from the south. The heavy guns continued to fire at long range: 'The last salvo of all straddled us in the dark at a range of about four miles.'

Now that the MGB had evaded the enemy, she reduced speed in the hope that Fenton's ML 156, passed further up the river, might catch up. At this moment, with the MGB so close to reaching the sea, disaster struck. Looming up in the darkness ahead was the outline of a boat. Assuming that it was one of the MLs, the MGB steered towards her. Realizing at the last moment that it was in fact a German patrol vessel, the MGB hove sharply away. The enemy vessel opened fire on the gunboat with a machine gun. 'A long burst of tracer passed right into the petrol compartment by our stern but by the Grace of God we were not set on fire.' The MGB increased to full speed and raked the German patrol boat with shot from the 2-pounder as she sped off into the night. Tragically, in this last, sudden, fierce exchange of fire Able Seaman Savage was killed having served the MGB's forward 2-pounder so courageously and so skilfully throughout the entire action.

Having shaken off the enemy patrol boat, the MGB reduced speed to 10 knots, shortly afterwards being joined by Irwin's ML 270. Together they steamed out to the rendezvous at sea with the destroyers. It was now about 0330.[30] Looking back towards land, the 'rosy glow of great fires coming from the dock area of St Nazaire' lit up the night sky. Occasional flashes suggested explosions and 'one big one at about 4 a.m. which ... Ryder, still on the bridge, thought might be the *Campbeltown* going up.'[31]

The two vessels steamed slowly out to sea. The gunboat was badly holed and shipping water alarmingly. One rating counted no fewer than fifty-two shot holes in the starboard side of her hull and found several feet of water in her forward magazine. The other danger, very much to the forefront of Ryder's mind, was the possibility of encountering the German destroyers known to be patrolling off St Nazaire. At around 0700, in broad daylight, Ryder and Curtis were overjoyed to see the destroyers *Atherstone* and *Tynedale* coming up astern. By now two other MLs, 446 and 156, were in view and at 0720 the six vessels hove to and stopped together.

In fact, the German destroyers had, unbeknown to Ryder, already encountered the British out at sea. At about 0530 the five destroyers of the 5th Flotilla were making their way back to St Nazaire when they came upon Ian Henderson's ML 306 about 45 miles out to sea. She was one of the MLs of the port column which had been forced to retire down the river without landing her Commandos. One of the German destroyers, *Jaguar*, was detached to deal with the ML. As the destroyer bore down on the motor launch, Henderson determined, despite the immense disparity in size between the two vessels – the destroyer weighed 800 tons, the ML less than 100, while the destroyer mounted three 4.1in guns, the ML had only one serviceable Oerlikon – that his boat would give a good account of itself. The crew and Commandos fought bravely, especially Sergeant Tommy Durrant, but ultimately vainly. By 0600 with most of the crew dead or wounded and the ML badly damaged, she surrendered. The casualties and survivors were transferred to *Jaguar* before being taken into St Nazaire.[32]

Atherstone and *Tynedale* had also had a brush with the four German destroyers returning to St Nazaire. At about 0630 *Tynedale* had exchanged shots with the German flotilla but suffered no damage. Surprisingly, given his numerical superiority, the German commander, discontinued the action to run for port.[33] This was fortunate for the British ships as, had the German destroyers retained contact, they would not only have posed a serious threat but would also have prevented the transfer of the wounded from the MLs. At 0730 *Atherstone* and *Tynedale* started transferring the wounded and others from the MLs to the destroyers. Fenton's ML 156 was clearly finished so all her crew were taken off. At this stage, the other three vessels, MGB 314, and MLs 270 and 446, were expecting to make the voyage home. Ryder and his staff decided to transfer to *Atherstone*, the better to conduct the withdrawal. Robin Jenks, commanding

Atherstone, was delighted that Ryder had transferred to his ship since 'we regard him as a talisman. He has had a charmed life both in this war and before it.'[34]

At 0830 *Cleveland* and *Brocklesby*, the two destroyers dispatched by the Admiralty to reinforce *Chariot* swept into view over the horizon with their battle ensigns flying. The new arrivals joined Ryder's little fleet as it steamed out into the Atlantic. With the arrival of *Cleveland*, Ryder relinquished command of the squadron as her captain, Commander G.B. Sayer, was now the senior officer. After two days of unremitting tension and activity, Ryder could now rest while someone else made the decisions. The four destroyers in company with the three small craft set course for England. However, with the two damaged MLs and the gunboat slowing the squadron down, Sayer became anxious. The wounded needed to be got home as soon as possible and his ships were still within range of the *Luftwaffe*'s fighter-bombers. Indeed, they had been attacked several times by shadowing enemy aircraft. At about 1300 he decided to abandon the gunboat and the two MLs. Their crews were taken off and the boats sunk by gunfire.[35] The destroyers then continued at 25 knots. That evening *Cleveland* and *Brocklesby* peeled off to search for the other MLs known to be making their way home from St Nazaire. *Atherstone* and *Tynedale* arrived at Plymouth at 0230 on 29 March.[36]

*   *   *

MGB 314 with Ryder on board was the last ship of the *Chariot* force to leave St Nazaire. Ryder departed because, as we have seen, he was in a hopeless position. Most of all, there was nothing he could do to rescue the Commandos who were fighting so gallantly in the dockyard, as both the planned embarkation points, the Old Mole and the Old Entrance, were in enemy hands. He related years later how, having disembarked from *Atherstone* in the early hours of the morning, he stood on the quayside at Plymouth feeling 'very conscious that we had failed to re-embark our comrades-in-arms and had left them to their fate.' It weighed particularly heavily as 'I felt personally responsible for the decision to leave without them.'

The 370 or so Commandos were divided, according to their targets, into three groups. Group One's primary target was to capture the heavily-defended Old Mole and hold it as the main re-embarkation point. The troops carrying out this task were to storm ashore from the port column of MLs at the Old Mole itself. The Commandos of Group Two, led by Captain Michael Burn, were charged with clearing, capturing and holding the ground to the west of the dry dock. These troops entered St Nazaire aboard the MLs of the starboard column, intending to land in the Old Entrance. Group Three, disembarking from *Campbeltown* herself, were detailed to complete the destruction of the dry dock installations: the pumping house at the south end of the dock, the winding houses for the caissons at either end and the north caisson itself. That was the plan.

In the event, much of this carefully-laid plan miscarried with terrible results. As we have seen, the MLs of both columns were shot to pieces by the well-armed defenders before they could land the Commandos. The planners, Hughes-Hallett and Luce, knew that the wooden MLs were extremely vulnerable to gunfire, as did Ryder and Newman, and so it proved. Once the German defences were alerted to the threat, there was little hope for the frail motor launches, their crews and Commandos. *Campbeltown* was able, at great cost, to plough through the hail of shot to ram the caisson but the MLs were doomed.

The Commandos on *Campbeltown* suffered many casualties during the run-in but were able to get ashore in sufficient numbers to carry out their allotted tasks most successfully. Stuart Chant's party destroyed the pumping house, while Christopher Smalley's party blew up the winding house at the southern end of the dock – raining Ryder with debris in the process. Corran Purdon's team wrecked the northern winding house, while Gerard Brett's men detonated charges against the inner caisson gate. Other Commandos from *Campbeltown*, charged with protecting the demolition parties, performed heroically, too.

The Commandos carried in the MLs never stood a chance of achieving their objects. Only one ML in each column managed successfully to land its troops. Of the starboard column only the men in Rodier's ML177 got ashore in the Old Entrance. Likewise, in the port column the only troops to land were those brought in to the Old Mole by Tom Collier in ML 457. The starboard column landed only fourteen Commandos from the more than fifty who came up the river; only fifteen of eighty-nine Commandos came ashore from the MLs of the port column. In all, no more than forty per cent of the Commandos embarked landed at St Nazaire.[37] The troops intended to take and hold the Old Mole never got ashore, so the intended point of re-embarkation was never captured.

Those that did get ashore fought heroically but soon realized that they were marooned. Once the MLs had been destroyed or, unable to put in to the harbour, had been driven off and MGB 314 had departed, the Commandos were on their own. With great courage and resolution they fought their way out of the dockyard – in which they could have been completely cut off by the enemy – into the town proper. Newman's intention was that they would then fight their way past the Germans out into the countryside and head for Spain. Most of the Commandos never penetrated beyond St Nazaire. Exhausted, out of ammunition and many of them wounded, they surrendered or were rounded up by the Germans. Five of their number did manage, after many an adventure, to get to Spain and thence to England.

The majority of Newman's men had been rounded up by 1030 on the morning of 28 March, nine hours or so after *Campbeltown* had rammed the dry dock. They were beginning to wonder whether the old ship would blow up, when, suddenly, there was a huge explosion. It could only be one thing: *Campbeltown* had gone up. A great cheer went up from the captured British soldiers and sailors. A large number, possibly hundreds, of Germans, soldiers and sailors of all ranks, souvenir hunters and the plain curious were aboard *Campbeltown* when she exploded. They were all blown to smithereens along with many onlookers. The dry dock's outer caisson was completely destroyed, a fact confirmed by aerial reconnaissance shortly after the raid. The force of the blast was such that the stern half of *Campbeltown* was washed halfway up the dock by the weight of water rushing in through the ruptured caisson. The dock was out of commission for the rest of the war. The failure of the force to carry out any of its subsidiary objects in no way diminished its achievement. As Hughes-Hallett, who conceived and planned the operation put it, 'the raid as a whole achieved its immediate objective of rendering the great lock useless for the rest of the war.'[38]

Ryder was, of course, completely unaware that *Campbeltown* had exploded – albeit later than expected. But it made certain the raid had achieved its primary object, the destruction of the great dry dock, thus denying its use to *Tirpitz*. This in turn altered the balance of the Battle of the Atlantic by ensuring that Hitler would never risk *Tirpitz* in Atlantic waters. The Prime Minister described the raid as a 'brilliant and heroic exploit', 'a deed of glory intimately involved in high strategy.'[39]

The men of Operation *Chariot* paid a high price for this 'deed of glory'. Of the 611 officers and men, soldiers and sailors, who took part in the raid 169 were killed, 64 Commandos and 105 naval personnel, 28 per cent of the force; 200 were taken prisoner, many of them wounded. In total the force suffered 60 per cent casualties. Of the 15 MLs that steamed up the Loire only three returned to England; Wynn's MTB 74 was sunk on her way down the river and MGB 314 scuttled out at sea.

The raid had other, perhaps less immediate, but no less important consequences. It prompted the Germans to start constructing their Atlantic Wall, at immense cost of materials and labour. It persuaded them to keep back in France divisions that might otherwise have been sent to the Eastern Front. But perhaps the raid's greatest impact was on morale.

In the early months of 1942, the war was going very badly for Britain and the news seemed universally grim. On 12 February 1942 the Royal Navy had been humiliated when the German battleships *Scharnhorst*, *Gneisenau* and the cruiser *Prinz Eugen* left Brest to run up the Channel for their home ports. The fact that the enemy's principal battle squadron could pass virtually unmolested through the Straits of Dover in broad daylight did nothing for the reputation of either the Navy or the Royal Air Force. But this was a mere pinprick in comparison with the disaster that befell British arms three days later: the fall of Singapore. The loss of Singapore was not only a military calamity but also a huge blow to Britain's prestige and her standing as an Imperial power. The raid on St Nazaire was both a tactical and a strategic coup for Britain, a much-needed fillip for national morale at a time when all around seemed dark indeed.

The raid gave the French hope, too. Paul Ramadier, the French Prime Minister, speaking at the unveiling of the St Nazaire monument in 1947, said:

At a time when we were shut in, imprisoned, battered down by traitors and the enemy we had begun to doubt whether we should ever see the light of day again. And then, for the first time, men came from England and landed on our soil, and throughout all France confidence and enthusiasm came flooding back.[40]

Chapter 13

Combined Operations, Dieppe and D-Day (1942–44)

In the early hours of the morning of 29 March Ryder was standing on a quay in Plymouth harbour supervising the disembarkation of the wounded from *Atherstone*. As the wounded men were ferried away in ambulances Ryder looked on, exhausted, wondering 'what the reaction would be to all this?'. He felt sure (although not at this stage knowing) that *Campbeltown* had exploded as planned, and so was elated 'at having struck a blow'. At the same time he felt responsible, as we have seen, for the decision to abandon Newman and his Commandos to their fate.

At that moment a Wren dispatch rider, breaking hard, drew up beside him on her motorcycle. 'She looked rather attractive, I thought, all spattered with mud.' 'Commander Ryder?', she asked, handing him a buff envelope. Ryder, thinking that it might be a congratulatory note from the Commander-in-Chief or perhaps Mountbatten, opened it. It was a letter from the Admiralty confirming the award of their Lordships' displeasure at his part in the loss of *Prince Philippe* the previous summer.[1] Once again, he had been brought down to earth.

The next few days passed in a whirl of activity writing up official reports and dealing with casualty returns. There was the sorrowful business of informing the families of those killed and the happier task of drawing up a list of names to be recommended for decorations. Almost at once this work was interrupted by a summons to London to report to the Chief of Combined Operations, Lord Mountbatten. Ryder was also summoned to see the First Sea Lord, Sir Dudley Pound, and A. V. Alexander, the First Lord of the Admiralty. No sooner had Ryder returned to Plymouth than he was called to London once again, this time to attend a press conference on Monday, 30 March organized by the Ministry of Information.

Earlier that day the news for which Ryder had been waiting on tenterhooks arrived. The Admiralty's Upper War Room announced at 0830 that aerial reconnaissance photographs taken the previous evening 'show that the seaward gate of the large lock is apparently missing and the lock is flooded.' So now he knew that *Campbeltown* had blown up, wrecking the dry dock. The raid had achieved its main object. Operation *Chariot* had not been in vain.[2]

There was a large gathering of reporters, 'several hundred', according to Ryder, at the Ministry for the press conference. Their appetites had been whetted by an official communiqué issued on Saturday night as the force was nearing home, which formed the basis of the first reports of the raid in the Sunday newspapers. Ryder took the platform to give a detailed account of the raid before answering a battery of questions. It being wartime, however, 'I had to be careful not to disclose any secret information.'

'I felt that I must pay a handsome tribute to Sam Beattie who, after all, had contributed more to the success of the raid than anyone. Immediately one of the Ministry of Information's officials jumped up to say that it was not permitted to publish names.' However, Ryder insisted that, since Beattie was either dead or a prisoner – it was not yet known which – the publication of his name would make no difference. So Beattie took his rightful place in all the reports of the raid, apart from Ryder and Newman, the only participant mentioned by name in the early press coverage of the operation. This was 'very warmly received, except of course by the poor MOI official whom I had snubbed. There was no comeback.'[3]

The press coverage was widespread and enthusiastic, but, as one might expect in wartime, rather limited. Gordon Holman, who returned to Plymouth in *Atherstone*, immediately settled down at his typewriter, his account of the raid appearing in the *Daily Mail* and other morning newspapers on 30 March. The headlines did not hold back: 'New Glory at St Nazaire', boomed the *News of the World*; 'Daring Raid on Nazi U-Boat Base', thundered *The People*, the wrong end of the stick clenched firmly in its jaws.[4]

The following day's papers contained reports of Ryder's description of the raid at the press conference. Several of them carried photographs of Ryder, including a rather dashing, informal one from the *Tai-Mo-Shan* days. The *Daily Express*, in its eagerness to jump on the bandwagon, published another photograph above the caption 'Ryder, R.N. Led the naval forces'. Unfortunately, it was a picture of Martyn Sherwood. Many of the papers carried potted biographies of Ryder, mentioning his adventures in *Tai-Mo-Shan* and *Penola*. He was rapidly becoming a national hero.[5]

Many of the papers had got in touch with Hilaré to report her reaction to the news. 'I'm terribly proud', she told the *Express*.[6] Several sent photographers to Lovel Hill to get a picture of the new hero's pretty young wife. One of them shows Hilaré knitting, another reading a book. Hilaré had, of course, no idea of what Ryder had been up to since he was suddenly called away from his comfortable billet as a staff officer at Wilton in late February. His letters to her during the month before the raid are models of of self-censoring, blandly uninformative banality. Although he could not tell her anything, she had a shrewd idea that something was afoot. 'I guessed there was something in the wind', she told the *Express*. 'I had a feeling he was on a special job.' The first she heard of the raid was when Ryder telephoned her at Lovel Hill soon after his arrival at Plymouth early on Sunday morning. 'I'm safe and well, darling', he told her.[7]

After Ryder had finished with the press conference at the Ministry of Information he went to meet Hilaré. As Ryder left the Ministry some eager press photographers gathered round to ask if they could come and photograph us celebrating that evening. This was the last thing I wanted.

'What gave you the idea that it is my wife I will be celebrating with?' Awkward silence.

'You are the sort of people who will get me into trouble,' I continued.

They looked a bit sheepish. 'Oh, if that's the case, we quite understand.'

So we had a quiet evening together.[8]

They had been treated to a night in the Berkeley Hotel on Piccadilly by her sisters to celebrate Ryder's safe return. It was a memorable experience: 'It was marvellous, just like being a film star ... Bob and I felt as though we were on the set of some play!' He was 'looking much thinner but very well & brown', she thought, seeing him after the press conference. As they talked he told her, bit by bit, of the raid.

I can't begin to describe all he has told me of the raid, it would take far too long. I can only say it is nothing short of a miracle he escaped unhurt, or in fact escaped at all ... It absolutely gives me the cold shudders when I think what dangers he's been in.

In the morning 'We had our breakfast served there on a trolley and felt terribly grand.'[9]

Once Ryder had finished tying up the loose ends of the St Nazaire operation and had taken some well-deserved leave he joined COHQ in late April. He was now involved in the planning of Combined Operations' raids on a number of different targets, including Ushant, Houlagat, Berk-sur-Mer and Alderney. Ryder, his stock riding high after St Nazaire, was in the enviable position of being 'first call' for many of the small and medium-sized operations. 'In a number of them I was to be the Naval Force commander or alternatively commanding the immediate assault or "cutting out" party.' It was a strange, mildly unsettling existence.

Armed with some plan or other I would go down to the Solent, Portsmouth, Hayling Island or the Isle of Wight with some strange assortment of boats and stand by for the executive signal. Each time I went flat out with all the detailed preparations and braced myself for the event only to be deflated when it was cancelled on account of the weather.[10]

It was not an easy role. Operations were complicated by inter-service rivalries and difficulties in procuring equipment, compounded by the need for absolute secrecy. Nor did Ryder have any of the usual apparatus of command: an office, a staff, a car or even a telephone. During the mounting of one of these operations Ryder was staying in a naval mess at Cowes when, on 21 May, the *London Gazette* announced that he had been awarded the Victoria Cross for his leadership and gallantry at St Nazaire. 'Poor darling', Hilaré told her mother,

> he heard the news in a rather odd way – apparently he hadn't been feeling very well, it must have been a chill I think, and had gone to bed early when almost the entire mess, including two Commodores, burst into his room and woke him up to tell him the news.[11]

Hilaré had heard the announcement on the radio, although she already knew of it as journalists had been telephoning her all evening. The citation read:

> For great gallantry in the attack on St. Nazaire. He commanded a force of small unprotected ships in an attack on a heavily defended port and led H.M.S. *Campbeltown* in under intense fire from short-range weapons at point blank range. Though the main object of the expedition had been accomplished in the beaching of *Campbeltown*, he remained on the spot conducting operations, evacuating men from *Campbeltown* and dealing with strong points and close-range weapons while exposed to heavy fire for one hour and sixteen minutes, and did not withdraw till it was certain that his ship could be of no use in rescuing any of the Commando Troops who were still ashore. That his Motor Gun Boat, now full of dead and wounded, should have survived and should have been able to withdraw through an intense barrage of close range fire was almost a miracle.

The same issue announced the award of the Victoria Cross to Beattie and to Able Seaman Savage, the MGB's astonishingly courageous gunlayer who had been killed almost as the boat reached safety. It also contained the announcements of many of the other decorations for the men of the Naval Force.[12]

Congratulations flooded in, by letter and by telegram, from every side: from family and friends, from fellow officers and admirals, from as far afield as the Middle East, Australia and the Falkland Islands. 'He has had masses of letters', Hilaré told her mother, 'the nicest being from Evans of the *Broke* and Mountbatten'. Lord Mountbatten's letter was fulsome indeed.

> I have never had more pleasure in writing to congratulate anybody than in writing to you for your grandly earned Victoria Cross. Alas, so few of the V.C.s of this war have been given to living people and it is essential for the younger officers and men coming along to have a few heroes to look up to who are still in the land of the living. I consider your V.C. will have achieved a double purpose: firstly, it is the greatest compliment that could be paid to the whole of your force; secondly, it will centre round it all the enthusiasm for the fighting spirit which is only awaiting an outlet in this country.[13]

Most of the letters were serious, sincere and admiring notes of congratulation. Only Philip Francis, Ryder's old friend from *Tai-Mo-Shan*, felt able to introduce a note of levity.

> I think the great thing about having a V.C. is that you can be as eccentric as you like, such as farting in railway trains, kissing girls in hotel lobbies, etc., and get away with it!!![14]

The following day the national newspapers gave the announcements blanket coverage. Particular play was made of the fact that Beattie's and Savage's VCs marked the valour of others who took part in the raid. In Beattie's case, it recognized the gallantry of *Campbeltown*'s crew and in Savage's of the ratings who manned the MLs, the MGB and MTB 74. Charles Newman and Sergeant Tommy Durrant were both awarded the Victoria Cross, Durrant posthumously, in 1945. Durrant's VC was for his courage against overwhelming odds during ML 306's fight with the German destroyer *Jaguar*.

Ryder was now, as Mountbatten had made clear, a national hero and public property, whether he liked it or not. True to character, all the indications were that he did not. He was a very private man who hated the publicity and adulation that was bound to come his way as a result of the VC. As Hilaré realized, 'Bob's opinion of himself seems to be much like that of Mr Thornton [that is, low] but he is really terribly thrilled though he says he gets sick of people coming up and congratulating him.'[15] Ryder's servant scoured Cowes for the VC's crimson medal ribbon which he then sewed on to Ryder's uniform. It made a striking – and unique – contrast to the white ribbon of the Polar Medal; Ryder was and remains the only holder of the Polar Medal to win the VC.[16]

Ryder's dislike of publicity and fuss was never better illustrated than at his investiture which took place at Buckingham Palace on 14 July. The King pinned the Victoria Cross on to Ryder's chest after which they talked about *Campbeltown* and the raid. After the investiture, Ryder slipped away by a side door in the hope of avoiding the crowds as well as his own family. As the *Daily Herald* reported, 'Twenty members of the Ryder family had to run to catch him. They did this in Green Park and there they had a family reunion.' Ryder explained to the newspaper that he was in a hurry: 'He wanted to dodge the crowd and get back to work.' Two days later he wrote to Hilaré to apologize.

> I am sorry I couldn't revel & wallow in the proceedings etc. as perhaps my Mother would have liked, but I do so dislike that sort of thing. I hope I didn't appear very surly. I didn't mean to. It was really sweet of everyone to come up & I felt honoured & flattered.[17]

During the summer of 1942 the planners at COHQ were busy men. As well as planning and mounting a number of small raids, almost all of which never took place, they were concentrating on a much larger operation: an attack on Dieppe. The Dieppe raid was and remains one of the more controversial episodes of the Second World War. The fact that it was a disastrous failure, achieved at a very heavy cost in casualties in pursuit of ill-defined aims has ensured its historical notoriety.

Part of the Allied strategy for 1942 was that British forces should stage a limited re-entry to the Continent. Operation *Sledgehammer*, as this was codenamed, would, it was hoped, provide a measure of relief for the hard-pressed Russians and offer the Americans evidence of Britain's fighting spirit. However, as it became obvious that Britain was not yet ready for such a major campaign, *Sledgehammer* was quietly dropped. By mid-1942 the raid on Dieppe was, as one historian has put it, 'all that was left to satisfy the Americans and the Russians of British aggressive intentions against the Continent.'[18] The historian Corelli Barnett distinguished between the 'ostensible' and the 'ulterior' aims of the Dieppe raid. The 'ostensible' aim of the operation was to take the port and town of Dieppe and hold them for a few hours, destroying everything of military value, before withdrawing in an orderly fashion. The 'ulterior' aim was to test the German coastal defences in the West.[19]

This was in marked contrast to the raid on St Nazaire, which had a specific object and an identifiable target. Indeed, the very success of the raid on St Nazaire convinced the Prime Minister, among others, that the Dieppe plan could work. Rear Admiral Baillie-Grohman, who was appointed Naval Force Commander in the initial planning stages of the raid, claimed that Churchill 'was largely influenced by the success of the bold St Nazaire raid which had been contrary to the gloomy predictions of many of his able advisors.'[20] Indeed, there is scope for arguing that the Dieppe raid would not have taken place were it not for the brilliant success at St Nazaire, a coup that did much for COHQ's reputation and that of its chief planner, John Hughes-Hallett. Hughes-Hallett was the driving force behind the Dieppe operation. He was involved in the planning from the first and took over as Naval Force Commander when Baillie-Grohman withdrew.

The operation, codenamed *Rutter*, was originally planned for early July but was called off on 7 July due to bad weather. It was then, controversially and in great secrecy, remounted along identical lines as Operation *Jubilee*. The plan specified a series of flanking attacks landing along the coast from the town, both to the east and to the west, combined with a direct thrust into the town itself from landings on the seafront. The Canadian 2nd Division, commanded by Major General Roberts, known as 'Ham', was given the honour of making the attack. The Canadians, who had been in Britain training for more than two years, were champing at the bit to get to grips with the enemy. The division provided two brigades of infantry to be joined by a Canadian tank battalion, the Royal Marine 'A' Commando and a handful of US Rangers, 6,100 troops in all. The assault troops were to cross the Channel in seven troopships before transferring to 150 landing craft for the run-in to the beaches. The Royal Navy provided an escort of seven destroyers and the RAF very substantial air cover.[21]

There remained serious flaws in the plan as finally resolved. The original plan had provided for a heavy preliminary bombing raid on the town. This was abandoned on 5 June on the grounds that the damage it was likely to cause would impede the tanks' progress through the streets of Dieppe. Likewise, the Admiralty refused to sanction the use of a capital ship in the Channel to provide heavy-calibre fire support to the landing forces. When Mountbatten asked Sir Dudley Pound, the First Sea Lord, for a ship for this purpose, he is supposed to have replied: 'Battleships by daylight off the French coast? You must be mad, Dickie!'[22]

Ryder was appointed to the command of the cutting-out party, whose job it was to enter Dieppe harbour to take or destroy as many invasion barges as possible. Ryder had never been enthusiastic about the plan. 'My heart rather sank', he wrote many years later.

> I didn't really like this plan much. I felt that there was no really adequate or clear objective. 'A training exercise', a 'diversion' to 'test the enemy's defences'; these were all rather abstract as far as the troops were concerned especially as it was planned to withdraw so soon.

However, Ryder's reservations were partly laid to rest by the appointment of Hughes-Hallett as Naval Force Commander. 'He had planned the raid ... and was a driving force, known as "Hughes-Hitler" he was not one to be put off by the weather or for any other reason.'[23]

Dieppe harbour could be entered only through the jaws of two dog-legged jetties, the mouth of which was 110 yards wide. From the area enclosed by these jetties there was a channel leading to the outer and the inner harbour beyond. The problem with this plan was that the harbour and its entrance were dominated by a powerful enemy artillery battery on the Eastern Headland. It was intended that the landing infantry would subdue the battery. If they failed to do so, Ryder's task would be little short of suicidal. Not surprisingly, he was very worried about this possibility. Indeed, he raised the matter at a briefing before the raid.

> I asked what my orders were should the harbour entrance not be captured. The answer was typically explicit, from Hughes-Hallett. 'If the harbour entrance is not captured you are not to go in. Next question?' Later I was glad to have had that clear.[24]

Ryder was allocated an old China river gunboat, HMS *Locust*, a battalion of Royal Marines, commanded by Lieutenant Colonel Picton-Phillipps, and a detachment of naval ratings to commandeer the enemy barges and to attack dockyard installations. The Marines would enter the harbour in *chasseurs*, a type of French fast, armoured landing craft, from where they would take the German defenders in the rear.

The raiding force sailed from the south coast during the evening of 18 August 1942. *Locust*, commanded by Lieutenant Commander Stride – promoted from the lower deck, he was 'a robust and unflappable officer' – with Ryder on board, was unable to keep up with the large flotilla of ships so fell behind. By the time *Locust* arrived off the French coast at first light Ryder could see that the landings had started. This is not the place to describe in full the several attacks that made up the Dieppe raid. I shall concentrate on Ryder's important role in the operation. Suffice it to say, that with the exception of the two Commando attacks on the extreme flanks, the entire operation was a catastrophic and bloody failure.

Locust's first task was to provide supporting fire for the Canadian Essex Scottish Regiment landing at 0520 at the eastern end of Red Beach, which comprised the eastern half of the mile-long shingle beach fronting the town and harbour of Dieppe. However, having slipped behind the main force, *Locust* did not arrive in time to take part in the initial bombardment. Her principal task was as spearhead for Ryder's cutting–out party so, at about 0545, Stride took her in towards the harbour mouth. However, smoke laid to protect the landing craft and other vessels also obscured the heads of the dog-legged jetties that formed the harbour mouth so *Locust* was obliged to withdraw.

Fifteen minutes later, by about 0600, the smoke had cleared so *Locust* approached the harbour entrance once more. At once she came under accurate fire from the heavy anti-aircraft batteries on the East Cliff and another battery to the east of the harbour. She was hit by a shell on the rear of the bridge, killing two men. The resourceful Stride had taken the precaution before leaving England of having the back of the bridge boarded up with railway sleepers which almost certainly saved Ryder's life. Having withdrawn, Ryder received a signal instructing him not enter the harbour 'till the situation to the East of the harbour had improved.' Ryder himself recalled that *Locust* had made three attempts to enter the harbour before this signal arrived.[25]

At about 0630 Hughes-Hallett signalled to Ryder instructing him to come aboard HMS *Calpe*, the headquarters ship. 'In view of the failure of the Blue Beach landing [to the east of Dieppe]', Hughes-Hallett recorded in his official report, 'and hence the plan to capture the East Cliff I felt doubtful whether HMS *Locust*'s proposed entry into the harbour would be either practicable or profitable.'[26]

At about 0645 Ryder went aboard *Calpe* where he discussed *Locust*'s task with Hughes-Hallett, who later recalled what had passed between them.

With great moral courage he [Ryder] told me that he felt certain that any attempt to enter the harbour would be attended by the loss of all the ships concerned, since they would have to run the gauntlet at point blank range of batteries of medium calibre guns concealed in caves dug into the side of the cliffs.[27]

Hughes-Hallett, having consulted Major General Roberts, called off the cutting-out expedition. Since the Royal Marines were now no longer required to accompany Ryder into the harbour Roberts ordered them to reinforce the hard-pressed troops on White Beach in front of the town. Ryder was detailed to organize the transhipment of the Marines from the *chasseurs* into landing craft for the run-in.

Having received his orders, Ryder sprang into action. At 0700 he signalled the *chasseurs* to close with *Locust* for transhipment to the landing craft. With his directing operations through a megaphone, this took some time. The Marines were not formed up for the assault until 0815 when the landing craft began to go inshore through the smoke screen. The landing took place at 0840.[28] Once the landing craft emerged from the smokescreen off White Beach they ran into an unrelenting hail of mortar and machine-gun fire. A Marine officer remembered that, 'As the range shortened the fire increased until there was no doubt that any attempt to reach the town over that beach would mean certain death.'[29]

Picton-Phillipps, leading his men in in the foremost landing craft, realized as he neared the beach that the position was hopeless and so 'he stood up in full view of us and pulled on pair of white gloves and semaphored to the other assault boats to turn back. He was shot and killed in a matter of seconds.' 'It was', the marine concluded, 'the bravest act I have ever seen.'[30] Ryder recorded sadly that 'Colonel Picton-Phillipps ... led his men gallantly into a hopeless situation.' Writing years later, he agreed with most commentators before and since that 'This was a classic example of the futility of reinforcing a failure.'[31]

The withdrawal began at 1100 and for the next two hours the gallant landing craft crews came into the beaches often under heavy fire to bring off the stranded soldiers. During this time Ryder, aboard *Locust*, attempted to provide covering fire for the withdrawal. For much of this period she was under attack from enemy aeroplanes: between 1012 and 1100 *Locust* was attacked four times by enemy dive bombers. The Navy did everything that it possibly could to rescue the soldiers from the beaches. *Calpe* got so close that she momentarily grounded. *Locust*, too, with her shallow draught, went perilously close inshore; as late at 1248 she closed to shell enemy positions on the East Cliff for five minutes but was forced by accurate return fire to retire into the smoke.[32] Hughes-Hallett and Ryder were discussing sending *Locust* inshore once more when the news came through that the Canadians on the beaches had surrendered.[33] The withdrawal was called off at 1300.

The flotilla, laden with wounded, made its way back to England. Ryder arrived at Portsmouth in *Locust* soon after midnight. 'Coming back from Dieppe', he wrote later,

I had a nagging feeling that I had not lived up to my hopes and ambitions ... We had made three attempts on the harbour entrance and had received an explicit signal not to continue. And yet in view of what the Canadians suffered should I not have pressed home our attack with more resolution? We would certainly have been sunk before reaching the entrance and one had to think of the many casualties it would have involved. It would have been a forlorn hope but might have helped others.[34]

There is little doubt that any attempt to enter Dieppe harbour while the batteries on the East Headland were unsubdued would have been suicidal. *Locust*, her crew and any troops accompanying her would have been shot to pieces long before they could have reached the enemy's barges in the harbour, let alone set about commandeering them (even supposing that to be a worthwhile sacrifice). It is hard to see how *Locust*'s sacrificing herself on the run-in to the harbour could have significantly lessened the plight of the Canadian infantry on the beaches. As Hughes-Hallett recognized, it takes great moral courage to admit the futility of a proposed course of action, as Ryder did. No one, least of all a holder of the Victoria Cross, wishes to be thought lily-livered. On 2 October Ryder was mentioned in dispatches for 'gallantry, daring and skill' during the Dieppe operation.

Once he had returned from Dieppe he resumed his duties at COHQ as a planner. It was an interesting time to be in the planning room as all manner of schemes, some less eccentric than others, came up for consideration. Major 'Blondie' Hasler's plan for attacking blockade-running ships at Bordeaux in tiny two-man canoes was one that was supported by COHQ. The raid came off successfully on 7 December 1942, although Hasler and Corporal Bill Sparks were the only two of the twelve participants who returned, having escaped overland to Spain. Hasler was awarded the DSO. The exploit was later immortalized in the film *The Cockleshell Heroes*. Other, less practicable proposals arrived on Ryder's desk.

Papers advertising ... an underwater pistol which had been produced. Was [this] an operational requirement? Then the folding bicycle which made smoke. The cart really had got before the horse, it seemed. The instruments were being invented around which operations were to be planned instead of the other way round.[35]

Of greater operational value was Ryder's role in the raising of two Commando units, both for a special purpose. The first was No.14 Commando, raised to carry out an attack on *Tirpitz* as she passed along the Norwegian coast between Trondheim and her operational base at Altenfjord. She made this journey in part using the Inner Lead, a passage along the coast sheltered by off-shore islands and reefs. The idea was that by repositioning or hiding the navigation lights and buoys along the Inner Lead, *Tirpitz* could be lured on to a reef. The plan would be carried out by small groups of Commandos laying up on the outer islands. Clearly men with experience of polar conditions would be needed, and who better than Ryder to raise the Commando? He recruited a number of men with polar experience, including Augustine Courtauld, an old friend and veteran of Gino Watkins's expeditions to Greenland, and Quintin Riley, who had been on the BGLE. Ryder was allocated Balta Sound on the Shetland island of Unsa as a training area, almost the most northerly point of the United Kingdom, a spot bleak and bare enough to stand comparison with sub-arctic Norway. They did a great deal of training in the use of canoes and kayaks as well as in the techniques of Commando fighting.

Frequently in such top-secret plans, laid and practised in deadly earnest, the absurd was never far from the surface. So it was here. Having rounded up a large number of canoes Ryder was advised,

> that it was a good idea to fill the ends of these folding canoes with ping-pong balls before going into action. Lillywhites came to the rescue. They had a good reserve stock. Did I want the 9d. sort or those costing One Shilling? I felt where lives were concerned we shouldn't be cheeseparing.

A few days later Ryder was telephoned at COHQ by an official from the Admiralty's Stores Department and asked to confirm that there was an operational requirement for £3,000 worth of ping-pong balls and, if so, that it would have to be sanctioned by higher authority. The officer at the next-door desk said at once, 'If they are going to be sticky I can authorize anything up to £300,000.' 'So', Ryder recalled, 'we got them that way and I politely told the Naval Stores officer he could go and get stuffed.' In the event, after months of training, the plan came to nothing in the face of objections raised by Admiralty lawyers that tampering with navigation lights was contrary to the Geneva Convention.[36]

Of much greater value and long-term significance was Ryder's role in raising 30 Assault Unit (30AU). This was the brainchild of Admiral Godfrey, the Director of Naval Intelligence (DNI), and his assistant Ian Fleming, serving as a Commander RNVR. Fleming's idea was to emulate the Germans' intelligence successes during the Greek and Balkan campaigns of 1941 where they had used small, self-contained units alongside the assault formations to capture intact enemy equipment and documents. Fleming's original proposal for a British intelligence assault unit was dated 20 March 1942. The proposal ground slowly along, encountering entrenched opposition from the Army until, at the end of July 1942, it was put on a permanent footing under COHQ with a title of 'Intelligence Assault Unit' (IAU). On 16 September Ryder was appointed the first commanding officer of Fleming's IAU. On 19 September a memo from the DNI announced Ryder's appointment 'to supervise the creation and training of a Naval Intelligence Assault Unit.'[37]

Ryder and Fleming made an oddly contrasting pair. Born within a few months of each other in 1908 they were of the same age but of very different characters. The reserved, self-disciplined Ryder would have looked askance at Fleming's rackety private life, his fondness for drink and gambling, while Fleming would perhaps have considered Ryder worthy but staid. Where the comparison between the two men becomes more interesting is that both had something the other wanted but could not attain. Ryder was the man of action, with a long record of adventure and death-defying derring-do to his credit (and a VC to prove it), whereas Fleming was the man-about-town, the urbane, golfing, bridge-playing, lounge lizard with an important job in naval intelligence. Fleming yearned to be the man of action – consider the character of James Bond; Ryder longed for an opening in naval intelligence, work which fascinated him. Indeed, Ryder tried intermittently but unsuccessfully to land a job in naval intelligence. In 1953 they both published first novels, too, one with rather greater success than the other.

On the day that Ryder was formally appointed to the command of IAU, Fleming sent him a long letter giving details of the proposed training programme for the new unit. It was intended that the forthcoming Allied landings in North Africa – codenamed Operation *Torch* – would be IAU's first taste of action. As the landings were expected to take place in November and IAU's training was likely to take six weeks, there was not a moment to lose.

IAU was divided into three sections: the Royal Navy troop, the Royal Marine troop and the Army troop. The Navy troop was recruited by Ryder from 'RNVR officers chosen from volunteers for hazardous service'. According to the official history, many of those originally selected were unsuited to the IAU's work. However, two of Ryder's original recruits, Dunstan Curtis and Quintin Riley, distinguished themselves in the service of IAU. Both were well known to Ryder. Curtis, who had taken Ryder to St Nazaire in MGB 314, spoke French and German so was ideally suited to the work. He, with a party of six Marines, took part in the *Torch* landings, IAU's baptism of fire. Quintin Riley, who had been a member of Ryder's other Commando unit, became commanding officer of IAU in April 1943. Ryder ceased to be the commanding officer of IAU towards the end of 1942 returning, it seems, to his duties at COHQ.[38] Fleming's IAU, after performing creditably in North Africa, played an important role in intelligence gathering for the rest of the war.

The year between St Nazaire and the spring of 1943 was a happy period for Ryder and Hilaré. In May 1942 Hilaré discovered that she was pregnant – the baby seemingly conceived on Ryder's return from St Nazaire. Their son Lisle was born on 3 January 1943.[39] In the middle of February, Hilaré, Ryder and the new-born Lisle moved into 10 Cloisters, a house in the precincts of Windsor Castle. In June 1943, with Ryder firmly in his new job at Southampton, the family took a cottage at Hythe, with a fine view over Southampton Water. Hilaré was 'indefatigable in finding accommodation, which was very endearing', Ryder remembered. It also meant that they could be together as a family when he was not at sea.[40]

On 1 May Ryder joined the staff of the Senior Officer of Force J. Force J had been established after the Dieppe raid as a permanent naval assault force. It arose from the conviction of John Hughes-Hallett and others after Dieppe that the Navy should never again rely on assembling ad hoc forces for large, complex operations. Ryder had expressed the same idea following his experiences at

St Nazaire, but had been ignored. Hughes-Hallett was appointed to the command of Force J, establishing his headquarters in HMS *Vectis*, a shore establishment ('stone frigate') at Cowes on the Isle of Wight, in October 1942. His chief of staff was David Luce, also from COHQ, so Ryder was surrounded by familiar faces.

By the time he joined Force J the Allies had started planning the invasion of the Continent. The Casablanca Conference of January 1943 had led to the appointment of Lieutenant General F.E. Morgan as Chief of Staff to the Supreme Allied Commander, a ponderous title soon reduced to the rather catchier acronym COSSAC. He was charged with drawing up the initial invasion plans. By November 1943, when Hughes-Hallett was superseded by Rear Admiral Philip Vian, Force J had grown enormously. It comprised more than 15,000 officers and men and was, according to Hughes-Hallett, 'the largest single administrative unit in the Navy'. More importantly, it was the only completely formed naval assault group and would constitute the core of the invasion force the following year.[41]

Ryder's job with Force J was as senior officer of the Support Group, charged, as the name suggests, with providing fire support for the assaulting troops. This was one of the major lessons of the debacle at Dieppe, where the troops had been denied significant fire support while landing with calamitous consequences. His principal responsibility was training the crews of the vessels which would provide the supporting fire. Ryder had at his disposal several types of craft. First there were the Landing Craft, Gun (LCG), landing craft mounted with a 6-pounder gun. These were intended to go in with the infantry landing craft so that they could engage enemy pillboxes at close range. Behind them were the Landing Craft, Rocket (LCR), and then the Army's ordinary artillery firing from their landing craft, which were the first to open fire. There were also Landing Craft, Flak (LCF) for anti-aircraft protection. Ryder himself, with the infantry's commanding officer, would go in in a Landing Craft Headquarters (LCH).

It was Ryder's task to train the crews of these variously modified craft so that they could fit into the intricate set-piece attack planned to take place on D-Day. The first step was to teach the crews some elementary skills such as night station-keeping at sea. But it was the LCRs that required the most practice. According to Ryder, the LCRs, mounted with 1,000 5in rockets, were 'one shot weapons, highly vulnerable and aimed by pointing the ship in the right direction'. They fired their rockets over the heads of the infantry at a range of around 6,000 yards. In September 1943 Force J's Support Group, having taken delivery of an early model of an LCR, was conducting firing practice at its training area, Studland Bay in Dorset. The report on the exercise shows that improvements to the specifications of the vessels, such as better voice-pipes and louder alarm bells, were needed. The practice also showed that around 25 of every 500 rockets misfired, a rate considered unacceptably high. The report concluded that the training had been 'most valuable' and that the crews concerned 'are now much more keen, confident and competent than they were before'. There was, however, no cause for complacency. There was 'still room for improvement and the more firings and dummy runs they do the better.'[42]

Force J had been training with the Canadian 3rd Division since that formation had returned from the Mediterranean in September 1943. A full-scale landing exercise – Operation *Pirate* – was organized for mid-October in which the entire Canadian division and all Force J would take part, accompanied by live fire from the artillery and rocket support vessels. The force was embarked at Spithead before sailing to Studland Bay for the landing. A specially reinforced concrete bunker was built on the beach to allow an array of high-ranking observers to witness the exercise at first hand. Despite a last-minute change of plan imposed by the weather, *Pirate* went well, according to Hughes-Hallett, demonstrating how far Force J had progressed with its training. Indeed, by the time he handed over command to Vian, he reckoned that Force J was 'three-quarters of the way to being completely trained' with 'over six months to run before *Overlord*'.[43]

In January 1944 the command structure of Operation *Overlord* was changed. Rear Admiral Vian became commander of the Eastern Task Force, which comprised the two British assault formations, Forces J and S. At the beginning of February Ryder was appointed as Training Officer on Vian's staff on top of his responsibility as commanding officer of the Support Group for Force J. The American formation, the Western Task Force, was commanded by Rear Admiral Kirk. The third British assault formation, Force G, was created in March 1944 as a direct result of the decision to have five assaulting divisions not three. From the early spring of 1944 it was full steam ahead for D-Day.

As preparations for D-Day gathered pace, work crowded in on Ryder. In January Hilaré and Lisle had moved from the cottage at Hythe back to the Cloisters in Windsor Castle. Here, on 14 March 1944, Susan was born. Ryder was, naturally, delighted with his daughter, but, as he confessed to Hilaré three months later, 'I look forward to Susan growing up a bit. I'm afraid that at the moment she is rather outclassed by her brother.' The move meant that, with the pressure of work, it was more difficult for Ryder to get home: 'I miss you so much and hate living in a mess again.' But there were still moments of bliss, stolen from the strain of war.

What a joy it was seeing you, my love, at Haslemere. I did so enjoy every moment of it. You looked so sweet and attractive – more so than when I first fell in love with you. I will always have the happiest recollections of our weekend together.[44]

On 12 April there was a full-scale landing exercise for Force J and the Canadian 3rd Division, codenamed *Trousers*. The landing was to be at Slapton Sands after a 100-mile sea passage from the Solent. According to Ryder, in a strong ebb tide many of the flotilla's craft got snared in the anti-submarine boom across the Solent, 'like herrings in a drift net'. All was eventually sorted out but the exercise was delayed.

As well as training and exercises, there were conferences, endless conferences. On 17 April there was a conference of Force J's Naval staff at the Royal Yacht Squadron at Cowes, a post mortem on *Trousers*. The following day there was another discussion of the lessons of *Trousers*, this time at Southampton, with Force J commanders and the top brass of the Canadian 3rd Division in attendance.[45]

There were also visits from VIPs, inquisitive politicians, senior generals and the like. Sir Archibald Sinclair, the Secretary of State for Air, watched *Trousers* from Force J's headquarters ship. A fortnight or so before D-Day the Commonwealth Prime Ministers, escorted by Winston Churchill, were taken round the invasion fleet by members of Admiral Vian's staff, including Ryder. This important visit was a dress rehearsal for an even more significant one: the King's inspection of Force J at HMS *Vectis* at Cowes on 24 May. Ryder had a starring role.

A Fairmile ML was detailed for the purpose and my job apart from being at Admiral Vian's right hand was to write out an operation order for the day's event with detailed timing at our various starting and stopping places. I felt rather responsible.

Fortunately, the royal visit, which started with a stroll through the magnificent azaleas in the gardens of Exbury House, passed off smoothly.[46]

A few days before the invasion was scheduled to start, Ryder attended General Montgomery's briefing for all commanding officers. It was held at General Eisenhower's headquarter at Southwick House near Portsmouth. 'I remember', Ryder recalled, 'being rather impressed by Monty whom I otherwise always disliked and could see how he imparted a feeling of confidence.'

Now everything was ready. The largest invasion fleet the world had ever seen, 175,000 soldiers, nearly 5,000 landing craft and 566 battleships, cruisers, destroyers, escort vessels and minesweepers had assembled in ports all along the south coast of England.[47] Two years of intense planning and training were about to be put into action. Ryder, with countless others, had been working for this moment since he had joined Force J more than a year earlier. As he walked down towards his embarkation jetty at Southampton, he noticed as he passed through the ancient city walls a plaque commemorating Henry V and his army's departure for France before Agincourt, five centuries earlier. 'I remember feeling rather inspired by this historical precedent.' Ryder returned to his LCH, which was berthed at Netley, near the top of Southampton Water, where 'we settled down in a state of high expectation and suppressed excitement.' The 'whole of the Solent and Southampton Water', he recalled, 'was packed with ships and Landing Craft rafted together.'

The only question now was the weather. After a fine spell in May the weather had broken, giving way to storms in the Channel. At dusk on Sunday, 4 June Ryder's LCH slipped its mooring to take its place at the head of the Force J formation. Ryder was in command of the leading waves of the Canadian

8 Brigade, detailed to attack the left-hand, eastern sector of Juno Beach. But the flotilla had not gone very far down Southampton Water towards the open sea – probably not further than Calshot Castle, only five or six miles away – when the order came through that General Eisenhower had postponed the operation by twenty-four hours on account of the weather. So 'back we all had to go to repeat exactly the same thing the next day.'[48]

The following day, 5 June, the weather was hardly better but the forecast had improved greatly. Eisenhower had decided that the operation could be delayed no longer so the invasion fleet left its moorings and steered for France. Ryder's formation consisted of his LCH with the Canadian battalion commander and the artillery control officer on board. The assaulting infantry battalion was the Queen's Own Rifles (QOR), a distinguished Canadian regiment, commanded by its colonel, John Spragge. The QOR, one of 8 Brigade's two assault battalions, was to come ashore on the right of the brigade's front at Bernieres. Behind them were the LCTs with the DD 'swimming' tanks on board; then came the LCRs and the artillery.

The troops transhipped to their landing craft, one platoon per craft, 7 miles offshore. The conditions off the Normandy coast were rough and completely unsuitable for the small, open landing craft that were to carry the troops into the beaches. There was a north-easterly wind blowing onshore, Ryder recalled, at about force 5 to 6, whipping up 4 or 5 foot waves which tossed the landing craft about, slowing them down. For the hapless infantrymen it was a ghastly experience: by the time they were required to storm ashore, they were soaked to the skin, cold, cramped and, in many cases, enfeebled by seasickness. And there was worse. The sea was 'far too rough', Ryder remembered, 'to launch the DD ['swimming'] tanks which were only kept afloat by a sort of canvas boat.' As the tanks were supposed to provide support and cover for the first wave of infantry, this was a serious setback.[49] In the event 8 Brigade's tanks were landed 'dryshod' on the beaches.

The difficulties and delays experienced by the in-coming landing craft were compounded in the Canadian sector by the presence of dangerous offshore reefs. So that the landing craft would have sufficient water to clear these hazards, H-Hour (the time of landing) was put back by ten minutes to 0740. But delayed by the rough conditions, the leading landing craft touched down on the beaches at about 0800, twenty minutes late.

'At Bernieres the fight was sharp while it lasted', was Chester Wilmot's verdict. Although the men of the QOR had to land without tanks, the rocket and artillery support that Ryder had worked on so hard came up to expectation. The rockets, he remembered, 'were sensational': 'The whole beach was deluged in explosions lasting for some 60 or so seconds. There was virtually no opposition left.' This was not quite true. Thanks to their late arrival, the QOR were carried in their landing craft much further up the beach than had been intended. As a result, they had only 100 yards to run to the cover of the sea wall at the back of the beach. But this

100 yards was covered by enemy fire; one company of QOR lost half its strength in the dash for the wall. The most dangerous enemy strongpoint was silenced by an LCF running very close inshore. Once the tanks had landed they were able to blast the defences at close range, clearing the way for the infantry to fan out from the beach into Bernieres itself. By the time that the French-Canadians of the Régiment de la Chaudiere began to land fifteen minutes later, the only fire on the beach was from isolated snipers. By 0930 Bernieres had been reported clear.[50]

The assault troops, having landed and brushed aside the enemy defences with such magnificent élan, had now gone inland, but those, including Ryder, remaining on the beach had much to worry them. The fact that the QOR had landed late in much higher water than planned had meant that the teams detailed to deal with the enemy's obstacles had been unable to clear the beaches. As these obstacles were mined, they were lethal to incoming landing craft, many of which were holed. Ryder took his LCH close in to direct traffic: 'Through loud hailers incoming craft were told to keep all hands well aft and to take the beach at speed. They got there all right. Getting them off was another matter.'

Half an hour after the assault had gone in Ryder himself went ashore to contact the Beach Master. As he walked along the beach he greeted an elderly French couple. *'Quelle force, monsieur'*, replied the husband, looking out to sea with tears in his eyes at the invasion fleet coming in. As far as the eye could see, to east, west and north, were ships. Ryder continued on along the beach until he came to a pillbox guarding the entrance to the small harbour of Courseulles. Here he was greeted cheerily by Colin Maude, a fellow Commander RN. Maude, who 'had a very gallant record as a destroyer CO but had been in trouble', had, on landing, with tremendous sangfroid, kitted the pillbox out as a bar. 'There laid out on shelves was ... everything from beer to pink gin. With shells still bursting in the vicinity this was his way of establishing confidence and it was quite effective.'[51]

As the bridgehead at Bernieres had been so swiftly established, Major General Keller, commanding the Canadian 3rd Division, decided to land his reserve brigade over the same beach. The brigade's three battalions were ashore by 1230, but the beach and town were so packed with armour and transport that they could not move inland for several hours. As the tide went out the scale of the damage suffered by the landing craft on the beach at Bernieres became apparent. '[O]ur 600 yards of shore', Ryder recalled, 'was littered and virtually blocked by damaged craft.'

But despite the difficulties they experienced on landing and the resulting congestion, the Canadian 3rd Division had made better progress than any other Allied division on D-Day. By nightfall, the most advanced Canadian formations had penetrated 7 miles inland and were only 3 miles from the outskirts of Caen.[52] The liberation of Europe had started well, but there was much hard fighting yet to be done.

Chapter 14

The Arctic Convoys, Peace and Politics (1944–50)

With the assault landings finished and the troops now fighting their way inland, Ryder's part in the great invasion saga was complete. He had little else to do. Within a week of the landings, Bernieres was so peaceful that, as he told Hilaré, 'I went for a lovely walk this forenoon up to the summit of a low hill overlooking the surrounding country, looking all green and peaceful with cows grazing.' The locals, he reported, 'are very glad to see us and give one a smile and greeting everywhere.'[1] Ryder was later mentioned in dispatches for 'gallantry, skill and devotion to duty' during the landings.

Ryder was soon back in England enjoying some leave. On 23 June he applied unsuccessfully to the Admiralty for a posting to Naval Intelligence. He was refused on the grounds that the Navy was short of officers of his rank in general service but he was not left unemployed for long. Appointed to the command of a destroyer, HMS *Opportune*, he spent the latter half of July and the first half of August on courses. On 14 August he took up his new command.

HMS *Opportune* was an O-Class fleet destroyer, which had been commissioned after a long-delayed construction in August 1942. Displacing 1,540 tons she mounted four 4.7in guns, a four-barrelled pom-pom and eight torpedo tubes. Despite the fact that she was only recently built, Ryder complained that she was 'handicapped by having a very obsolete armament of very old 4 inch guns and an outdated radar.' Nevertheless, it was a welcome change after his long stint at Combined Operations: 'It was', he recalled, 'good to be back with the real Navy and even better to be in a destroyer.'[2]

When Ryder joined his new command she was based at Portsmouth, engaged in screening patrols against enemy E-boats attempting to attack cross-Channel shipping from the east. Within three days, Ryder was in action. On 17 August *Opportune* in company with another destroyer HMS *Walpole* and some MTBs, engaged some enemy E-boats off Dover. Ryder's typically laconic summary of his early weeks in *Opportune* said simply that 'We had one or two inconclusive engagements with E-boats ducking in and out of smoke screens.'[3] He was later mentioned in dispatches for 'courage, skill and determination in light coastal craft in engagements with the enemy in the Channel'.

On 6 September *Opportune* was released from her deployment in the Channel and, after a boiler clean, joined the Home Fleet at Scapa Flow, arriving on 15 September. From now on she was earmarked for escort duty with the Russian convoys. 'This was', Ryder wrote, 'indeed what might be termed a proper job of work.' The convoys had started in the late summer of 1941 to supply the Russian war effort. Some of the earlier convoys suffered very heavy losses, the worst being to convoy PQ17 in June 1942, which lost twenty-four ships, two-thirds of the convoy. By the time Ryder began escort duty, although the worst had passed, the convoys were still subject to regular attack, notably from enemy air bases in northern Norway and from U-boats lurking off Murmansk. If by this stage of the war the convoys were better organized and suffered fewer losses, they remained a very tough assignment with the ever-present menace of the enemy, frequently in appalling weather.

During the convoys, as Ryder was second-in-command of the destroyer screen, *Opportune*'s position was as 'tail-end Charlie' at the rear of the convoy. Each had a small escort carrier equipped with Wildcat fighters. *Opportune*'s role was threefold. Her first job was as a sheep dog, making sure that stragglers kept up with the convoy; the second was to make occasional forays astern, usually at dusk, in the hope of surprising any shadowing U-boats, rejoining the convoy by an indirect route in an attempt to throw the submarine off in the wrong direction. The third job was rescuing ditched fighter pilots. As flying conditions were often very bad, landing a plane on a small, pitching carrier at night, with the pilot's view of the deck frequently obscured by snow flurries was no joke. Many pilots were forced to ditch. The sea was, of course, very cold so they had to be rescued quickly before hypothermia set in. *Opportune* had only a few minutes to locate the ditched pilots, not easy in the dark in often heavy seas. After his own experiences in 1940, this was a task to which Ryder attached particular importance. On 2 November 1944 *Opportune*'s log recorded proudly that 'This ship has managed to rescue a lot of crashed airmen even in severe seas.'[4]

In all Ryder made five journeys to Russia, often in poor weather. In early October he told Hilaré, who had reproved him for failing to write to her regularly,

I wonder if you realise what kind of life we lead ... the weather has been pretty atrocious. Blowing hard generally, with a heavy sea and driving rain and spray, not very easy at night and not the conditions quite for trying to write a letter. Last trip we had both our boats smashed with heavy seas coming inboard and six inches of water swilling about in the mess deck. The trip before one man was flung against a stanchion and broke his leg above the knee.

But the worst conditions that *Opportune* encountered were during Convoy RA64 homeward bound in mid-February 1945. As the outward bound convoy from the Clyde, JW64, was coming in to Kola Inlet on 13 February, HM Corvette *Denbigh Castle* was torpedoed. At dusk on 16 February the escorts of RA64 were ordered to sea to clear the German blockade of Kola Inlet. During an Asdic sweep a U-boat, *U-425*, was located and sunk.

The following morning the merchantmen – which were empty and ballasted – formed up in Kola Inlet before setting sail for home. It quickly became apparent that the previous evening's attempts to disperse the enemy blockade had not been successful. At 1024 as the convoy moved into the open sea, the escort sloop *Lark* was torpedoed by *U-968*; crippled, she was beached and abandoned. At 1200 the same submarine struck again, torpedoing the US Liberty ship *Thomas Scott*. The crew abandoned ship. At 1600 the corvette *Bluebell* was hit by a torpedo from *U-711*. So quickly did she sink that there was only one survivor. After this inauspicious beginning, RA64 ran into some atrocious weather.

On 18 February storms were starting to develop; by midnight winds of up to 60 knots – almost hurricane force – were recorded. By the following morning the convoy was widely scattered, but as the storms moderated during the day the convoy began to reassemble. At 1000 on 20 February the convoy came under attack from more than forty enemy aircraft, Ju88s. Fighters flying off HMS *Nairana*, the convoy's escort carrier, inflicted some casualties on the enemy, as did accurate anti-aircraft fire from the destroyers. It was during this attack that Ryder rescued two aircrews who had ditched simultaneously. Ryder sent off the ship's whaler to pick the crew of a ditched Swordfish while he took *Opportune* across the carrier's wake to rescue the second crew. Having done so, Ryder swung the destroyer round to recover the whaler. To his horror, in the murk he lost sight of the whaler. 'We spent an exceedingly anxious half hour searching in the dark.' Eventually, assisted by HMS *Orwell*'s superior radar, the whaler was located and rescued. 'Was I relieved!' Ryder recorded. 'This was one of my worst moments of the war.' There was, however, a happy ending. Once the whaler had been recovered, *Opportune*'s surgeon succeeded in resuscitating the two airmen, who were suffering from hypothermia.

Over the next two days the storms continued to rise, reaching a pitch during the evening of 22 February, when the wind rose to speeds of 70 to 80 knots. *Opportune*'s barograph chart shows a spectacular depression during those hours, with the wind being recorded at force 12. He sent it to his father-in-law, remarking, 'There are on it some of the steepest curves I have ever seen and some very wild weather.' The conditions confronting RA64 were accounted to be the worst endured in the entire North Atlantic theatre during the whole war. Ryder, writing many years later, a lifetime's seafaring behind him, simply said it was 'terrible weather, the worst I have ever known'.

On 23 February the storms moderated to some degree, but the merchantman, *Henry Bacon*, sent out a distress signal, saying that she was under air attack from a large flight of enemy torpedo bombers. *Opportune* and two other escorts were sent to pick up survivors. On 1 March the majority of the convoy's vessels arrived in the Clyde. All the escorting destroyers reported defects and damage caused by the rough conditions. *Opportune* had lost both her ship's boats, smashed.[5]

The weather endured by Convoy RA64 was exceptionally bad, but not all convoys were buffeted by storms throughout their passages. There were calmer periods. 'We had some beautifully fine nights when the Aurora [Borealis] lit up the night sky with the most wonderful displays.' Ryder found the time to make two charcoal and chalk drawings of the convoys under the Northern Lights, which were published in the *Illustrated London News* in December 1944. Uplifting though these fine nights were, the light, clear skies did leave the ships alarmingly 'silhouetted for any lurking U-Boat or prowling torpedo bomber.' In early March 1945, after the tempestuous fury of RA64, Ryder was pleased to be able to tell Hilaré that

We have had a fine trip – flat calm for a change. It makes everything so much easier and the longer days help enormously. It's a still calm afternoon at the moment with quite a warm lazy feeling in the air even the gulls are sitting quietly on the water or perching on our yardarms.[6]

There was even, between convoys, the occasional opportunity for Ryder to let his hair down. In September he told Hilaré that 'I went sailing this afternoon. The first time for nearly seven years.' On one occasion the following spring, with *Opportune* in port in England, Ryder allowed himself an uncharacteristic flash of lower-deck humour.

We have just had a party of Wrens on board. And I must admit that I am full of whisky and bonhomie, but we have packed them off ashore, together I regret with most of my wardroom. It's the old story – 'anything will do so long as there is a hole in it'.[7]

Even the stops in Russia provided opportunities for distraction from the strain of convoy duty. 'I am glad to say', he wrote in March 1945, that

our allies are at last thawing and we had one very fine *prasnik* – which has made everyone very envious – oceans of vodka and champagne and a very fine concert afterwards including an act by a most attractive dancing girl.[8]

But these episodes were only brief respites in what was a stressful, lonely period of Ryder's career. He had little in common with *Opportune*'s officers who were generally much younger than he. 'This is a lonely life really', he told Hilaré in January, although '... I occasionally see some of the other COs which helps a bit.'[9] It was difficult too for Ryder and Hilaré to see one another. *Opportune* was based at Scapa Flow while Hilaré was living in Berkshire with the children, so even when his ship was in port Ryder was a long way from home.

They did manage to spend Christmas 1944 together at Cleethorpes while the ship was refitting. Being together over Christmas gave Hilaré the chance to help Ryder with the festivities aboard the destroyer. After church on Christmas Day Ryder did his rounds of the ship to 'be stood glasses of rum from the tots the men have been saving up for the past weeks.' Later there was a party in the ward room, as Hilaré told her mother.

> I think I told you I was going on board at noon to help Bob entertain the ship's company. As you can imagine he was dreading it and [was] quite convinced the men would all be drunk or tongue tied. Actually, it went off splendidly though some of the very young A.B.s were a bit sticky. Bob was in very good form and made them laugh a lot.[10]

Once this happy interlude was over, however, Ryder had little opportunity to see his wife and children.

The strain of the prolonged war is clearly reflected in their letters of the time. There is a taut sense of longing, of anxiety and of sexual frustration. In April 1945 Hilaré wrote to Ryder,

> On Saturday we heard an account by an officer who had been aboard the flagship during your last trip to Russia. Darling how kind and loving you are in your efforts to spare me anxiety. You told me so little of the dangers of the journey and now I hear it was more heavily attacked than any other convoy in the past two years.[11]

In a letter written at the end of the month Hilaré confessed that 'This long drawn out end to the war, with the foolish hopes it raises is getting almost more than I can bear.' Ryder likewise felt bereft,

> For all the good news and better weather I am lonely. Just plain lonely. Lonely for you my love. I can never be happy really away from you which is not altogether surprising as I was never happy for long until I fell in love with you.

Three weeks later he confessed 'I cling desperately to the future. The present is a rotten life for me with the girl I love eating her heart out with worry and anxiety, and getting worried and frightened.'[12]

Absence, they say, makes the heart grow fonder. In this instance, Ryder's prolonged spells away from home certainly sharpened Hilaré's and his mutual sexual desire. In April Hilaré confessed to Ryder that

> I can tell from even my small experience of men that you are exceptionally passionate and becoming increasingly so. I look on this as a gift which should be developed just as any other gift, where we are lucky is that I believe I share that gift to a certain extent, much more satisfactory than both being good at tennis, say!

A few days later Hilaré told Ryder that the present separation 'will be our longest parting, nine weeks is our record so far. I wonder if the longer time will make you even more energetic and eager for me?'[13]

By April the Germans were on their last legs as the Russians closed in on Berlin. When Hitler committed suicide on 30 April the end was nigh and on 8 May all remaining German forces in the Reich surrendered. Ryder was at sea when the news came.

> This is such a historic day that I felt I must start a letter to you. It is one of the glorious fine days when the sea really does look blue. Aided by an almost cloudless sky and a very calm sea there could hardly be a better day to be at sea. For the past 24 hours we have been steaming up and down off the enemy coasts. We have been listening to the wireless with all the announcements ... Thus for us the German war has come to an end.

The previous day, with the war about to end, Hilaré expressed her feelings to Ryder in a prolonged sigh of relief.

> It is hard to take in all it will mean. I can't really grasp yet that the door-bell need no longer mean to me a policeman with a telegram, the telephone ringing some friend of yours ringing up to break bad news to me gently before I read it in the papers. To be able to come back to the house without searching people's faces to see if they have heard anything while I've been out.[14]

The end of the war did not, of course, mean that Ryder could abandon his ship to return home, although the ship's company was given leave once she came into Rosyth on 11 May. However, on 24 May *Opportune* was off once more, this time across the North Sea to Kiel. Having spent the night of 25 May at Cuxhaven at the western end of the Kiel Canal, she passed through it the next day. It was, Ryder recalled, 'most interesting'.

> As we passed through the most lovely grazing fenland country I wished I had had you with me. At all places the people came to the banks to watch us pass. The women all waving in a most friendly way, often with their arm linked in their husbands, or even with couples out courting on the canal banks.

Opportune was the first British warship (bar a couple of MLs) to pass through the Canal since the end of the war. *Opportune* arrived at Kiel after dark whence she was immediately dispatched to the port of Flensburg. Ryder had understandable reservations about the dependability of the German pilot in coastal waters which had been heavily mined by the Allies during the final days of the war. But on a foggy night the pilot led *Opportune* safely along the narrow, twisting channel, passing the occasional wreck on the way. 'Flensburg', Ryder told Hilaré, 'is the most lovely old Baltic town ... It is full of colour with rich red brown tiled roofs.'

In Flensburg Ryder was ordered to inspect all the vessels in the harbour. 'There was', he remembered, 'a good deal of surliness but I had a very smart and efficient German boat's crew to take me round and a Petty Officer to issue the necessary orders.' Once Ryder had confirmed that none of the vessels was booby-trapped he began allocating prize crews for the German naval yachts. These were then sailed home, claimed as the booty of war, for use by various service sailing associations.[15] Ryder was also able to do some sightseeing while in Flensburg. Grand Admiral Doenitz, who had taken over as Führer from Hitler, had made his headquarters in the town. Ryder was able to wander round his offices, even sitting in the Führer's chair.

Opportune, her stint in the Baltic over, returned to England at the end of the first week of June. Ryder was by now seriously ill, with a high temperature. Immediately on arrival in England he was admitted to Haslar naval hospital at Gosport. He was examined by no fewer than nine specialists, none of whom could diagnose the cause of his illness. His daughter is convinced that it was a reaction to the ending of the war. All the stress, responsibility and anxiety of command, all the privations and frustrations of the Russian convoys, on top of five years of unremitting strain, had taken their toll. Always lurking in the back of his mind was the memory of his four days in the water in 1940, a permanent, terrifying reminder of the harsh reality of naval warfare. Suddenly released from all this by the outbreak of peace, Ryder's system temporarily shut down. This theory is borne out by letters written at the time. He told his father-in-law on his return to England:

> The end of the German war has left me feeling very tired and limp. I am in one of those moods when all the things I have really longed to do seem quite pointless … The only thing I still long for is to see Hilaré again and the children.[16]

Hilaré saw clearly the emotional strain that the war had imposed on her husband. The day before the German surrender, she wrote to him.

> Darling, I want to tell you how my heart has ached to think of you frightened and anxious, with everything depending on your steadiness and good example, your handling of the ship and of the men in her … I knew you could never fail but I couldn't bear to think of how hard it must often be to go on, to go back to the same dangers again knowing just what it would be like and with your terrible experience to make it so much harder for you than for most people to face the possibility of getting sunk. That is where you have shown the greatest courage my sweetheart, more than at St Nazaire and with no acknowledgement to reward you, in going back to sea again, forcing yourself to go on as though nothing had happened, after those four days in the Atlantic. No one would have blamed you if you had admitted to having lost your nerve, asked for shore jobs in the future, in fact anyone but you would have been a case for a nerve specialist for the rest of your life. Because you have gone on without any sign I know it doesn't mean the experience left no trace, I have known, and understood, the effort it has taken to remain steady and unafraid.[17]

* * *

The war was now over; Ryder had survived. St Nazaire had made him a national hero. His outstanding war record had given him wide renown in the Navy and beyond. 'Darling', Hilaré told him in June, 'you don't realize nearly enough how impressed people are by you, or what a great figure you have become.'[18] But it had come at a price. He had lost some of his best friends in the war: James Martin and Michael Seymour both perished when *Willamette Valley* was torpedoed. George Salt went down with his submarine *Triad* in the Adriatic in 1940. Both his brothers had been killed in the war. Lisle, as we have seen, was murdered by the *SS* in France in 1940. Ernle, who was nearer to Ryder in age but, as a Gurkha officer, had spent most of his military career in the East, was lost at sea off Sumatra in the spring of 1942 after the fall of Singapore. On 13 July 1945 his father, who had done so much to encourage him in his early career, died at the age of seventy-seven.

Once he had recovered Ryder was discharged from hospital but declared unfit for service at sea for a period of six months. Unable to go back to sea, he joined the Tactical & Staff Duties Division of the Naval Staff at the Admiralty at the beginning of October. In February 1946 Ryder and Hilaré rented Wheatbutts Cottage at Eton Wick, a pretty, rose-clad house that had once been home to David Niven. The rent was more than they could afford, but Hilaré, who loved the cottage, hid this uncomfortable fact from Ryder, resolving to make up the difference from her own resources.

Ryder enjoyed his spell at the Admiralty. It was 'pleasant and interesting work' but gave him both the time and the opportunity to write his book on the raid on St Nazaire. At this point little detail had been made public about the raid; the two official reports from 1942 on the raid, by Admiral Forbes and by Ryder himself, were not published until October 1947. He had started the book before the end of the war; in January 1945 Ryder thanked Hilaré for typing the first chapter. It was finished by February 1946, although the need to get official clearance before publication was a time-consuming business.

> My book I am told has to go now to the Air Ministry, War Office and Combined Operations Headquarters. Having taken 4 weeks at the Admiralty I see no hope of it being finished in under another ten now.

Ryder got so fed up with bureaucratic delays that he contemplated adding a note on the flyleaf stating that 'The Author wishes to make it clear that he has received no help from the Admiralty.'[19] The book was accepted for publication by John Murray & Co in April 1946. In his letter accepting the book for publication Sir John Murray told Ryder that

> Undoubtedly, you tell the story of a very fine affair but, as was only to be expected, you suppress your own part in it far too much ... In fact it might seem that you were little more than a casual looker-on while others were doing

the hard fighting! I know that this presents a very difficult problem for you, as the last thing that you would want would be to put yourself forward.[20]

Murray was right, but it was wholly characteristic that Ryder should write the book in that way. *The Attack on St. Nazaire* was eventually published on 28 March 1947, six months before the official reports on the raid appeared in the *London Gazette*. In its first three months the book sold more than 4,000 copies, making Ryder more than £120 (including a £75 advance) in the same period, although thereafter sales tailed off sharply. The reviews were generally favourable, even laudatory. A 'piece of first-class wartime reporting', thought the *Southern Times*. *The Times Literary Supplement* considered that 'Commander Ryder's story of the raid is clear and objective.' Brigadier Derek Mills-Roberts, a man with his own distinguished war record, told the *Liverpool Daily Post*'s readers that this 'admirable book' 'includes no trimmings of any kind. The story is good enough to live for all time without any embellishments.'[21]

However, many critics echoed Murray's opinion that Ryder was unduly modest, to the point of being positively unforthcoming about his own part in the raid. 'The raid', wrote the *Liverpool Echo*'s critic, 'was one of those exploits that combine practical warfare with the daring spirit of knight-errantry. Yet Commander Ryder writes with extreme modesty.' *The Listener* told its readers that 'Commander Ryder is a … sober writer. He keeps close to the log of events, and denies us, for instance, almost any clue to the exploits which won him the Victoria Cross at St Nazaire.' *The Recorder*'s critic considered the book 'brilliantly written', its 'place in the annals of naval history … assured' but added that 'The author is almost irritatingly self-effacing, and the reader is left to fill in from his own imagination much that Commander Ryder could much better have supplied.'[22]

Despite Ryder's excessive self-effacement, the book did accomplish one important task. As an article in the *RNSS Journal* in July 1947 pointed out, for a time after news of the raid had been made public 'the German propaganda machine was worked to such good effect, in complete contrast to our own', that many neutrals concluded that the raid was a resounding success for the Germans.

> Until now the full effect of this invidious distortion of the facts has never completely died down, so that the publication of Commander Ryder's book should do much to dispel the widespread misapprehension which may still exist in the minds of many people.

Brigadier Mills-Roberts, in his review, reinforced the point.

> I myself, like most other people who were not there, relied for my knowledge of this raid on the Press reports and information given by the BBC. The German propaganda was most effective and it was not generally appreciated

that the main object of the raid, namely the destruction of the large dry dock at St Nazaire, was completely fulfilled.[23]

Ryder's book had set the record straight. Any doubts about the value or triumphant success of Operation *Chariot* and the brave men who took part in it had been dispelled, once and for all.

The other major event for Ryder in 1947 was the return to St Nazaire. In August 150 Charioteers returned to St Nazaire aboard HMS *Sirius*, lent by the Admiralty for the occasion, to witness the unveiling of the memorial to those who had died in the raid. The unveiling, which took place on 2 August, was a full day of ceremonies, receptions, services and dinners. The proceedings began with *Sirius* and the French cruiser *Kléber* exchanging a 21-gun salute. At around 9 am the French Prime Minister, Paul Ramadier, arrived to be greeted by the British Ambassador, Mr Duff Cooper, and his wife Lady Diana. With the former Commandos drawn up in line on the quay alongside *Sirius*, M. Ramadier decorated Ryder and Newman with the Legion d'Honneur and the Croix de Guerre. There is newsreel footage of a stoic-looking Ryder being kissed on both cheeks by the French Prime Minister as he pinned the medals to his chest.

The Commandos 'now demobilized and in civilian clothes but marching smartly' as *The Times*'s correspondent observed, then led the way to the memorial, a tall, roughly-shaped obelisk of granite, on the seafront. The French Prime Minister, unveiling the monument, made a speech in which he said that the Charioteers 'were the first to bring us hope.' The memorial was the initiative, jointly, of the St Nazaire Society and the townspeople of St Nazaire itself, who had contributed 400,000 francs towards its cost. Once the memorial had been unveiled, wreaths were laid for the dead and a bronze plaque brought from England was deposited to be fixed to the stone. The plaque was inscribed with the words 'They achieved much, having dared all.'

There followed a service at La Baule cemetery, where the casualties of the raid are buried. At lunchtime the British contingent gave a reception aboard *Sirius* to which the government contributed five cases of gin and three of vermouth. The party went, we are assured, 'with the swing that is usual in HM Ships.' In the evening the French gave a *diner intime* for 125 people in the casino at La Baule. At the dinner Ryder gave a short, impromptu speech paying tribute to the courage of the people of St Nazaire and the losses they suffered during and after the raid. 'We hope', he said, 'that it will be yet another bond of friendship between our two countries and one never to be forgotten.'[24]

This memorable occasion was not the Charioteers' first reunion. The first Annual Reunion Dinner took place on the anniversary of the raid following the end of the war, 28 March 1946. It was held at Chez Auguste, a restaurant in Soho. A year later the second reunion took place at Mecca's Restaurant in Liverpool, thereafter becoming an annual event. Ryder, naturally, always attended the dinners, but almost always found them awkward occasions. He was not by nature a gregarious man; indeed, his daughter describes him as 'shy, uncomfortable in society' and an old friend likewise as 'a shy, retiring man.'[25] At the St Nazaire reunions his awkwardness was increased by the fact that naturally everyone knew who he was whereas there were many of the Charioteers, particularly the Commandos, whom he hardly knew at all. He also felt that many of the Charioteers had got to know one another well during their long incarceration as PoWs. Hilaré did her best to help him but he never found the reunions easy.

Ryder finished his posting on the Admiralty staff in September 1947. On 1 March 1948 he arrived in Norway to take up his appointment as Naval Attaché to the British Embassy in Oslo. He arrived in Oslo at a time of acute and rising tension between the West and the Soviet Union. In February the Communists had engineered a coup in Czechoslovakia. The Prague coup was 'of enormous significance, precisely because it came in a more or less democratic country that had seemed so friendly to Moscow.'[26] On 10 March Jan Masaryk, the Czech Foreign Minister, died in suspicious circumstances, allegedly after a fall from his window at the Foreign Ministry in Prague. Many in the West blamed the Communists. In April Finland signed a 'Friendship Treaty' with the Soviet Union. In June Stalin cut the lines of communication into West Berlin forcing the Allies to supply the city from the air; the Berlin Airlift lasted until May 1949. To the anxious Allies it was proof that Communism was bent on expansion westwards. Norway, it seemed, might be the next brick to slip from the wall.

In the spring of 1948 Norway was under considerable pressure from Stalin to align itself to the Communist bloc by signing a 'non-aggression' pact with the Soviet Union. Equally, Western diplomats were anxious to persuade Norway's socialist government to sign up to the proposed North Atlantic Treaty Organization, founded in 1949. Norway and Russia had a common border in the extreme north where there was a good deal of infiltration by the Russians. Teams of Russian communist agents, masquerading as war graves inspectors, were fomenting trouble in Norway's northern provinces. 'It was our principal task as diplomats', Ryder wrote, 'both officially and behind the scenes, to stiffen the attitude of the Norwegian Government.'[27] Norway was on the front line of the struggle between East and West, communism and democracy, oppression and freedom.

It was a fascinating moment for Ryder to take up his new job and, arriving in Oslo ahead of Hilaré and the children, he flung himself into it. Naval intelligence work had always, as we have seen, been greatly to his taste. He immediately discovered, however, that there was more to being an accredited naval attaché than drafting intelligence reports, as he told his father-in-law after three weeks at the Embassy,

I am not sure yet how much I am really going to like this job, owing to the number and formality of the parties. Otherwise the work is most interesting. I see looking at my little book that I have been to 25 major parties in 19 days.[28]

Apart from his intelligence role and the diplomatic cocktail parties, the main strand of Ryder's job consisted of making the arrangements for naval visits. These ranged from a single minesweeper to HMS *Medway* and four submarines. At one point, Ryder's old command, HMS *Fleetwood*, put into Oslo. These visits required much organization on Ryder's part: berthing and fuelling arrangements, the exchange of diplomatic courtesies, and well as the inevitable recreation and entertainment. To share the administrative load, he had one secretary, Enid Coulson. Both the British Military and Air Attachés, by contrast, had a larger staff, but, Ryder noted, 'Neither of them had fleet visits to arrange.'[29]

Ryder had been living in a hotel, but once Hilaré and the children had arrived in Oslo, they moved into more permanent accommodation. They rented a house in Bestun which had belonged to a collaborationist politician but had been requisitioned by the Norwegian government after the war. Externally, it was a modest brick house with shutters and a tiled roof. Internally, it was rather grander, boasting a fine marble fireplace, gilt chairs and tapestries on the drawing room walls. 'It was a strange house for Norway', Ryder remembered, 'more like a Parisian Salon, but it suited well.' For weekends they rented a *hytte*, a wooden chalet with a turf roof, on the edge of a lake in a forest about 40 miles outside Oslo. It was an idyllic spot. 'After a lot of diplomatic parties it was wonderfully invigorating to get away into the freshness of the mountain air'. In the winter there was skiing, in the summer sunbathing. 'We drink the lake water and cook on a dear little range', wrote Hilaré. 'The children adore it as you can imagine.'[30]

It was a happy interlude for the family. They were away from the gloom of post-war Britain. Food was rationed in Norway – as in Britain – but as diplomats the Ryders were entitled to a double allowance. More importantly, Hilaré had for the first time a worthwhile role in helping Ryder in his job. Ryder, in turn, felt that he was now living his own life and was pleased to have been able to allow Hilaré to escape from Lovel Hill and her parents. And there was much for Hilaré to do. For one naval visit the Ryders gave a big cocktail party, which, Hilaré told a friend, 'involves a good deal of preparation as Norwegians expect plenty to eat and always stay a full 2 hours.' She and her sister made '600 eats for our 150 guests and it all disappeared, not to mention 4 vast iced cakes!' In May 1948 Churchill visited Norway, which 'kept us horribly busy on a very grand scale.'[31]

On 30 June 1948 Ryder was promoted Captain. This was something of a surprise as he had been told that taking the Oslo job would hinder his promotion prospects. He had nevertheless taken it in the hope that it might lead to a more permanent berth in naval intelligence. For others, it was long overdue. One newspaper announced that Ryder's promotion 'will appear to many a belated recognition of one of the most remarkable episodes of the war.' Belated or not, it did mean that his spell as Naval Attaché, a commander's appointment, would soon come to an end, but the Ambassador, Sir Lawrence Collier, obtained for him a temporary extension.

However, by now Ryder was beginning to consider his future. In the 1930s Ryder had looked askance at the prospect of prolonged service in the peacetime Navy, but had, to a large extent, managed to plough his own furrow. Now, with the war over, the same worries returned, 'I can see so clearly now why I just can't stomach the peacetime navy', he wrote a month after the war had ended.[32] But he needed something else to do, a new challenge.

'In a foreign embassy one is in a unique position to see one's own country in perspective', he wrote years later. He noticed that Britain was no longer so greatly admired by foreigners, 'Within an incredibly short time from "Our Finest Hour" we were rapidly falling from grace.' To a man as intensely patriotic as Ryder this was deeply unpalatable. Brooding on the problem, it seemed to him that the Labour government elected so sweepingly in 1945 was the root cause of the decline. 'It seemed to me that we should try and get Churchill back', Ryder wrote. Enid Coulson, his secretary in Oslo, maintained that Ryder's 'taste of the diplomatic life whetted his appetite for politics – as he said, the battle for peace was now in the hands of the politicians.' He duly began to look for a seat to contest as a Conservative candidate.[33]

This was not, in fact, the first time that Ryder had considered a career in politics. In early 1945, while Ryder was away at sea, Hilaré had been asked to put his name forward as Conservative candidate for the constituency of Slough and Eton. It was a decision which she had to take without being able to consult Ryder directly, but, as her letters clearly show, she was under no illusions about his political ambitions. 'I know that you are in two minds about a political career. As I see it you would probably dislike the electioneering with all its publicity but find the life as a member very interesting and worthwhile.' But she could see that 'Your shyness is the great bar, and might make it a miserable life for you.'[34] Ryder himself also harboured other doubts about a political career. He was worried about the financial difficulties that election to Parliament might pose and also about how life as an MP could coexist with his naval career. In the end his name was withdrawn.

By 1948, however, things were different. This time, encouraged by Churchill, perhaps during his visit to Oslo, Ryder was determined to carry it through. Financially, too, Ryder's position had improved since 1945. Once he passed his fortieth birthday – in February 1948 – he was entitled to retire on half-pay, which, of course, increased on his promotion in June. As he explained to his father-in-law in January 1949, being elected to Parliament would make little difference to the family's income. His naval pay was £1,500 a year which, with Hilaré's £300 produced a total income of £1,800. As an MP he would draw £1,000 a year and with his naval pension of £450 and Hilaré's £300 would amount to roughly the same. 'In addition, I hope to get some part-time job like most MPs or else write.'[35] Hilaré, however, was less sanguine about the financial consequences of becoming an MP. '[W]e shall', she told a friend at the same time, 'be pretty badly off if he does get into Parliament. £1,000 a year is a good deal less than his present pay and his expenses will be much greater, especially as he will have to have a room in London.'[36]

Ryder was soon travelling back and forth between Oslo and London – 'thumbing lifts in various aeroplanes', as he put it – to attend interviews at Central Office and with constituency selection committees. He was offered a place on the shortlist at Chertsey, a safe Conservative seat, but declined it because it would have involved ousting the sitting Member, a brother naval officer. He was then offered Merton and Morden, his name to go forward for adoption on its own.

Chapter 15

The House of Commons (1950–55)

On 25 January 1949 Robert Ryder was formally adopted as Conservative candidate for the new constituency of Merton and Morden in south-west London. The adoption meeting, which took place in Merton Public Hall, was attended by members of the local Conservative Association who ratified the decision made the previous month to select Ryder to contest the seat. He had travelled from Oslo to attend the meeting but had been nervous beforehand. 'It will be rather an awe-inspiring business as I will be speaking to some 250 people and the local press will probably report my speech. So I have to mind my P&Qs.'[1]

Ryder's speech to the meeting set out his solidly conservative, anti-socialist principles. 'I am not interested', he said

in any policy which sets itself the task of levelling people down to a common level. I am much more interested in seeing that everyone gets a chance of rising up in his profession.

Warming to his theme, he added,

This is not a policy to make the rich richer or the poor poorer, nor is it a defence of privilege. This is a policy of opportunity for all who wish it, and promotion by merit.[2]

Merton and Morden, which had been created by splitting the old Wimbledon division, was thought likely to be a Labour-supporting constituency. It included the St Helier housing estate, the largest of the London County Council's pre-war slum-clearance schemes, 'very red', as Ryder described it. Indeed, Arthur Palmer, who had sensationally won Wimbledon itself for Labour in the 1945 landslide, had chosen to fight the new division as he considered it had constituted his power base within the old Wimbledon seat. His theory was partly confirmed at the 1950 election when the Conservative candidate won the rump of the Wimbledon constituency with a huge majority. Conservative Central Office told Ryder that he had a 50:50 chance of victory. Certainly, he would have a fight on his hands, 'Merton and Morden is of course far from being a safe seat.' He reckoned that as the floating vote would be important, perhaps decisive, 'a great deal depends on how one puts one's case across and how the pendulum swings.'[3]

Once the adoption meeting was over, Ryder returned to Norway. At that time as there were a number of serving officers sitting in the House of Commons, the Admiralty was content to allow Ryder to continue in his post. The Foreign Office, however, was not, so Ryder was replaced as Naval Attaché. 'This brought to an end a most interesting and happy period of my life', he wrote later. He, Hilaré and the children returned to England in the spring of 1949. Ryder was appointed by the Admiralty to a course at Greenwich which allowed him to nurse his constituency at weekends.

Once back in England, Ryder and Hilaré threw themselves wholeheartedly into political life in the constituency. We 'shall spend the week-ends at bazaars and whist drives when Bob isn't speaking at meetings', Hilaré predicted. 'Bob is in tremendous form and really heart and soul in the job', she told a friend. 'He is filled with a crusading spirit and prepared to do anything, even kissing babies!' Ryder's obvious sincerity and conviction made a favourable impression in the constituency.[4] There is a photograph of the Ryders at the constituency 1949 summer fete. They are standing with the constituency chairman and his wife at a trestle table draped in the Union Jack and hung with bunting, Hilaré in a floral summer dress and hat, Ryder in a suit and tie, looking every inch the dutiful, aspiring, political couple. Also there, no doubt drumming up support for Ryder's cause, was Brendan Bracken, wartime Minister of Information, confidante of Churchill and then MP for Bournemouth East and Christchurch.

With the Labour government now in the final year of its term, everyone knew that there would have to be an election within twelve months. As always, the question was, when, precisely? And, as always, the answer lay with the Prime Minister. Clement Attlee announced on 10 January 1950 that the nation would go to the polls on 23 February. It was to be the first winter election since 1910.

'The election itself was very exciting', Ryder remembered. The months he had spent in the constituency addressing public meetings, attending fetes, visiting hospitals and so on had not been wasted. Most importantly, he had improved his public speaking, teaching himself to cope with hecklers and other tricks of the politician's trade. On 11 February the candidates handed in their nomination papers at the town hall: Ryder, dapper and fit-looking, for the Conservatives; Arthur Palmer, slight and donnish, for Labour; and Roy Douglas, tweedily earnest, for the Liberals. Ryder used the occasion to clarify the future of his naval career. Hitherto, serving officers had been permitted to sit as MPs but now the rules had changed. 'If I get in, I get out', he said.

> Mr AV Alexander [Defence Secretary] has been very fair. He agreed that Naval personnel may be nominated as candidates, but if they are elected they must at once retire from the Royal Navy. Thus if I am elected as the first MP for Merton and Morden Division, my Naval career is at an end.[5]

Ryder campaigned vigorously, Hilaré at his side, touring the constituency in an old military jeep and clad in a duffle coat addressing voters through a megaphone. His election literature was characteristically self-effacing, 'Having to advertise myself in this way is most distasteful but I am told that it is necessary.' It makes no mention of any of the specifics of his war record, let alone his VC, a far cry from the self-aggrandizing, slick campaigns of modern politics. Ryder's low-key, modest approach to campaigning did not however mean that he ducked the political issues of the day. He entered the debate about food subsidies and rationing, both emotive topics at the time. He was clearly opposed to the Socialist policy of public ownership, which had formed such an important plank of the Attlee government's policy. 'Nationalization has fallen on bad days and the people of this country no longer want it.'[6] He was in favour of reducing taxation. In the years after the war housing was a pressing problem, and, according to Ryder, the most important element of any government's social policy. 'I am not at all satisfied that the Socialist government has tackled this correctly or with the necessary drive.' But most of all, he was his own man, 'not a mere mouthpiece of some party caucus', who supported Conservative policy 'in a spirit of sincerity and conviction'.

After the polls closed on 23 February Ryder and his opponents attended the count at the Merton Public Hall. There had been a high turnout of eighty-eight per cent from an electorate of 55,749. Ryder paced around the hall, watching the votes being counted. First the ballot boxes were emptied and the papers bundled into hundreds before being delivered to a long table under the watchful eye of the Returning Officer. Hilaré remembered the candidates examining spoilt ballot papers to see if they disclosed a voting intention. As many of them had scrawled against Ryder's name 'I love you' or 'Our hero', Arthur Palmer had little option but to allow them to be counted.[7]

> Watching the stacks advance along the table in three columns Palmer led off from the beginning with myself way behind about level with the Liberal. Then I began to catch up but it seemed certain that Palmer would win by several thousand votes. The last big bundle was brought along. They were all for me, my pile shot ahead and I won.[8]

The result was declared at 2.45 in the morning. For Ryder it was a triumphant beginning to his political career, although he preferred to think of it as 'a pleasant surprise'. He had won a seat that had at best been regarded before the election as a marginal. He polled 23,928 votes, a majority over Labour of 2,793; the Liberal lost his deposit. He and a beaming Hilaré were photographed surrounded by jubilant supporters after the declaration. Ryder received a congratulatory telegram from Winston Churchill. Lord Woolton, the party chairman, also sent Ryder a telegram. 'Congratulations', it read, 'on your most important success. You had a difficult task. Your hard work and that of your supporters has been well rewarded.'

Ryder's success was symptomatic of the broader picture: Labour did especially badly in London, where its failure to take Merton and Morden was part of a wider decline. Attlee had enjoyed a parliamentary majority of 136 but the election reduced it to a mere five, partly the result of boundary changes and partly the inevitable consequence of improving conditions. The Conservatives had come close to overturning Labour's huge majority won in 1945. They had won 298 seats to Labour's 315. For the Conservatives, it was the start of a new era. The Labour landslide of 1945 had swept away the ten-year-old Parliament elected in 1935, greatly thinning the Tory ranks. The election of 1950 returned a new generation of future luminaries to the Conservative benches. Edward Heath, who scraped home in Bexley by 133 votes, Enoch Powell, Iain Macleod and Reginald Maudling were all elected for the first time in 1950. Another new Conservative Member was Lord Halifax's son, Richard Wood (later created Lord Holderness), who was to become a great friend of Ryder's. Ryder was also joined on the Conservative benches by another VC, Brigadier J.G. Smyth and by the young fighter ace, 'Laddie' Lucas.

On the day that he was elected, Ryder, true to his word, moved on to the Navy's retired list. His active naval career was now over, a poignant moment after twenty-five years of distinguished service. His publisher, Sir John Murray, wrote congratulating him on his election, but added

I suppose that means the end of your naval career which must be rather a wrench – especially considering how distinguished you have made that career, & the visions which your friends have rightly had of your flying an Admiral's flag in future.[9]

His father-in-law, too, had his reservations, 'I think the navy must badly need such a wonderful leader as Bob', he wrote, 'and to me it seems a tragic loss to the country to lose such a man from the profession he has been trained for with such outstanding success ...'[10]

Ryder himself had mixed feelings about leaving the Navy. On the one hand there was the natural sadness at leaving a profession that had nurtured him throughout his adult life. On the other, as we have seen, he did not relish the prospect of the longueurs of peacetime service. He also resented the fact that he had not been promoted captain before the end of the war as he considered that his record would have justified it. Indeed, Rear Admiral Vian had stated in June 1944 that Ryder, 'Should make an admirable Captain'. He was inclined to attribute this lack of promotion to the fact that he had done a good deal of special service and that he had never acquired the patronage of an important admiral. There remain, however, lingering doubts about whether he would have progressed to the upper echelons of the service. In one version, at least, his tendency to flap and his lack of presence would have marked him as unsuitable material for high command.[11]

The new Parliament sat for the first time on 1 March 1950. It met in the chamber of the House of Lords as the repairs to the Commons chamber following wartime bomb damage were not yet complete. The King opened the restored House of Commons on 26 October. Ryder made his maiden speech on 16 March in the debate on the Defence White Paper, speaking for sixteen minutes. Both Enoch Powell and J.G. Smyth also made their maiden speeches in the same debate.

With a notable election success under his belt and an early maiden speech – fellow 'new boy' Edward Heath did not make his maiden speech until 26 June – the auguries for Ryder's political career looked favourable. This early promise was never properly fulfilled. Ryder himself wrote that 'I do not feel that my Parliamentary career calls for much mention. It was not distinguished.' He had enjoyed the excitement of the election and relished being at the centre of the nation's political life but

I soon felt out of my element in the debating chamber. I was outclassed by lifelong politicians … and by barristers trained in debate. Nor had I been to Eton, at that time rather more than just an advantage, nor indeed was I a member of White's nor likely to be.

There was, too, a more fundamental problem – one that Hilaré had so perceptively put her finger on five years previously – that Ryder simply disliked being a public figure. '[A]ll in all, it was not surprising that I made little or no headway.' He was not even asked to be Parliamentary Private Secretary to a minister, the first rung on the ladder for an ambitious MP. According to one friend who knew him at the time, Ryder was 'an appalling speaker in Parliament'.[12] Almost inevitably, he was regarded as an expert on naval affairs and did make some weighty contributions to the debate about the future role of the Royal Navy. As the senior naval Member, he was voted joint-chairman of the 1922 Defence Committee and chairman of its naval sub-committee. He was also elected chairman of the islands sub-committee, which looked out for the interests of places such as Cyprus, Malta and Gibraltar. But beyond naval matters he was not taken seriously.

Ryder may not have made much impact in Parliament, but he was a diligent constituency member as the list of his engagements shows. He threw himself into the multifarious duties expected of an MP. He visited factories and hospitals, spoke at public and private meetings, attended garden parties, lunches, dinners and receptions, opened fetes, and conducted parties of constituents round the Palace of Westminster. Hilaré played her part to the full, representing Ryder at all manner of functions in the constituency. He took up the cudgels on behalf of his constituents, campaigning for an inquiry into the running of London Transport, pressing for the extension to London Underground's Northern Line and for a new bus station at Morden. He asked questions about raising the value of disability pensions for Great War veterans, about compensation for bomb damage and took a keen interest in the progress of the Korean War, which broke out in June 1950.

The Labour government, with its majority greatly reduced, limped on until the autumn of 1951. Parliament was dissolved in the first week of October, with polling day fixed for 25 October. Ryder's diligence at constituency work paid dividends in the campaign. He was opposed once more by Arthur Palmer who had set his stall out within a fortnight of his defeat in February 1950.

> I cannot believe that the forward thinking people of Merton and Morden will be content to accept reactionary Conservative representation in the House of Commons as part of the natural order of things for long ... Merton and Morden's Tory MP has gone in on a minority vote with one of the smallest majorities in Surrey ...[13]

A week before polling day *The Times* reported on the campaign in Merton and Morden. In the 1950 election, the newspaper reported, Surrey went 'uniformly Conservative', but with two seats – one of which was Ryder's – being won on a minority vote. 'The Labour Party view is that they had no business to go that way.' 'The Labour Party headquarters', the newspaper continued,

> are sparing no effort to win back the seat. In addition to Sir Hartley Shawcross, the imported talent includes a selection of the Labour nobility. A couple of peers are also speaking for Captain Ryder, but he is relying largely on personal contact with the electors. As he tours the streets with his 'circus' of helpers, he is encouraged by the fact that Conservative bills are appearing in districts where once it would have been regarded as highly eccentric to display them.[14]

Ryder once again campaigned hard, Hilaré at his side. As he had in the previous election, he toured the constituency in his old jeep, clad in his duffle coat, addressing the crowds through a loudspeaker. His campaign slogan – 'Engage the enemy – and good luck' – had a suitably naval ring to it. He rallied his supporters with a stirring call to arms: 'The Socialist ship is sinking fast. The steep rise in the cost of living, for which they are to blame, will lose them untold votes.' The local evening paper reported on the day before polling that

> The Tories are canvassing hard on the St Helier estate, where Labour has six supporters for every two of theirs. But it is a Tory joke that while the 'old man' is away at work his wife changes the 'Vote for Palmer' poster in her window to 'Vote for Ryder'.[15]

When the result was declared Ryder had polled 26,488 votes to Palmer's 22,086. This time there was no Liberal candidate. He had increased both his share of the vote and his majority, which now stood at 4,402. This was a tremendous result for

Ryder, just reward for all his and Hilaré's hard work in the constituency. Overall, the election returned the Conservatives to power, headed by the ageing Winston Churchill. Ryder's original reason for entering politics – to return Churchill to Downing Street – had been achieved. The Tories won 321 seats to Labour's 295, giving them a majority of seventeen, although Labour polled a marginally greater proportion of the popular vote.

The highlight of Ryder's second term in Parliament was his trip to Canada as a Conservative member of the British delegation to the Commonwealth Parliamentary Association Conference at Ottawa in August and September 1952. The British delegation, led by Lord Llewellin, consisted of eleven Conservative and Labour MPs, including Ryder. One assumes that he was selected because of his wartime association with the Canadians, at Dieppe and later during the build-up to D-Day. On arrival in Canada, the delegates were taken on a tour of the country's eastern provinces, Quebec, Nova Scotia, New Brunswick and Prince Edward Island. The conference's formal proceedings opened in Ottawa on 9 September beneath the splendid Victorian Gothic arches and crenellations of the Canadian Parliament's Senate Chamber. Ryder made a speech about British defence policy, during the course of which he made some trenchant remarks about the status of Northern Ireland (an issue raised by the Irish delegation).[16] Once the conference had closed the delegates were taken on a tour of Canada's western provinces. Ryder and his fellow delegates were

> greatly impressed with the immense industrial development which they saw taking place in Canada. There was no doubt Canada would be a most powerful country in the near future. They were showing immense energy, initiative, enterprise and technical ingenuity in the development of hydro–electric power and mineral resources.[17]

Ryder's trip to Canada brought back to Hilaré memories of his long, worrying absences during the war.

> I feel completely bereft when you are out of touch & far away. I'm fairly used to living alone but it's different when you are just at the other end of a telephone. We really are rather silly about each other but it's nicer that way, isn't it?[18]

Before going to Oslo, the Ryders had bought Castle Farm House, near Windsor. It was the first house that they had owned in their married life, a welcome relief after the endless peregrinations of the war years. Gabled, with low-ceilinged interiors, it had a large garden in which Hilaré toiled tirelessly. They also had the use of a large mansion flat in Ennismore Gardens, South Kensington. This had been bought by Hilaré's father after his wife's death early in 1949 and the subsequent sale of Lovel Hill. He did not live to enjoy his return to London for very long, dying on 27 September 1949. Hilaré had lost both her parents in the same year.

In April 1952, Ryder was co-opted on to the management committee of the Royal National Lifeboat Institution (RNLI). It was a worthy cause which, after his own experiences during the war, was close to Ryder's heart. The RNLI, for its part, was no doubt glad to have a distinguished Naval VC and MP adorning its writing paper. Ryder served on the RNLI's Boat and Construction committee until 1966. He resigned from the committee of management in 1974 after which he was appointed a Life Vice-President of the Institution.[19]

In August 1952 Ryder sent the typescript of a novel, *Coverplan*, to John Murray. Murray declined it but it was published by Allan Wingate in October 1953. Ryder had hoped that he would be able to combine authorship with his parliamentary activities in order to provide much needed extra income. Indeed, much of *Coverplan* was written on the benches of the House of Commons during late night sittings. The initial print-run was 3,000 copies, of which 2,230 had sold by the end of the year.

Coverplan is a gentle thriller about the smuggling of nylon tights set against a background of boats and the sea. It is clearly influenced by Erskine Childers's *The Riddle of the Sands*, a favourite novel of Ryder's youth. It attracted some reviews but made few waves in the national press. *Yachting World* thought that 'Robert Ryder writes with a lightness of touch, an easy style and with a sense of humour.' *Motor Boat & Yachting* was delighted by 'a book which shows inferentially that the best thing in the world is to be afloat.' *The Catholic Herald* had certain reservations: there are 'some patches of dialogue so unreal that one wonders just how well the author got to know the lower deck during his Service career.'[20]

Coverplan may not have achieved the success that Ryder had hoped for but he did receive some encouragement from an unexpected quarter. Ian Fleming, his co-conspirator in AIU during the war, wrote to Ryder in November,

> I think it is splendid that you have found time to write a book and I am certain that it is a good one. I, also, produced a thriller earlier this year, called *Casino Royale*, which did quite well, and I sympathize with you over the pains of authorship.

Fleming may or may not have read *Coverplan* but he did offer Ryder some advice on being a novelist. 'You must write one every year, and then suddenly you will find that you have hit the jackpot.' Ryder attempted to follow this advice; in August 1954 he sent the typescript of a second novel, *Jane*, to Wingate, who declined it.[21]

Money was now becoming a worry for Ryder. *Coverplan* was not the financial success that he had hoped. Although it was reprinted and then published in paperback, he made only about £120 from the book. Although he had been sanguine about the financial consequences of entering Parliament, Hilaré's doubts proved nearer the mark. Ryder had hoped – and Central Office had done nothing to dampen these hopes – that he would find part-time work which could be combined with his parliamentary duties. But nothing suitable had materialized. Hilaré was reduced to taking in paying guests in the Ennismore Gardens flat in order to help make ends meet.

By 1953 MPs' salaries were a subject of frequent discussion. They had been paid £1,000 a year since 1946, but inflation had eroded the value of the salary by about a third by the end of 1953. Moreover, as a committee appointed to inquire into the question found, MPs on average paid £750 a year in expenses incurred in pursuit of their duties. This left £250 to support a family. In Ryder's case, with only his naval pension and Hilaré's small investment income to supplement his parliamentary salary, this was not remotely adequate. Lisle, who was at prep school, was down for Eton, so Ryder had school fees to consider, too. When Lisle went to Eton in January 1956 the fees were £360 a year, by the time he left in 1961 they were £490. With Susan's education also to provide for, let alone his and Hilaré's daily needs, continuing as an MP was clearly unsustainable.[22]

The impossibility of supporting a family on an MP's salary and Ryder's failure to make his mark in the Commons made his decision to leave Parliament almost inevitable. On 10 November 1953 he announced his decision to the Merton and Morden Conservative Association. He felt that the country's position had improved greatly since the Conservatives had been returned to power in 1951, 'The country is now well led and well set on the right course. I feel, therefore, that the time has come when I must take some thought for my family and the means whereby I can support them.'[23]

It was a dispiriting end to a political career which had promised much. Ryder's successes in the elections of 1950 and 1951 were noteworthy, demonstrating that, despite his shy, retiring nature, he was an effective campaigner. He was a diligent and popular MP, 'Here, people will be very sorry to see Captain Ryder go', his successor said. The local newspaper wrote in a valedictory article that during the 1951 election Ryder had 'received a hero's welcome wherever he went. Captain Ryder's decision to retire is bound to lose the Conservatives some prestige.' Hilaré was offered the candidacy in succession to Ryder - a resounding vote of confidence in her abilities - but she declined it.

Labour's new prospective candidate, Bob Edwards, rather gracelessly demanded that Ryder depart at once, precipitating a by-election. This he declined to do. His successor was Humphrey Atkins, who was to reach Cabinet rank – and the peerage – under Mrs Thatcher. He too had served in the Royal Navy during the war as a young lieutenant and joked to the Conservative Association during the hand-over period that

I have the utmost difficulty, when talking to your present Member of Parliament, in restraining myself from standing stiffly to attention, saluting and calling him 'Sir'.[24]

Ryder stepped down as MP for Merton and Morden in April 1955.

Epilogue

Ryder was only forty-seven years old when he left Parliament, extremely fit and widely respected, even revered. Nevertheless, writing about his life in old age, he recorded that 'I do not think that the rest of my life will be of much if any lasting interest.' To say that he was haunted by a sense of failure would be too strong. Nevertheless, he was undoubtedly acutely aware that the rest of his life fell short of his wartime achievements and the ambition of the early adventures. Things were never quite the same again. His daughter, for one, is convinced of it. But even allowing for Ryder's highly-developed sense of self-effacement, this might at the time have seemed an unduly pessimistic view of the future. He was a national hero as a result of St Nazaire, with an enviable war record and many an adventure to his credit. He was still youngish, had been twice elected to Parliament and was very happily married. But he had now reached a critical point in his life. He had forsaken his chosen career, in which he had served with such distinction, for politics, a change which had not proved a success. It is tempting to conclude that leaving Parliament was the watershed in Ryder's life.

It is more accurate, however, to see the war as the important fault line in Ryder's life, as for so many other men of his generation. The factors, personal and financial, which compelled him to leave Parliament without having made his mark were already present before he was elected. Hilaré had seen them clearly. It was the war that changed Ryder's life. In 1939 he was thirty-one, serving rather reluctantly – and only for the sake of his future naval career – in *Warspite*. He had spent four of the previous six years away from general service in his own small commands in far-flung parts of the world. He was a man who thrived on adventure. Furthermore, there was every prospect that Ryder would soon have been off again, as Colin Bertram had offered him the command of his expedition's ship. Once the war came, however, there was no doubt in Ryder's mind where his duty lay.

In many respects, the war made Ryder but it changed his life, too. He had lost many of his best friends and seen countless horrors. The strain it imposed exhausted him and at its end he became seriously ill. By 1945 Ryder was thirty-seven, a married man (and glad to be) with two children. He now had a family to support; his days as a Polar explorer were over. He was no longer the carefree adventurer of the 1930s, domestic bliss and the peaceful joys of home now had greater appeal.

In 2010 his daughter Susan Bates retraced his travels with the BGLE in the Antarctic. She found the experience moving and revealing. She had always regarded her father as a self-centred man, particularly in the way that he indulged his passion for sailing when he knew that Hilaré was at best only lukewarm about it. The trip to Antarctica provoked a change of heart. Here, in the wild polar wastes, she recognized that perhaps he had forsaken much for Hilaré: he 'gave up his sense of adventure for her.' 'He didn't go off, as other explorers do, for months on end, leaving their wives at home.' Seen in that light, having 'a small boat, with an engine, nosing in and out of Brittany harbours with the family' was indeed a sacrifice. Certainly, for a man used to the excitements of life on a *Tai-Mo-Shan* or a *Penola* it was tame stuff.[1]

Although Ryder was prepared to write off the last thirty years of his life in one, dismissive, self-disparaging sentence, he did not descend into a long period of dull decline. Far from it. The first problem he had to resolve was the lack of income that had forced him from Parliament. In March 1955 the John Lewis Partnership advertized two senior vacancies, one for Managing Director, at a starting salary of £5,000 a year, with the promise of annual rises of £1,000 to a minimum of £10,000. In the mid-1950s, this was a very substantial sum. Not surprisingly, there were nearly 700 applications but nevertheless Ryder was appointed to the post.[2] He started his period of training in July 1955. It seemed to be the answer to his prayers: a steady job with a salary five times the size of his MP's stipend, and rising, without the concomitant expenses. However, he was a fish out of water, 'I was not cut out for a life-long career in the Drapery Trade of Oxford Street.' In January 1959 he resigned, after only three years.

After the John Lewis debacle Ryder's morale was at a low ebb, so, characteristically, he and Hilaré went sailing in the Baltic for three months. Back in London, with his spirits restored, he cast around for ways to earn a living before settling on opening a newsagency. By 1961 the business, Robert & Co., had four leasehold shops in west London. In that year he was joined by Duncan Beardmore Gray, a young accountant. Together they expanded the business, adding six further shops, taking the annual turnover to £500,000. However, dishonesty among the managers was a constant problem so when, in 1965, they were made an offer for the shops which doubled their capital, they accepted with alacrity.[3] Ryder had always felt that it was a demeaning, rather sordid line of business, 'selling porn and cigarettes' as he put it.

Demeaning it may have been, but it did make Ryder a handsome profit of about £55,000. With this money in the bank, he and Hilaré were able to retire. In 1964 they bought the Old Rectory at Wolferton in Norfolk for £7,500. The house came with a lodge which they sold on for £2,000. Wolferton lies in the midst of the Sandringham estate, protected by the enfolding beneficence of the Royal patrimony. The Old Rectory is an attractive, handsomely-proportioned early Victorian house of local carstone and mellow brick with elegant bays and good-sized rooms. Nestling in trees, the house looks out over the Wash, to fine sunsets under wide skies.

The Ryders lived there very happily until 1977. Ryder and Hilaré had been acquainted with the Queen (or Princess Elizabeth, as she then was) since the war when they had lived periodically in Windsor Castle. They were now occasionally invited to shoot at Sandringham, as Ryder told his sister.

> Great fun really but of course I am terribly out of practice but it didn't seem to matter very much. Fortunately I didn't pepper Prince Charles or anything like that & Prince Philip was warned that I was a bad shot.

Shortly before, he continued, he and Hilaré had been invited to dinner at Sandringham,

> I sat on the Queen's left with the Queen Mother on my other side so I had a Queen each side and Hilare next to Pr. Philip. All very alarming ...[4]

But it was sailing and the sea that dominated Ryder's later life – and that of his family – as they had his earlier years. In 1952 Ryder bought *Foresight*, a 45 foot converted, Scottish herring drifter, cruising in her almost·every summer until he sold her in 1969. In the earlier years she cruised mainly in home and French waters. After their long trip in the summer of 1959, the Baltic became the Ryders' favourite cruising ground. They were usually accompanied by friends and other members of the family. Ryder was, of course, a vastly experienced sailor. Aboard he was intensely practical; he loved working on his boats, scrubbing, painting, polishing, and repairing as well as the never-ending task of correcting his charts. He was also very frugal, a trait no doubt ingrained by his experiences on *Tai-Mo-Shan* and *Penola*. Anything brought on board, he decreed, had to have two uses; the boat's water supply was strictly rationed, hair-washing greatly discouraged.

In 1970 Ryder took delivery of *Millfleet*, a 36 foot, Dutch-built sailing cruiser. She was handier than *Foresight*, more seaworthy as well as being cheaper and easier to maintain. In the seven years between 1970 and 1976, Ryder was at sea for at least twelve weeks each summer. In 1971 he and Hilaré cruised off the west coast of Ireland; in the summer of 1973 Ryder took *Millfleet* from England to Corfu, a trip of more than sixteen weeks. For the next two summers they sailed in the Mediterranean. In 1977 Ryder suffered two heart attacks, whereupon, thinking his sailing days to be over, he sold *Millfleet*. However, he soon recovered his strength and promptly acquired another boat, *Watchdog of Wareham*. The call of the sea was too strong to be ignored.

Meanwhile, Ryder's family was growing up. Lisle, having finished Eton, followed his father into the Navy. Hardly surprisingly, he found it difficult to live up to his father's stellar reputation and did not prosper. However, during his brief spell in the service, Lisle discovered his vocation and left to train as a priest. He has now retired as a Canon of Worcester Cathedral.

Susan showed early promise as an artist, winning her first art prize at the age of five. Ryder, a self-taught but accomplished artist himself, did much to encourage her. Ryder used to take Susan to the Natural History Museum where they would draw stuffed creatures together. He persuaded her to go to art school at the Byam Shaw when all her friends were doing secretarial courses by asking, 'If you are forty and unmarried, would you rather be an artist or a secretary?' Susan's great break came when, in 1981, she was commissioned by the Prince of Wales to paint Princess Diana in her wedding dress. She has since developed a highly successful practice as a portraitist and painter.[5]

Ryder was devoted to his children and was, by all accounts, a wonderful father, 'very hands-on', strict but scrupulously fair. When they were younger, he was a patient teacher who instilled in both of them a love of the sea. Lisle remembers particularly how good his father was at teaching him seamanship and navigation. As they grew up they spent many a memorable holiday together on the boat, although Ryder expected them, once they were older, to shoulder their fair share of the work that sailing boats involve. During the 1950s, the Ryders took the children ski-ing in alternate years. In January 1953 they had a very lucky escape when the second of two coaches taking visitors up to Lech from the railhead was swept away by an avalanche. Everyone on board was killed. The Ryders had boarded the second coach but changed to the front coach when, at the last minute, spare seats were found on it. As money was always tight, most of these family holidays were conducted on a shoestring: the children slept on the luggage racks in the trains; Hilaré would heat up tins of soup on an up-turned iron.[6]

In 1965 Susan married Martin Bates. Characteristically, Ryder offered her and Martin £500 to elope in order to spare him the expense and social anguish of a wedding. The money was to compensate them for the wedding presents which they would thereby forfeit. It was declined. In due course, grandchildren appeared: Oliver (born 1969) and Susannah (1970), on whom Ryder doted. Lisle married Olivia Langton in 1977, giving Ryder further grandchildren, Harriet (born 1980) and Philip (1982).

But it was his marriage to Hilaré that was the keystone of Ryder's life, an almost perfect match of opposites. Ryder was an intensely private man, happiest in the company of his family: his brother-in-law said of him 'that left to his own devices he wouldn't have seen anybody', while another old friend described him as 'very anti-social', 'at parties he would hide in the corner.' Hilaré, by contrast, was gregarious, the life and soul of a party. One friend who knew them in later life remarked that they had 'A marvellous marriage ... they were good to each other.' Ryder to an extent surprising in so retiring a man, wore his heart on his sleeve far more obviously than the more outgoing Hilaré. Their daughter believes that her mother encouraged her father's self-centred nature by spoiling him. He would be upset if she did not enjoy something with the result that she spent a good deal of time playing up to him. She concluded that 'they had very little in common but loved each other deeply.'[7]

Ryder may have been ill at ease in society – despite having dined with queens – but he was devoted to his family and loved children, with whom he had great empathy, and dogs, especially springer spaniels. He was a great tease and practical joker. His granddaughter remembers him as a 'happy, hands-on grandfather, involved in a very positive way.' Ryder's late-flowering devotion to springers began while he and Hilaré were living in Norfolk in the late 1960s. He had one called Brutus and another Max, whom he trained for picking-up out shooting, a pastime he enjoyed rather more than the shooting itself. He was fond of dressing the dogs up for family occasions such as Christmas. His nephew Francis Peel recalls Ryder being 'very mischievous' with a 'boyish sense of fun lurking beneath the reserved exterior of the old-school naval captain.[8]

Ryder was a stocky, trim, muscular man of barely medium height, with a distinct, bouncing gait, the product perhaps of the years spent at sea. Square-jawed with a pronounced chin, his eyes were slightly hooded as if keeping watch on distant horizons against the glare of sun on sea. He kept himself in shape to the end of his life. A journalist who interviewed him at the age of seventy-five reported that 'he walks with the snap and bearing of a 50-year-old.' The wife of a sailing friend remembers admiringly that 'his upper arm was like a piece of oak.' His granddaughter recalls him doing hand-stands well into his sixties and has an indelible memory of his 'gnarled, weather-beaten hands'.[9]

He was both an immensely practical man, who loved nothing more than working on his boats, and an artist. On one occasion he reroofed an entire barn for his daughter and son-in-law, 'a massive undertaking'. He had been drawing since his schooldays and became an accomplished, self-taught painter. Ryder began painting in oils on a family holiday to the Costa Brava in 1952. As one might expect, he was at his strongest artistically in his depictions of the sea in all her many moods and painted many friends' boats. He was at heart 'a great romantic' who, according to his granddaughter, saw himself as the reincarnation of Carruthers, the hero of *The Riddle of the Sands*, an idealist devoid of materialistic impulses, who loved the English countryside and the natural world. His Christian faith was 'one of the lynch-pins of his life ... simple, undemonstrative and firm.' He served as churchwarden at Wolferton between 1965 and 1977, despite his habit of fleeing immediately after the end of the service to avoid churchyard chit-chat.[10]

In 1977 he and Hilaré moved from Norfolk to the village of Inkpen near Newbury. Sadly, it was not long before Hilaré was diagnosed with breast cancer but several operations and treatments failed to stem the advance of the disease. Ryder found it impossible to accept that his adored wife was terminally ill; that was not how he wanted to remember her but he was nevertheless with her at the end. Hilaré died on 19 September 1982, aged only sixty-four. For Ryder it was terrible blow – 'it was as if more than half his life was wrenched away' – one he faced with great courage although characteristically, 'he wouldn't show it.'[11]

Four years later, on 28 June 1986, Ryder left Wareham in *Watchdog* for a ten-day cruise along the coast of Brittany. He was accompanied by two other retired naval officers, John Marriott and Patrick Glennie. In the morning, after an anxious night caused by bad visibility while crossing the Channel, the weather deteriorated with a strengthening wind, rain, thunder and lightning. At 0645, at which point *Watchdog* was about 25 miles south-west of Guernsey and 15 miles off the French coast, Ryder went forward to secure the boat's rubber dinghy. This done he returned to the wheelhouse and having sat down to remove his safety harness suddenly pitched forward on to the deck. He had died instantaneously.

* * *

The tributes to Ryder were fulsome and admiring; both *The Times* and *The Telegraph* published obituaries. Ryder's funeral took place at St Michael's, Inkpen, on 10 July 1986, after which his body was cremated at Oxford. A memorial service was held at Holy Trinity Church, Prince Consort Road, South Kensington, on 2 October. The address at the service was delivered by Launcelot Fleming, formerly Bishop of Norwich, Ryder's old friend from the BGLE in the 1930s. Fleming was aware of the need to 'kerb any tendency to eulogy or extravagant praise which would have been anathema to Bob Ryder'. Noting that he was 'not only a supremely humble man, but in certain respects a very private one', Fleming thought it difficult to 'touch on those inner motives which shaped his life and his outlook'. He did, however, draw the congregation's attention to Ryder's 'enterprising and adventurous' nature and his 'rigorous self-discipline, ... strong sense of duty, ... resolution and great courage.' His friends, Fleming said, 'would testify to his straightforward integrity and honesty – and his single mindedness' as well as to his utter humility.

Outside the porch of St Peter's, Wolferton, overlooking the well-tended churchyard, is a bench, a gift of the St Nazaire Society, Ryder's comrades-in-arms. On it is a small plaque which reads:

> To the memory of Captain Robert Ryder, VC, RN.
> A skilled and daring seaman
> A true leader and a Christian Gentleman
> Churchwarden 1965–1977.

But the last word should go to Philip Francis, Ryder's shipmate and great friend on *Tai-Mo-Shan*, with whom he had shared so many adventures more than half a century earlier. Francis had pasted a cutting of Ryder's obituary into his scrapbook and next to it, under the heading 'Two friends I'll miss', he wrote:

> Red was short and stocky, modest and a man of few words. He was brave and very determined. A true leader. The sort of person to have with one in a tight corner.

Postscript

On Friday, 18 July 1986, three weeks after Ryder's death, Mr B.E. de Carteret visited the marina at St Peter Port, Guernsey, to inspect *Watchdog of Wareham* before taking her back across the Channel to her permanent berth. De Carteret found *Watchdog*, as one would have expected, 'in very good seamanlike order'. Early the following morning he set off in *Watchdog* bound for Wareham. After a short first leg to Alderney, where the fuel, engine oil and water were checked, de Carteret continued his passage to England, departing at 1100. The weather was fine and clear but a light north-westerly wind obliged *Watchdog* to motor the whole distance from Guernsey to the south coast of England.

By 1720 *Watchdog* was well within sight of the Dorset coast and the Isle of Wight. At this point de Carteret noticed a smell of burning and almost at once black smoke began to pour out from under the starboardside seat in the wheelhouse, followed by flames. De Carteret immediately turned off the engine and radioed to the Portland Coastguard. As the Coastguard was replying, the fire increased to such an intensity that de Carteret was forced to retreat from the wheelhouse. Having made a 'Mayday' call he attempted to launch the boat's life-raft. Suddenly there was an explosion in the wheelhouse, nearly knocking him off his feet. At this point he jumped over the side.

De Carteret was rescued by a passing yacht, *Sexy Knickers* – a name that would have amused and appalled Ryder in equal measure – after about ten or fifteen minutes minutes in the water. *Watchdog* burned fiercely until she sank. So a story that began with a burning vessel sinking comes full circle. It was as if *Watchdog of Wareham* was determined to avoid serving another master. Self-immolation was preferable to life without her skipper, the old naval hero.

Notes

Chapter 1: Family and Childhood: India and England
 1. Burke's *Peerage & Baronetage*, 105th edition, 1975.
 2. *The Times*, 16 July 1945.
 3. CHDR, letter, 23 Nov 1914.
 4. CHDR, letter, 27 April 1916.
 5. CHDR, letter, 19 July 1916.
 6. Sophie Darlington, letter, 26 Oct 1919.
 7. CHDR, letter, 25 June 1919.
 8. CHDR, letter, 21 Aug 1920.
 9. CHDR, MS note, 23 June 1923.
10. REDR, letter, n.d. [prob. 1922].
11. REDR, TS memoirs.
12. REDR, TS memoirs and J.W. Mercer, letter, 23 Dec 1925.
13. REDR, TS memoirs.

Chapter 2: Into the Navy (1926–31)
 1. REDR, letter, 16 Jan 1926.
 2. Admiral Phillimore, letter, 23 Aug 1926.
 3. The account that follows of Ryder's time as a Midshipman in *Ramillies*, etc. draws on the two volumes of his Midshipman's Logs.
 4. REDR, letter, 4 Dec 1927.
 5. REDR, letter, 14 Dec 1927.
 6. REDR, letter, 2 Jan 1928.
 7. REDR, letter, 23 Jan 1928.
 8. REDR, letter, 2 April 1928.
 9. REDR, TS memoirs.
10. REDR, letter, 7 July 1928.
11. REDR, letter, 14 Oct 1928.
12. REDR, TS memoirs.
13. REDR, TS memoirs.
14. P. Heaton, *Yachting: A History*, London, 1955, pp. 222–8.
15. REDR MS account of the 1929 races.
16. REDR, letter, 5 Sept 1929.
17. REDR, Letter, 31 Oct 1929.
18. REDR MS account of race and letter, 14 Aug 1930.
19. Heaton, op. cit.
20. REDR, letter, 1 Sept 1930.
21. REDR, TS memoirs.
22. REDR, letter, 29 Dec 1930.
23. REDR, letter, 1 Sept 1930.

Chapter 3: Hong Kong and the China Station (1931–33)
 1. REDR, letter, 29 Dec 1930.
 2. REDR, letter, 11 Jan 1931.
 3. REDR, letter, 8 Feb 1931.
 4. REDR, letter, 14 March 1931.

5. REDR, letter, 21 April 1931.
6. REDR, letter, 13 May 1931.
7. REDR, letter, 12 June 1931.
8. REDR, letter, 12 June 1931.
9. REDR, TS memoirs.
10. REDR, letters, 25 June and 17 Oct 1931.
11. REDR, letter, 7 Oct 1931.
12. REDR, letter, 30 Dec 1931.
13. REDR, letter, 15 Oct 1931.
14. REDR, TS memoirs.
15. *The Times*, 25 Aug 2007 and *Classic Boat*, Sept 2007.
16. REDR, TS memoirs.
17. REDR, letter, 17 Oct 1931.
18. Copy letters, H.R. Marrack, 18 Nov 1931 and Sir Howard Kelly, 2 Dec 1931, Ryder papers.
19. REDR, letter, 5 Dec 1931.
20. REDR, letter, 1 Feb 1932 and *Tai-Mo-Shan* TS diary, 28 March 1932.
21. *Tai-Mo-Shan* TS diary, 27 Jan 1932.
22. REDR, letter, 16 Jan 1932.
23. *Tai-Mo-Shan* TS diary, 2 April 1932 and REDR TS memoirs.
24. *Tai-Mo-Shan* TS diary, 2 and 5 April 1932; REDR, letter, 20 May 1932.
25. M. Sherwood, *The Voyage of the Tai-Mo-Shan*, London, 1942, pp. 7–8.
26. *Tai-Mo-Shan* TS diary, 9 Nov 1932; P. Francis, letter, 5 May 1932, Ryder papers.
27. Sherwood, *op. cit.*, p. 13.
28. REDR, letter, 7 July 1932.
29. *Tai-Mo-Shan* TS diary, 17 June, 10 Oct and 30 Nov 1932.
30. *Tai-Mo-Shan* TS diary, 17 and 25 Jan 1933.
31. *Tai-Mo-Shan* TS diary, 17 March 1933.
32. *Tai-Mo-Shan* TS diary, 28 April 1933.
33. *Tai-Mo-Shan* TS diary, 25 Oct 1932 and 16 Feb 1933.
34. REDR, letter, 7 Jan 1933.
35. *Tai-Mo-Shan* TS diary, 23 Nov 1931.
36. REDR, letter, 18 March 1933; *Tai-Mo-Shan* TS diary, 23 May 1933; Mrs Bridget Lamb to the author, Jan 2010.
37. *Tai-Mo-Shan* TS diary, 26 May 1933.
38. *Tai-Mo-Shan* TS diary, 26 May 1933.
39. *Tai-Mo-Shan* TS diary, 2 April 1932; REDR, TS memoirs; *ODNB*.
40. *Tai-Mo-Shan* TS diary, 17 and 25 Jan 1933.
41. *Tai-Mo-Shan* TS diary, 23, 29 and 30 May 1933.

Chapter 4: The Voyage of the *Tai-Mo-Shan* (1933–34): Japan, the North Pacific and the United States

1. *Classic Boat*, Sept 2007.
2. To avoid an unnecessary proliferation of endnotes, henceforth all quotations and information cited relating to the voyage of the *Tai-Mo-Shan* may be assumed to be drawn from Ryder's *Tai-Mo-Shan* TS diary unless otherwise stated.
3. REDR, TS memoirs.
4. *The Times*, 9 July 1944.
5. Sherwood, *op. cit.*, p. 41.
6. *Ibid.* p. 66.
7. REDR, letter, 7 Aug 1933.
8. Sherwood, *op. cit.*, p. 69.
9. *Ibid.*, p. 85.
10. *Ibid.*, p. 93.
11. REDR, letter, 16 Sept 1933.
12. *Ibid.*
13. *San Francisco Examiner*, 8 Oct 1933; Sherwood, *op. cit.*, p. 95.
14. Letter, possibly from P. Francis, 14 Oct 1933.
15. REDR, letter, 20 Oct 1933.
16. *Ibid.*

17. *Los Angeles Examiner* and *Los Angeles Times*, both 23 Oct 1933.
18. REDR, letter, 26 Oct 1933.
19. REDR, letter, 7 Nov 1933.
20. REDR, TS memoirs.

Chapter 5: The Voyage of the Tai-Mo-Shan (1933–34): Central America, the West Indies and Home
 1. Sherwood, *op. cit.*, p. 121.
 2. *Ibid.*, p. 123; REDR, TS memoirs.
 3. REDR, letter, 30 Nov 1933.
 4. Sherwood, *op. cit.*, p. 137.
 5. REDR, letter, 19 Dec 1933.
 6. *Ibid.*
 7. *Ibid.*
 8. *The Times*, 4 May 1935.
 9. REDR, letters, 7 Nov 1933 and 7 Jan 1934.
10. REDR, letter, 12 and 21 Feb 1934.
11. *Ibid.*
12. Sherwood, *op. cit.*, pp. 183 and 195.
13. REDR, letter, 11 March 1934.
14. Sherwood, *op. cit.*, p. 167.
15. *Ibid.*, p. 203.
16. *Ibid.*, p. 204.
17. REDR, letters, 5 and 10 April 1934.
18. REDR, letters, 25 April and 29 March.
19. REDR, letter, 16 Sept 1933.
20. REDR, letter, 21 April 1934.
21. *Ibid.*
22. Lady Drax, letter, 31 May 1934.
23. *The Times*, 9 July 1944.

Chapter 6: The Voyage of the *Penola* and the British Graham Land Expedition (1934–37): The First Year
 1. *Penola* MS diary, 5 Aug 1934. In the chapters about the BGLE, all quotations are from Ryder's contemporary diary unless otherwise stated.
 2. Obituary by Q. Riley, quoted in *Antarctica Sixty Years Ago: We the Obligate Pinnipedophagi*, by Colin Bertram in *Polar Record*, Vol. 32, No. 181, April 1996, p. 167.
 3. J. Rymill, *Southern Lights*, London, 1938, pp. 23–5.
 4. REDR, TS memoirs.
 5. Bertram, *op. cit.*, p. 101.
 6. REDR, TS memoirs.
 7. REDR, TS memoirs.
 8. Quoted in Bertram, *op. cit.*, p. 177.
 9. *Ibid.*
10. REDR, TS memoirs.
11. *Ibid.*; quoted in Bertram, *op. cit.*, p. 169.
12. Colin Bertram obit., *Daily Telegraph*, 17 Jan 2001; Bertram *op. cit.*, p. 179.
13. REDR, TS memoirs.
14. Rymill, *op. cit.*, p. 27; quoted in Bertram, *op. cit.*, p. 173.
15. Bertram, *op. cit.*, p. 169.
16. REDR, TS memoirs.
17. Quoted in Bertram, *op. cit.*, p. 167.
18. See Rymill, *op. cit.*, pp. 58–9.
19. REDR, TS memoirs.
20. REDR, TS memoirs.
21. Bertram, *op. cit.*, p. 139; Rymill, *op. cit.*, p. 61.
22. Rymill, *op. cit.*, p. 70.
23. *Ibid.*, pp. 73–4.
24. *Ibid.*, p. 72.

25. REDR, TS memoirs.
26. *Ibid.*

Chapter 7: The Voyage of the *Penola* and the British Graham Land Expedition (1934–37): The Second and the Third Year
1. REDR, TS memoirs.
2. Bertram, *op. cit.*, p 128.
3. *Ibid*, p. 130.
4. Rymill, *op. cit.*, p. 85.
5. *Ibid.*, p. 86.
6. *Ibid.*, p. 89.
7. Bertram, *op. cit.*, p. 107.
8. Rymill, *op. cit.*, p. 94.
9. Bertram, *op. cit.*, p 107.
10. REDR, TS memoirs.
11. Rymill, *op. cit.*, pp. 255–6.
12. *Ibid.*, p. 256.
13. REDR, letter, 16 May 1936.
14. *Ibid.*
15. REDR, TS memoirs.
16. REDR, letter, 20 May 1936.
17. REDR, letter, 16 May 1936.
18. Rymill, *op. cit.*, p. 257.
19. REDR, TS memoirs.
20. *Ibid.*
21. Rymill, *op. cit.*, p. 258.
22. REDR, letter, 13 Dec 1936.
23. REDR, TS memoirs. Interestingly, Ryder blacked out the relevant entries in the *Penola* diary but was nevertheless happy to describe the incident in the TS memoir.
24. *Ibid.*
25. Bertram, *op. cit.*, pp. 110–2.
26. REDR, TS memoirs.
27. *Ibid.*

Chapter 8: The Coming of War (1937–39)
1. REDR, TS memoirs.
2. *Ibid.*
3. REDR, letter, 16 Nov. 1936.
4. REDR, TS memoirs.
5. REDR, letter, 13 Dec 1936.
6. REDR, TS memoirs.
7. S.W. Roskill, *HMS* Warspite*: The Story of a Famous Battleship*, London, 1957, pp. 20, 84, 160–1.
8. *ODNB.*
9. REDR, TS memoirs.
10. The details of the incident of 30 June 1937, the report of the Court of Enquiry, the C-in-C, Portsmouth's letter and subsequent correspondence can all be found in ADM 178/190, NA.
11. *The British Graham Land Expedition, 1934–37*, Papers by members of the Expedition reprinted from *The Geographical Journal*, vol. XCI, April, May and June 1938, and vol. XCVI, September 1940, p. 28.
12. *Ibid.*, pp. 29 and 31.
13. REDR, TS memoirs.
14. Colin Bertram, letter, 17 August 1939.
15. REDR, letter, 28 Aug 1939 and TS memoirs.
16. REDR, letter, 9 Jan 1938.
17. REDR, TS memoirs.
18. Letter, Admiral Sir Dudley Pound, 26 May 1938.
19. REDR, TS memoirs.
20. REDR, letter, 1 July 1939.
21. Lt.-Cdr. Fred Smith, letter, 4 Jan 1941.

22. REDR, letter, 27 Sept 1938.
23. REDR, letter, 13 July 1938.
24. REDR, letter, 28 Sept 1938.
25. REDR, letter, 3 Feb 1939.
26. REDR, letter, 21 Sept 1938.
27. REDR, letter, 26 Sept 1938.
28. REDR, letter, 13 Oct 1938.
29. REDR, letter, 20 Oct 1938.
30. D. Mack Smith, *Mussolini*, London, 1983, p. 267.
31. W.S. Churchill, *The Gathering Storm*, Boston, 1948, p. 351.
32. REDR, letter, 9 April 1939 and TS memoirs.
33. REDR, TS memoirs.
34. F.G. Weber, *The Evasive Neutral*, U. of Missouri Press, 1979, p. 44.
35. *Ibid.*
36. REDR, letter, 4 Sept 1939.

Chapter 9: HMS *Willamette Valley* (1939–40)

 1. REDR, TS memoirs.
 2. *ODNB.*
 3. REDR, TS memoirs.
 4. *Ibid.*
 5. REDR, TS memoirs.
 6. *Ibid.*
 7. REDR letter to A. Cecil Hampshire, 25 March 1969.
 8. *Ibid.*
 9. REDR, TS memoirs.
10. Letter, Con Blake to REDR, 7 March 1986.
11. *Willamette Valley* 'Report of Proceedings', Ryder papers. These are copies of Ryder's reports to Admiral Campbell.
12. REDR, TS memoirs.
13. *W.V.*, Proceedings.
14. REDR, TS memoirs.
15. *W.V.*, Proceedings.
16. *Ibid.*
17. Letter, Admiral Gordon Campbell to REDR, undated.
18. The account of the final voyage and sinking of the *W.V.* and the survivors' experiences are drawn from the official reports preserved in Ryder's papers.
19. CHMR, letter, 28 May 1941.
20. REDR, TS memoirs.
21. REDR, letter, 5 July 1940 and TS memoirs.
22. *Ibid.*
23. Letter, A. Cecil Hampshire, 13 June 1969.
24. REDR, TS memoirs.

Chapter 10: HMS *Fleetwood*, HMS *Prince Philippe* and Marriage (1940–42)

 1. REDR, letter, 28 Dec 1940.
 2. J.R. Carew, *The Royal Norfolk Regiment*, London, 1967, ch.8.
 3. *The Times*, 9 Jan 1941.
 4. Copy of W.S. Churchill's memorandum, 4 July 1940, Ryder papers.
 5. REDR, TS memoirs.
 6. 'Report of Proceedings on HX 71', 21 September 1940, Ryder papers.
 7. 'Report of Proceedings on Convoy OA 222', Ryder papers.
 8. REDR, TS memoirs.
 9. REDR, letter, 13 Oct 1940.
10. REDR, letter, 21 Sept 1940.
11. REDR, letter, 28 Dec 1940.
12. REDR, letter, 3 Jan 1941.
13. REDR, TS memoirs.
14. Mrs Katherine Penley to the author, Jan 2010; John Green-Wilkinson to the author, Feb 2010; Susan Bates to the author, 2011.

15. REDR, letter, 17 March 1941.
16. CHMR, letter, 19 March 1941.
17. REDR, letter, 21 March 1941.
18. REDR, letter, 22 March 1941.
19. J. Green-Wilkinson, *Bishop Oliver: Letters & Reminiscences*, York, 1995, ch.1 and 2. Mrs Katherine Penley to the author, Jan 2010.
20. Neil Campbell, letter, 27 March 1941.
21. REDR, letter, 22 March 1941.
22. Neil Campbell, letter, 27 March 1941.
23. Archbishop Lang, letter, 29 March 1941.
24. Enid Ryder, letter, n.d. (Spring 1941).
25. REDR, letter, 21 March 1941.
26. Mrs Peter Cracroft to the author, June 2010.
27. *The Times*, 28 April 1941.
28. CHMR, letter, 9 April 1941.
29. REDR, letter, 30 April 1941.
30. REDR, TS memoirs.
31. REDR, letter, 18 Feb 1941.
32. REDR, TS memoirs.
33. REDR, letter, 1 June 1941; CHMR, letter, 30 April 1941.
34. REDR, letter, 1 June 1941.
35. ADM 267/129, NA.
36. REDR, TS memoirs.
37. The account of the collisions of HMS *Prince Philippe* with SS *Empire Wave* and MV *Lowick* is drawn from Ryder's official report on the incidents to the Admiralty and other documents in his papers.
38. CHMR, letter, 16 July 1941.
39. Admiralty letter NL.15617/41, 20 Oct 1941, Ryder papers.

Chapter 11: The Raid on St Nazaire, Operation *Chariot*: Hatching the Plot (February and March 1942)
 1. REDR, TS memoirs; Ryder's two unpublished accounts (1 TS [1942], 1 MS [prob. 1970s]) of the raid in his papers; Ryder recorded in 1974 BBC documentary about the raid. To reduce the number of endnotes in the two chapters about the raid on St Nazaire all quotations not otherwise acknowledged can be assumed to be from Ryder's three unpublished accounts of the raid.
 2. C.E. Lucas Phillips, *The Greatest Raid of All*, London, 1958, p. 36.
 3. CHMR, letter, 29 April 1949.
 4. C. Barnett, *Engage the Enemy More Closely: The Royal Navy in the Second World War*, London, 1991, p. 202.
 5. W.S. Churchill, *The Hinge of Fate*, Boston, 1950, p. 112.
 6. See 'Operation *Chariot*: The Raid on St. Nazaire' by T.W. Willans in Purnell's *History of the Second World War*, vol. 3, no.2, 1967.
 7. Memoir of Vice Admiral J. Hughes-Hallett, Mountbatten Papers, MB1/B47, Hartley Library, University of Southampton, p. 118.
 8. *Ibid.* p. 119.
 9. *Ibid.* pp. 121–2.
10. J.G. Dorrian, *Storming St Nazaire*, London, 1998, p. 18.
11. Minutes of Chiefs of Staff meeting 25 Feb 1942, CAB 79/18, NA.
12. Minutes of Chiefs of Staff meeting 2 March 1942, CAB 79/18, NA.
13. Dorrian, *op. cit.*, p. 40.
14. REDR letter to C.E. Lucas Phillips, late 1950s.
15. Lucas Phillips, *op. cit.*, pp. 72–4.
16. Lucas Phillips, *op. cit.*, p. 54.
17. Captain Michael Burn, quoted in *The Journal of the Victoria Cross Society*, 14th ed., March 2009.
18. Maj-Gen Purdon to the author, June 2010.
19. Dorrian, *op. cit.*, p. 57.
20. *Ibid.*, p. 55.
21. Dorrian, *op. cit.*, p. 65.

22. Hughes-Hallet, *op. cit.*, p. 124.
23. Lt Nigel Tibbits, 'Appreciation on the best method of placing the charge in *Campbeltown*', Ryder papers, and Ryder's unpublished TS account of the raid.
24. Hughes-Hallet, *op. cit.*, pp. 125–6 and 'Draft Memorandum to the Chiefs of Staff', Ryder papers.
25. Beattie recorded in 1974 BBC documentary about the raid.
26. REDR, letter, 22 March 1942.
27. Lucas Phillips, *op. cit.*, pp. 99–100.

Chapter 12: Operation *Chariot*: the Raid on St Nazaire (26–8 March 1942)

1. Dorrian, *op. cit.*, p. 77 and Lucas Phillips, *op. cit.*, p. 110.
2. Lucas Phillips, *op. cit.*, p. 110.
3. Dorrian, *op. cit.*, p. 77 and 1974 BBC documentary about the raid.
4. Lucas Phillips, *op. cit.*, p. 75.
5. Dorrian, *op. cit.*, p. 2.
6. *Ibid*, pp. 65–7.
7. Quoted in Lucas Phillips, *op. cit.*, p. 112.
8. Dorrian, *op. cit.*, p. 100.
9. The account of *Tynedale*'s action against the U-boat draws on Lucas Phillips, *op. cit.*, pp. 114–5 and 117.
10. Lucas Phillips, *op. cit.*, pp. 121–2 and Ryder's unpublished TS account of the raid.
11. Lucas Phillips, *op. cit.*, p. 123; G. Holman, *Commando Attack*, London, 1942, p. 115.
12. Ryder's unpublished TS account of the raid; Dorrian, *op. cit.*, p. 111; Green and Purdon recorded in 1995 BBC documentary about the raid.
13. Willans, *op. cit.*
14. Hughes-Hallettt, *op. cit.*, p. 126.
15. Willans, *op. cit.*
16. Ryder's unpublished TS account of the raid; Copland quoted in Dorrian, *op. cit.*, p. 115.
17. Ryder's unpublished TS account of the raid; Burn, Montgomery and Purdon recorded in the 1995 BBC documentary.
18. For details of the flotilla's timings and positions during the run up the estuary see the excellent plan in Dorrian, *op. cit.*, pp. 80–1.
19. Ryder's unpublished TS account of the raid, REDR TS memoirs and Lucas Phillips, *op. cit.*, pp. 132 and 134.
20. Lucas Phillips, *op. cit.*, pp. 134–5; Ryder recorded in 1974 BBC documentary.
21. Lucas Phillips, *op. cit.*, pp. 140–2.
22. Copland recorded in 1974 BBC documentary on the raid.
23. Ryder's unpublished TS account of the raid; Lucas Phillips, *op. cit.*, pp. 182–3.
24. Stephens recorded in 1995 BBC documentary on the raid.
25. For the account of the fate of the starboard column of MLs, see Lucas Phillips, *op. cit.*, pp. 171–8.
26. For the account of the fortunes of the port column of MLs, see Lucas Phillips, *op. cit.*, pp. 184–94.
27. Quoted in Lucas Phillips, *op. cit.*, p. 194.
28. Ryder recorded in 1974 BBC documentary on the raid.
29. Holman, *op. cit.*, p. 125.
30. Dorrian, *op. cit.*, p. 213.
31. Holman, *op. cit.*, p. 126.
32. Dorrian, *op. cit.*, pp. 243–6.
33. *Ibid.*, pp. 247–8.
34. Account the raid for the Weekly Intelligence Report, written by Lt. Cdr. Jenks, CO of *Atherstone*. Written in early April 1942. Ryder papers.
35. Dorrian, *op. cit.*, p. 265.
36. Jenks, *op. cit.*
37. J. Cooksey, *Operation Chariot: The Raid on St Nazaire*, Barnsley, 2005, p. 87 and generally for details of the planned Commando operations.
38. Hughes-Hallett, *op. cit.*, p. 126.
39. Churchill, *op. cit.*, p. 121.
40. See report of Naval Attaché to British Embassy, Paris, 15 Aug. 1947, Ryder papers.

Chapter 13: Combined Operations, Dieppe and D-Day (1942–44)

1. Ryder's unpublished MS account of the raid and REDR TS memoirs. I have harboured doubts as to the chronological accuracy of this story. The letter in question, a copy of which is in the TS memoirs, is dated 10 Apr 1942. It could not therefore have been delivered to Ryder on the Plymouth quay on 29 March. However, it may be that the letter of 10 Apr was a later, written confirmation of an earlier message, perhaps sent by telegram, delivered to Ryder by the sexy Wren on 29 March. I have included the story because it seems to have been firmly etched on Ryder's memory and is not the sort of thing one would invent. It is also rather a good tale.
2. PREM 3/376, NA.
3. Ryder's unpublished MS account of the raid.
4. *News of the World* and *The People*, 29 March 1942.
5. *Daily Express*, 30 March 1942.
6. *Ibid.*
7. *Ibid.*
8. Ryder's unpublished MS account of the raid.
9. CHMR, letters, 31 March 1942.
10. REDR, TS memoirs.
11. CHMR, letter, 26 May 1942.
12. *London Gazette*, 21 May 1942.
13. Lord Louis Mountbatten, letter, 21 May 1942.
14. Philip Francis, letter, 18 July 1942.
15. CHMR, letter, 26 May 1942.
16. I am grateful to Iain Stewart for confirming this fact.
17. *Daily Herald*, 15 July 1942; REDR, letter, 16 July 1942.
18. P. Ziegler, *Mountbatten*, London, 1985, p. 187.
19. Barnett, *op. cit.*, p. 547.
20. Quoted in T. Robertson, *Dieppe: The Shame and the Glory*, London 1963, p. 97.
21. Barnett, *op. cit.*, p. 547.
22. Ziegler, *op. cit.*, p. 189.
23. REDR, TS memoirs.
24. REDR, TS memoirs.
25. See 'Detailed Narrative' attached to *Naval Force Commander's Narrative*, ADM 199/1079 (Operation 'Jubilee'), NA; REDR, TS memoir.
26. *Naval Force Commander's Narrative*, ADM 199/1079 (Operation 'Jubilee'), NA.
27. Hughes-Hallett, *op. cit.*, p. 185.
28. *Naval Force Commander's Narrative* and attached reports.
29. R. Niellands, *The Dieppe Raid*, London, 2006, p. 239.
30. *Ibid.*
31. REDR, TS memoir.
32. Report of CO *Locust* attached to *Naval Force Commander's Narrative*.
33. *Naval Force Commander's Narrative*.
34. REDR, TS memoirs.
35. *Ibid.*
36. *Ibid* and A. Courtauld, *Man the Ropes*, London, 1957, ch.16.
37. See 'A History of 30 A.U.' HW 8/104, NA, and files relating to the formation of IAU, ADM 223/500, NA.
38. *Ibid.*
39. Lisle Ryder to the author, 2010.
40. REDR, TS memoirs.
41. Hughes Halllet, *op. cit.*, p. 298.
42. REDR, TS memoirs; Report of Capt Fisher, RM, ADM 116/4956, NA.
43. Hughes-Hallett, *op. cit.*, pp. 292–5 and 303.
44. REDR, letters, 2 June, 21 April and 19 May 1944.
45. 'Record of Air Staff, J Force', from *Operations Record Book Allied Expeditionary Air Force, Vol. 5, 1943–44*, AIR 2 4/32, NA; REDR, TS memoirs.
46. REDR, TS memoirs.
47. A. Beevor, *D-Day: The Battle for Normandy*, London, 2009, p. 74.
48. REDR, TS memoirs.
49. *Ibid.*

50. C. Wilmot, *The Struggle of Europe*, London, 1952, pp. 274–5; REDR, TS memoirs.
51. REDR, TS memoirs.
52. Wilmot, *op. cit.*, pp. 275–6.; REDR, TS memoirs.

Chapter 14: The Arctic Convoys, Peace and Politics (1944–50)
1. REDR, TS memoirs; REDR, letter, 12 June 1944.
2. HMS *Opportune's* Ship's Book, NA; REDR, TS memoirs.
3. Lt. Cdr G.B. Mason, RN, *Service Histories of Royal Navy Warships in World War 2*; REDR, TS memoirs.
4. REDR, TS memoirs; HMS *Opportune*, extract of log, Ryder papers.
5. R. Woodman, *The Arctic Convoys, 1941–1945*, London, 1994, pp. 424–32; REDR, letter, 1 March 1945 and TS memoirs.
6. REDR, letter, 11 March 1945.
7. REDR, letter, 28 April 1945.
8. REDR, letter, 12 March 1945.
9. REDR, letter, 29 Jan 1945.
10. CHMR, letters, 25 and 27 Dec 1944.
11. CHMR, letter, 2 April 1945.
12. CHMR, letter, 23 April 1945; REDR, letter, 28 April 1945.
13. CHMR, letters, 23 and 27 April 1945.
14. CHMR, letter, 7 May 1945; REDR, letter, 8 May 1945.
15. REDR, letter, 26 May 1945.
16. REDR, letter, 11 June 1945.
17. CHMR, letter, 7 May 1945.
18. CHMR, letter, 7 June 1945.
19. REDR, letter, 12 Feb 1945.
20. Sir John Murray, letter, 16 April 1946.
21. *Southern Times*, 18 Apr 1947; *TLS*, 26 Apr 1947; *Liverpool Daily Post*, 29 March 1947.
22. *Liverpool Echo*, 31 March 1947; *The Listener*, 26 June 1947; *Recorder*, 29 March 1947.
23. *R.N.S.S. Journal*, July 1947; *Liverpool Daily Post*, 29 March 1947.
24. Details from report of Naval Attaché to British Embassy, Paris, 15 Aug 1947, Ryder papers; *Times*, 4 Aug 1947; note of speech, Ryder papers.
25. Susan Bates and Moira Marriott to the author, 2010.
26. T. Judt, *Postwar*, London, 2007, p. 139.
27. REDR, TS memoirs.
28. REDR, letter, 19 March 1948.
29. REDR, TS memoirs.
30. REDR, TS memoirs; CHMR, letter, 5 June 1947.
31. CHMR, letter, 5 June 1948.
32. REDR, letter, 10 June 1945.
33. REDR, TS memoirs; Enid Henley (*née* Coulson) to the author, 2010.
34. CHMR, letter, 20 Jan 1945.
35. REDR, letter, 3 Jan 1949.
36. CHMR, letter, 31 Dec 1948.

Chapter 15: The House of Commons (1950–55)
1. REDR, letter, 3 Jan 1949.
2. Ryder's Adoption Address, Merton and Morden, undated.
3. REDR, letter, 3 Jan 1949.
4. CHMR, letter, 31 Dec 1948.
5. *Merton and Morden News*, 17 Feb 1950.
6. *Ibid.*, 13 Jan 1950.
7. Susan Bates to the author, 2011.
8. REDR, TS memoirs.
9. Sir John Murray, letter, 25 Feb 1950.
10. Lumley Green-Wilkinson, letter, 10 Nov 1948.
11. Lady Holderness to the author, 2010.
12. REDR, TS memoirs; Lady Holderness to the author, 2010.
13. *Merton and Morden News*, 3 March 1950.

14. *Times*, 17 Oct 1951.
15. *Evening News*, 24 October 1951.
16. *Report of the Proceedings of the Commonwealth Parliamentary Conference, 1952.*
17. *Times*, 14 Nov 1952.
18. CHMR, letter, 31 Aug 1952.
19. I am grateful to Barry Cox, Hon. Librarian, RNLI, for this information.
20. *Yachting World*, Dec 1953; *Motor Boat and Yachting*, Dec 1953; *Catholic Herald*, 18 Dec 1953.
21. Ian Fleming, letter, 23 Nov 1953.
22. *Keesing's Contemporary Archives*, 7–14 Aug 1954, 13719; Mrs P. Hatfield, College Archivist, Eton College.
23. *Sutton Times and Cheam Mail*, 13 Nov 1953.
24. *Merton and Morden News*, 22 April 1955 and 8 Oct 1954.

Epilogue
1. Susan Bates to the author, 2010.
2. *Gazette of the John Lewis Partnership*, 21 May 1955.
3. I am grateful to Duncan Beardmore Gray for details of Robert and Co.
4. REDR, letter, 25 Jan 1966 [prob.]
5. Lisle Ryder and Susan Bates to the author, 2010.
6. Susan Bates to the author, 2010.
7. John Green-Wilkinson, Diana Holderness, Sheena Skjöldesbrand and Susan Bates to the author, 2010.
8. Susannah Gurdon to the author, 2010 and Francis Peel to the author, 2011.
9. *Newbury Evening Advertiser*, 19 March 1983. Anne Head and Susannah Gurdon to the author, 2010.
10. Susannah Gurdon and Susan Bates to the author, 2010. Rt Revd Launcelot Fleming, address at REDR's memorial service.
11. Moira Marriot to the author, 2010.

Index